Losing Lou-Ann

Erb, Clinton A.
    Losing Lou-Ann
    1. Erb, Lou-Ann 2. Presenile dementia, Patients, Biography
3. Presenile dementia, Patients, Family relationships
    I. Erb, Clinton A. II. Title

RC523.E7 E7 1996

ISBN 0-9627232-6-6

Losing Lou-Ann

Clinton A. Erb

Holistic Education Press
Brandon, VT 05733-0328

This book is dedicated to
all those individuals and families who are,
or will be, engaged in the struggle of having to
live with dementia, in any of its forms.

Contents

Preface

Lou-Ann, my wife of 30 years, was an energetic and active person. She loved her family and was committed to her faith and a life of helping others. We moved to Burlington, Vermont, in 1971 with our two children, Maria and Keith, when I took a position as an assistant professor in the College of Education and Social Services at the University of Vermont.

In 1986, when she was 44 years old, her personality and behavior started to change in ways that were totally out of character. By the end of 1987, her mental capability had deteriorated to that of a three-year-old. This book is the story of that change, the search for the cause of what was happening, and the remaining years of her life in which the family was confronted with her decline and death as a result of Pick's disease.

As we were going through the diagnostic stage of Lou-Ann's illness — I tried to educate myself about this disease. My research at the Dana Medical Library of the University of Vermont's Medical College showed little written on Pick's. There wasn't much information that described what we were facing or what we could expect as the disease progressed. As a result, I thought Lou-Ann's case could provide the medical community with an opportunity to add to its research base in a way that could prove useful to others who face similar situations. Through this she could make a final contribution to her life's commitment of helping others.

As time went on it became apparent no one was going to use her situation to educate others about Pick's disease. Losing this unique opportunity of closely documenting the course of this disease frustrated me. It was at this time that the idea of writing a case study myself first entered my mind. I began to keep a journal and collect physicians' reports so I could act on this idea of describing the progression of Pick's disease. As I became more involved with our local support group, the Green Mountain Chapter of the Alzheimer's Association, and was invited to speak to various groups — the freshman class of the Medical College, the staffs of several nursing homes, the Visiting Nurses Association — it seemed to me that there were many people who were also searching for information about dementia and its effects on families. At most of these talks, I was teamed with a representative of the medical community, either a physician, a nurse, or a social worker. The family perspective always provoked great interest during these discussions. This expanded my vision from a case study to a book that documented, not just what happened to Lou-Ann, but what was happening to me as the principal caregiver, as well as to our children and extended family.

I found some books describing personal experiences as the authors traveled down the road of dementia. They were very helpful, but I would have liked to have known more about what was going on inside the writers—their emotions, feelings, and frustrations. In our support group, it was always meaningful when people shared their inner feelings, thoughts, and reactions with the rest of the group. Many times another member of our group would respond by saying, "I'm glad to hear someone else feels that way. I thought something was wrong with me because I had those same thoughts and emotions." In the movie *Shadowlands*, a similar outlook is stated: "We need to know we are not alone." It is critical that people confronting dementia know that they are not alone. The motto of the Alzheimer's Association, "Someone to Stand by You" conveys the same message. Consequently, this project took on a second purpose—to try to give others a glimpse of my inner feelings, thoughts, and personal situations that might portray a fuller picture of living with dementia.

There was also a third purpose behind writing this book. For those people who genuinely want to help someone in dealing with dementia, I hope this stimulates their thinking as to how to be most useful. Many people backed away from us as they learned about our plight, some immediately, others later, but I heard the statement, "Perhaps they don't know what to do," given as a reason for this behavior. It is my hope that after reading this, people will have a clearer view of what could be helpful to the afflicted person as well as the caregivers.

What one finds in this manuscript is my perception and interpretation of what happened during these seven years of our lives. I do not claim my interpretation is always a totally accurate description of what transpired, but it is how I saw and understood what went on around me. I have tried to be accurate in telling what happened and relate my reactions to those events. Since I do not wish to discredit anyone by this book, I have changed the names of some individuals.

My desire is that this book be an aid to people, helping them cope with this devastating disease. Lou-Ann's life centered around being of service to others. It is my hope that even in death she can continue to help and inspire.

Chapter 1

The End Draws Near

January 19, 1993

The spring semester at the University of Vermont begins tomorrow. I always get nervous and uptight when a new semester starts. I guess it will be time to retire when I'm not on edge before I meet my new classes. Maria and Keith always used to say that they knew when it was time for a new semester because I was so hard to live with. This semester is no different, even after 22 years of teaching at UVM. As I get ready for bed, I picture Lou-Ann in the nursing home and reflect upon the last couple of months. She has been doing well. I would find it hard to concentrate on the first few days of classes if my mind were always on her. Even though she can only roll her head from side to side, and sometimes follow you with her eyes, she has been able to have her meals without choking too much, and hasn't had a high fever. The past two to three months have been relatively calm. It is amazing that she's been able to survive for so long. Now, more than seven years since Pick's disease started its relentless course, she can no longer move any part of her body, except her head, and even then she needs a neck roll for support. She hasn't stood or walked with assistance in over six months. I exercise her arms and legs every night to keep her as limber as possible. She has been mute for more than three years, and she hasn't had facial expressions since at least a year before that. But she is still Lou-Ann, my wife and closest friend for the past 30 years. She's been at the Starr Farm Nursing Center for almost 56 months now. I spend two to three hours with her every day. I always look forward to being with her. I can hold her and be close. The touch of her skin, holding her hand, kissing her, even though she hasn't puckered in four years, is something that still brings me pleasure. No one can hold my hand like Lou-Ann. My first class tomorrow starts at 9 a.m. and my last one doesn't end until 7 p.m. It will be relaxing to be with her after a long first day.

January 20, 1993

The telephone rings as I'm about to leave for school. Who would be calling at 7:45 in the morning?

"Lou-Ann woke up congested with a temp of 103°, and we want to let you know."

It is the charge nurse at the Starr Farm nursing home. Lou-Ann has had higher temperatures than this before, but they've always been able to bring it down. "We'll give her Tylenol as we've done in the past. Do you want us to start her on an antibiotic?"

"I guess it wouldn't hurt to put her on the antibiotic. I've got a class at nine so I'll call back after that to see how she's doing."

I made the decision two years earlier not to give antibiotics or to initiate any other means of prolonging her life, such as a feeding tube, if she were in critical condition. The nurses know of my decision, and in fact, we had not gone ahead with aggressive treatment twice before when they thought she was coming down with pneumonia. This must not be a similar situation since they asked about using an antibiotic. By noon she should be starting to feel better, and we can still have a good evening together.

The first class is always somewhat crazy. Students are coming and going. Some want to get in when there is no more room, others on the class list do not show up, and a lot of students show up at my office after the first class. As a result, I am not able to call until around 11 a.m. "She's on oxygen, her temp is still up, but we've just started the antibiotic so that should help. We've put cold compresses under her arms, neck, and head to try to cool her off and to keep her comfortable. She hasn't shown any improvement since I first called you."

By now there should have been some indication that her temperature was on the decline. It has always started down by this time in the past. They didn't say she was in trouble and the nurse's voice didn't seem to indicate they were overly concerned, so hopefully she will be better when I call later.

After lunch

She's been on my mind since my last call. I'd like to cancel my 4-7 p.m. class, but some students travel quite a distance to get here. There is no way we can get in touch with everyone anyway since some students don't register until the first class.

Getting organized for a three-hour class when your mind is somewhere else does not help calm the nerves for a first class. I can't concentrate on what I am supposed to be doing. How can I teach when I don't want to be here?

3 p.m., I call again

"There's no change in her condition. Her temp is 104.8°. She's still very congested. She wouldn't swallow any of her lunch, but did take a full glass of water. She's had a pretty hard day."

What to do? Class starts in less than an hour. The nurses didn't say that I should come, and they know my desire to be with her if she becomes really sick. I decide to start class and call during our break.

5:30 p.m., Break time

What a lousy start! I couldn't concentrate on what we were doing in class. I'm sure the students have second thoughts about taking this course. Most of them are working on their MSW, the Masters Degree in Social Work, and are required to take a statistics class. Many are not too confident about their ability in math, so a good start is important to their self-confidence. I could not take my eyes off the clock while teaching. All I could think of was Lou-Ann and wanting to get to a telephone.

"Her temp has come down some, but she's still very congested. Her pulse is 130, and her respiratory rate is 38. This is the worst I've ever seen her. She took some apple juice and water, but we had to suction her mouth to help her breath." There is no way I can continue this class. I have to get to the nursing home to be with Lou-Ann. I'm not sure what to expect now.

I'd better call Pastor Coffey right away. I won't be able to reach him later because of prayer meeting. He says he'll come as soon as the meeting begins and he can get someone else to lead it.

6:30 p.m.

The drive to the nursing home seems to take twice as long as usual.

I feel the concern as I enter the nursing home. People glance at me as I walk down the hall but say nothing. There are not the friendly hellos and smiles I usually get when I arrive.

Lou-Ann has had a standing order for morphine since her last episode of severe congestion. She was given 2 mg which seems to have given her some relief. No stethoscope is needed to hear the rasping in her lungs. Even though her temperature is so high, she feels cool to the touch. She is lying in her bed with her eyes closed. The only movement I can see is the rise and fall of her chest as she struggles for each breath. She looks so helpless. Her regular doctor is not on call tonight, but the doctor taking his place is visiting residents at the nursing home. At 7 p.m. he comes to check her.

"Lou-Ann's condition is very serious. I am afraid she is not going to make it."

Did he say what I think he said? Did he really mean she was dying?

"How much time do you think she has?"

"It's hard to say. Each person is different, but I don't think she'll make it through the next 24 hours."

As I look down at her, I cannot believe this may be our last night together.

"What about the antibiotic? If I knew her situation was this serious, I wouldn't have agreed to put her on it."

"The antibiotic is not having any impact on her condition. It won't make any difference one way or another."

After seven years of struggling with this disease, this day has arrived. In my mind I have lived this moment over and over, but I'm still not prepared for it. I have less than 24 hours to be with my wife of 30 years.

How can I say good-bye? The doctor leaves. I'm struck by how quiet it is in the room. The earth should quake at such an announcement. The heavens should clap with thunder and lightning. Angels should cry out in sorrow and mourning. Instead there is silence. My wife is about to die, and life goes on around us. Other residents continue to walk up and down the halls oblivious to what is happening to us. People are shopping at the local grocery store, the national evening news comes on TV; around the world little children are playing. I want to scream, "STOP! My wife is dying. Our life together is coming to an end. Show some respect." Instead there is silence. It is so quiet in the room.

I remember the first time Lou-Ann and I met. I was a sophomore at Clarkson University, then Clarkson College of Technology, which at that time was all male. My roommate, George, and I were studying at the Potsdam State library, where the scenery was better than at Clarkson. Anita, the older sister of a high school classmate of mine and a resident adviser in a freshman dorm, came over and said she wanted to introduce me to someone. That someone was Lou-Ann. She was wearing a dark brown jumper with a light brown blouse, had long dark hair, warm brown eyes, and a pleasant smile. We only talked for a minute or two before I went back to the table where I was studying. I then did something I had never done before. I wrote her name, spelled it wrong, in the math textbook I had with me at the time. That is as romantic as an engineering student can get, writing a girl's name in his differential equations text. I don't know why I did that because I knew I didn't have the nerve to call her afterward. I didn't see her again until our paths crossed early the next year when she was a sophomore. We met when she started to come to Inter-Varsity Christian Fellowship meetings. Some of us from I-V also started attending the same church. We became active in the church and formed a mixed quartet that sang at many services. Lou-Ann and I were a part of that quartet so we started to see quite a bit of each other. One thing led to another; we started to pair off as the semester went along and then began to date, which mainly consisted of studying together in the library. We almost broke up toward the end of her sophomore year because I was quiet and didn't talk a lot. She felt frustrated in trying to develop our relationship. She told me I had to open up and share more, or else our relationship was over. It was then that I realized how much she meant to me, that I didn't want to live the rest of my life without her. I thank God our relationship didn't end at that time. A little over a year later, on her birthday in April of her junior year, we became engaged. One month after her graduation, on July 7, 1962, we were married.

We made a major decision about our family before we were married. We decided that we would adopt some of our children. During college summers, Lou-Ann had worked as a counselor at a Baptist camp for inner-city children from New York City. At that time, she came in contact with many children, and some counselors, who were from extremely poor family situations. As we talked and made plans for our future, we decided we wanted to include children who weren't born into a situation where they could grow up as part of a family. We purposely waited to start our family so we could solidify our marriage before we had to face the responsibilities of child-rearing. At the time we were married, I was working as an engineer for the General Electric Company in Syracuse, New York, and Lou-Ann had accepted a position teaching fifth grade at the Mattydale Elementary School in North Syracuse. Three months after we were married, I left GE to enter Syracuse University to obtain my master's degree in education and become certified to teach secondary school mathematics. The following year, after I obtained my degree, I taught math and coached the wrestling team at North Syracuse High School.

Two years later my father had major surgery for cancer. The prognosis was not encouraging, but he was able to return to work and did much better than expected. A year later, the first signs that the cancer had returned appeared on the evening I called to tell Mom and Dad they were going to be grandparents. The birth of Maria on April 17, 1967, was a poignant time since my father had survived the cancer long enough to see his first grandchild. He died seven months later on November 22, 1967, at the age of 48. That year I applied for, and was granted, a one-year National Science Foundation Fellowship for high school mathematics teachers at the Ohio State University. We moved to Columbus three months before my father died. We decided to stay at Ohio State for an additional three years so I could complete study for my doctorate in mathematics education. Knowing Maria would be five years old when I finished my Ph.D. degree, we had to make some important decisions regarding our family. We didn't want our children to be five or six years apart, so we decided to add to our family through adoption while we were in Columbus. The more we talked and investigated what it would take to adopt, the more we became convinced we should adopt a child that might not have a good chance of having a home. At the time the waiting list for a white, blue-eyed baby was quite long. It was pretty certain that those children would find homes. What about the child who was handicapped, older, or of mixed race? We read as much as we could about the subject. We found people who had already adopted children from out of the mainstream and invited ourselves over to talk about their experiences. Everyone we contacted welcomed us to their homes, and spoke openly of their experiences. Through this we came to question whether we would have the resolve and the emotional and financial resources to give a physically handicapped child the care s/he deserved. That narrowed our options to a mixed-race or foreign-born child. We also wanted a baby, preferably directly from the hospital. We continued to become as knowledgeable as we could about adopting a child of another race. Once someone goes ahead with something like this, there is no turning back, so we wanted to be as sure as possible that this was right for us and the child. We visited a support group consisting of people who had recently adopted "hard to place children," as they were called then. We weren't doing this to make a social statement or to further civil rights. What we wanted was to give a child a home who might not otherwise have had one.

After much prayer and talk between the two of us and with others, we decided to go ahead. We eventually contacted three local adoption agencies in the Columbus area.

Two days before Christmas, with a list of questions in hand, I called each agency to see if we could proceed. One was a private group who didn't want anything to do with us. At that time, placing a child of another race with a white family was relatively new, and many agencies didn't want to become involved with anything that radical. I next called the agency associated with the Department of Social Services for Franklin County in Ohio. I started by saying we were interested in adopting a child. Before I could say much of anything else, the person I was talking to went into a long explanation of how difficult and time-consuming the process would be. Their waiting list was so long they wouldn't accept an application for at least six months, and it would probably be a couple of years before a child would become available. I waited until she was finished before asking my questions. My first was whether they placed "hard to place" children. With that our conversation turned completely around. They couldn't begin the process fast enough once they knew of our interest. A week later we met with a representative of the agency, and two other couples who also had an interest like ours. The other couples were just beginning to investigate adoption as a means of expanding their families, so the first meeting did not give us much new information, but it did give the agency a first impression of us. We answered many of the other couple's questions, and it became evident to agency personnel how much we had thought through what we were about to do.

We submitted our application and were approved less than three months from the time we made that initial telephone call. Our only stipulation was that we wanted a baby boy, preferably under a month old. When they notified us that our request had been approved, we were told of a little boy who might match our family, who was born on December 19th, four days before our initial call. We said we would wait since a three-month old was older than we would like. The process was also moving much faster than expected, and we had a few things to do before our family could expand. We expected the process to take at least a year, but now we could have a child only three months after our first call.

The agency said they would contact us only in the event a child was available, but we could call any time we wished. After two months of silence we called to inquire about the status of our adoption. There was no change. A few days later the agency called back and talked with Lou-Ann. The social worker didn't want to put pressure on us, but wanted us to know that the little boy born on December 19th was still with them. As I returned from school that night, the first thing I saw when the bus door opened was Lou-Ann. She had never met me at the bus stop before. As my foot hit the sidewalk, she asked if I would like to have a son. It took us all of ten minutes to decide that a 5½-month-old little boy was just as nice as a three-week-old child. The call was made, the match was done, and the last week in May we went to meet our new son. We were to spend half an hour with him at the agency, to get acquainted, before they brought him to our home to officially place him. We were with him over an hour. A week later, Keith Allen, a 5½-month-old, biracial boy, permanently entered our lives.

Chapter 2

The First Signs

Who was Lou-Ann? She was a loving, caring, compassionate, generous, hospitable, intelligent, independent, and stubborn person. She was energetic and active and always had to be doing something. Don Goff, her boss and Director of the Champlain Valley Office of Economic Opportunity (CVOEO) described her as a "complex bundle of paradoxes in life."

> Lou-Ann did not believe in wasting time. She would come to work with her bag of goodies, always in there was a book of some description, she loved books. It was as though there was not to be a single idle moment in her life, as though there was a measured amount of time in life, and it should be filled up to the brim and used and loved. She was a steward of time.

She couldn't stand injustice and the abuse of power whether it be by individuals or institutions. She fought for what she believed in and arrived at her positions through study, thought, discussion, and prayer. She would not change her opinion simply because someone said she should, but only if she could be shown the logic of that position. A person who wanted to change Lou-Ann's mind had better have a rationale for their opinions because she would argue her point. She set high standards for herself and expected no less of those around her. Her mind and intellectual pursuits were an integral part of who she was. She was an avid reader, a lover of books. She was a teacher and a role model, not only to her fifth-grade students, but to everyone who came in contact with her. She taught me a lot over the course of our life together, including the seven years of her illness. Her life centered around her love of her family, friends and her faith. Her faith was the focal point of her life. It defined who she was and how she lived. It was an active, dynamic faith, evolving and growing. That faith was the foundation of our relationship and marriage. Scripture talks about a husband and wife molding together, becoming one — "the two shall become one" (Genesis 2:24). Our marriage was far from perfect, but I never realized the fullness and depth of that statement, or the extent to which our relationship became and reflected this oneness until her death.

She had her flaws. She was impatient, opinionated, and stubborn. She was also an organizer, sometimes to the chagrin of the family. "I see your refrigerator with the list of who's cooking, who's cleaning and who's shopping." (Helen Chappatis) She organized a Bible study every place we lived. She formed a book group among friends to read and discuss books on a variety of topics. When we joined the local food co-op, it didn't take long for her to become a member of the Board of Directors. Together we became the youth group advisors at churches in two of the cities where we lived, and she also taught Sunday School. Lou-Ann was an excellent knitter and seamstress, always working on some project, outfitting the entire family in clothes and sweaters. She could knit the most intricate pattern while her attention was on something else, knitting as she watched TV, when visiting friends, or during Bible studies. Music also played an important role in her life. Her mother was a piano teacher, so by the time Lou-Ann graduated from high school, she had been playing piano for 14 years. In high school she played flute in the band and was the accompanist for the chorus and other singing groups. She played for some of the churches we attended, and for a number of years accompanied a singing group in Burlington, until her illness made that impossible. Lou-Ann entered college as a music education major, but at the end of her first year, transferred into elementary education. She felt she could have more of an influence on her students if she had them for a full day as their grade level teacher rather than for a few hours each week as a music teacher.

Work was important to her and was always people-oriented. After we were married, she taught in an elementary school that was in one of the older, blue-collar sections of town. She left teaching after four years when we decided to start our family. She was out of the work force for ten years before attempting to reenter. Obtaining a job after ten years was not an easy proposition. She tried substitute teaching, but was frustrated with students who did not want to learn. While searching for a permanent position she volunteered in Vermont's office of consumer protection. She worked at two local colleges before obtaining the position of Executive Secretary at the Champlain Valley Office of Economic Opportunity (CVOEO). This agency was one of the last remnants of President Johnson's Great Society. As time passed, she was given more responsibility and promoted to Administrative Officer. Support for the office became a critical issue as President Reagan cut funds for programs that aided the poor. These cutbacks eventually took her job. After three and one-half years of working for CVOEO, she was again looking for work. At the time she was leaving CVOEO, the Governor of Vermont was establishing a task force to investigate the problems of hunger within the state. She was asked to become the coordinator of their efforts. It was a one-year position that was to end in June of 1986. During this year, Pick's disease started its relentless journey.

This is an insidious disease. You don't know when it starts, and by the time you're aware of its presence, it has already had a major effect, profoundly changing the person you knew. Little things happened that could be easily explained by other reasons. Even looking back, it is hard to determine when the first signs began to appear. At times everyone exhibits some of these signs, but they are not permanent and are generally only evident during periods of emotional stress and strain. But with Pick's and other dementing illnesses, once these signs start, they don't vanish. They continue to get worse. Her behavior started to change in the early months of 1986. She did not acknowledge any changes, and we felt they were due to stress and other events in her life. Work was very important to her, and her job was coming to an end. Our daughter Maria, in her first year at the University of Vermont, was starting to become serious with Tim, a young man she met at school. Hence, her allegiance to the family was beginning to undergo a change. Our son Keith, a junior in high school, was soon to start off on his own. The "empty nest syndrome," we reasoned, could have been affecting her behavior. She was also in her mid-forties, the start of menopause was not out of the realm of possibility. It was a stressful time in her life, a time of transition. I thought things would eventually work themselves out, but as time went on they were not getting better. The stress that was seemingly affecting her was now attacking the family. Our family was starting to disintegrate. Her first strange behaviors were just exaggerations of normal activities. We recycled our vegetable scraps and other degradable kitchen leftovers in a compost pile for our garden. Lou-Ann became a fanatic in composting leftovers. She would even compost the few remaining drops of milk in the bottom of the glass after someone had finished drinking, by adding a little water to increase the volume of liquid, then throw the milk and water mixture into the compost pile. She became a conserver of everything. When she drove, she would try to take the shortest distance possible. If there was a bend in the road she would cut the corner as close as she could, even if that meant driving on the shoulder. On the interstate highway she would move into the far left lane if the road turned to the left, and the far right lane if it went to the right. I was thankful she didn't do that on a two-lane highway.

If house lights were on that she felt were not necessary, she would turn them off. One day while I was shaving, she walked by the bathroom and said, "You don't need all those lights," then turned them off. I was left standing in the dark with a razor in my hand and shaving cream on my face. When I objected she was nonchalant about the whole matter and simply passed it off as unimportant. She got to the point where she would not use lights, even in the most extreme conditions. I would come home at night and she would be using a flashlight instead of turning on house lights.

In March, Maria invited Tim to dinner to introduce him to our family. He brought flowers as a thank-you for dinner, and no doubt to help with the first impression. They worked. Lou-Ann called every day to thank him for the flowers, but she also reported on how many were still alive and how many had died. This went on for over a week. At the time I was unaware she was doing this. No one's life is seen whole by any single individual. All those who know the person see a part, and each person then develops his or her own individual interpretation of the unusual behaviors. Each person who knew and interacted with Lou-Ann saw behaviors that were abnormal. No one saw the whole of her life, so the full extent of her actions were not known to any one person. The most significant change at this time focused on her personality. Her emotions and feelings became flat. This occurred quickly, over a period of only a few months. She became distant and detached from the entire family. In those few months she went from a loving person, whose life centered around her family and others, to a person who didn't seem to care about anyone, even her husband and children. She no longer seemed to want to be involved in our lives. She would return a hug or a kiss if someone initiated it, but no longer showed any spontaneous affection. Her whole life tended to turn inward. She seemed to have difficulty seeing anything from someone else's perspective.

As her job with the Task Force on Hunger was coming to an end, she would talk about her desire for another job but did very little to look for a new one. Her supervisor from the Task Force wanted to hire her for another position, but Lou-Ann would come up with excuses for not accepting it. Here was a person who was usually forthright and confident, who never backed away from challenges, giving lame excuses for not wanting something she claimed to desire. She would peruse the paper for openings, but would make only one or two calls per week. She wanted a job, but was doing everything she could to not get one, then claim her problem was that she was soon going to be out of work. I tried to encourage her to become more active in her search, but kept getting rebuffed. I was becoming very frustrated because I couldn't understand her actions.

She added other strange behaviors as spring turned into summer. She began to watch *Sesame Street* on a regular basis. She videotaped segments of the program she found enjoyable and would watch them throughout the day. She taped another educational TV show, *A Man Who Loved Bears*, which was about a person who raised a grizzly cub to maturity, then let her go in the wild. She watched that video a couple of times every day. I had copied the movies of our children on videotape and that was also added to her viewing repertoire. When someone came to visit she would immediately begin to tell the bear story and want them to go downstairs to see the tape. She also gathered a collection of old postcards and pictures and would constantly look through the stack.

She became less informed about what was going on in each of the family member's lives. She didn't know what each of us was doing and didn't seem to care. When we tried to involve her with something important to us, she would ignore us and turn to her taped programs. Even though Lou-Ann's behavior had become strange, we did not fully comprehend the impact of what was happening. We were rationalizing her actions, in many ways hoping our rationalizations were true. It was not easy to admit that drastic changes were taking place that could result in dire consequences to the family and our way of life. Some individuals and families take a long time to accept what is happening to their loved one. The result is that families lose valuable time to enjoy each other while there can still be some meaningful interaction. I've learned with dementia, the best day a person has is today. Tomorrow will be a little less, even though the decline may be unmeasurable. The disease continually diminishes the capabilities of the person, slowly but unrelentingly.

Chapter 3

The First Six Months

As summer began, Lou-Ann got progressively worse. She reached the point where she could not tolerate noise. At first she would turn off the sound on the TV when ads came on. She would go back and forth to the television set during a program to turn the volume up and down, irritating those who were watching with her. We tried to convince her to remain seated, but reasoning with her was fruitless. She was not a fan of president Reagan. Everytime he was on TV, she would hold her hand in front of her face to block out the President's image and say, "I can't stand that man." Without warning, she would turn off the kids' music saying it was too loud, but later would listen to her own programs just as loud. Once, we were sitting in the living room, about ten feet apart. I was using earphones, listening to soft music on my walkman, while she was looking through her stack of pictures and postcards. Even though she could not hear what was being played, she asked me to turn off the music because it distracted her and she could not concentrate on her pictures.

Compromise was no longer in her vocabulary. Our large television was in the basement, directly under our bedroom. She could not sleep when someone was watching that set. She would go downstairs and announce that it had to be turned off at once! No matter how soft it was, she would insist that it kept her awake. No radio could be played in the living room when she wanted to go to bed, which by now was sometimes as early as 8:30 or 9:00. Besides becoming sensitive to sound, she also started to react to light. We had a small TV in the kitchen on which we watched the evening news as we ate our dessert. If I turned on the overhead light while watching the news, she would put on a baseball cap to shield her eyes. She would no longer lie with her head on my shoulder as we went to sleep. She claimed she could hear my heartbeat, and it made too much noise for her to go to sleep. I couldn't believe that the times of snuggling together and going to sleep in each other's arms were over simply because my heart made too much noise! She rolled on her side with her back to me. I was rejected because of the sound of my heart! I started to resent her even being next to me at night. I began to stay up later and later. Keith and Maria were staying away from home more and more. Summer used to be a time when our family did things together, but this year the family was being torn apart by a wife and mother who didn't seem to care about anyone in her family. All of us began to keep our distance from each other, and that started to take its toll on everyone.

She started a habit that would continue for the next few years. She wouldn't swallow her saliva: instead, she carried a mug with her, and spit into it about every minute. I learned to accept a lot, but never got used to this. Sometimes her "phlegm mug," as we called it, would spill, or get knocked over, and have to be cleaned up. She would either quickly bend down, suck up the spill, then spit it back into the mug, or else she'd just ignore it. No one in the family ever got used to her doing this, even though there were other more unpleasant things to come, which we accepted better. She never did this in public, outside the home, which we considered a blessing. Her phlegm mug went with us in the car, but always stayed there when we got out.

We had a close friend visit during the summer who had been teaching in China for two years. She wasn't here more than five minutes when she asked what was wrong with Lou-Ann. None of us had an answer. A friend had quickly noticed her odd behavior, when I still had not acknowledged the increasingly strange nature of her actions. I did not grasp the magnitude of Lou-Ann's problem. I tried to get her to see her doctor but she would not go, saying there was no need since she felt fine. No matter what I said or did, she absolutely refused. She claimed she was not depressed, that things would change when she got a job. When I talked to her about what she was doing that bothered the family she would listen, but not react, and then continue to behave in the same manner as before. It was as if she willfully ignored everything I had said. She started to lock the house, even when she was not alone. She also began to carry a long boning knife. She wouldn't make a big issue of it, but would just have it with her if she was sitting or walking around the house. She even carried it when she went out for a walk in the neighborhood. I know some neighbors became nervous, but no one ever said anything. Also, if I went to the basement she would ask if it was me when I came back upstairs.

In June, her work with the Task Force on Hunger ended. Lou-Ann applied to two temporary employment agencies and was getting work on a daily or weekly basis. She kept getting called back for employment so her performance must have been reasonably satisfactory.

We celebrated our 24th wedding anniversary July 7th, but I began to question how committed she was to continuing our relationship. I believe two of the most important ingredients of any marriage are trust and commitment, and we had enjoyed both. I always felt our relationship was a team endeavor. We didn't try to upstage one another, but took pride in each other's successes. We had our ups and downs, but there was never a time when either of us thought of tossing in the towel. Both of us had always been totally committed to making our marriage work. The trust was still there, but now it seemed as if her commitment was missing. I was reaching a point where the idea of a separation was the only way I could see to save my sanity, and any hope the relationship I had with our children could be salvaged. Even if I could live under the pressure of her behavior, I knew that unless she changed, we would hardly see our children once they left home and started a life for themselves. The split between our children and ourselves was widening every day. She would not, or could not, acknowledge that anything was wrong. In her view, since nothing was wrong, nothing needed to be changed. I was being placed in a position where I would have to choose between my wife and my children. No person should have to make, or even consider, such a choice. I was being torn apart by what I saw happening to our family, and there was nothing I could do about it. Everytime I tried to talk to her, I got nowhere. She made more fuss over the main character in her bear story than she did over me. I thought if I shared my thoughts about separation, it might shock her into action to save our marriage. I was convinced she would not throw out 24 years of married life without a fight to save it. So I told her if things kept on going as they were, I could not continue to take it, and we would have to separate. I would not risk living a life of hell with her, possibly growing old without seeing my grandchildren. We had reached a point that something had to be done. I was willing to do anything I could to save what we had, but I couldn't do it alone. She would have to come to a decision as to whether she felt our marriage was important enough to save.

Sometimes when I brought up this subject she would have no reaction. It was as if I had asked her if she wanted her eggs fried or scrambled. What I said didn't seem to register with her. Other times she would say that she could not live without me, but then there would be no change in her behavior. She didn't seem willing to work on our relationship. I don't think I had ever been at a lower point in my life. The person I loved with all my heart, the person whom I would have given my life for, the person who was the mother of my children, the person who was my strength and life was not able to acknowledge that there was a problem between us. She didn't care! I could not accept that. I could not give up yet. I would give my last ounce of effort to save what we had before I would turn my back on her. On the other hand, I would not spend the rest of my life trying to make it work. We might reach a time when it was indeed all over. I prayed to God that I would never see that day.

I wanted the two of us to see a counselor. She refused to go, and I could not talk her into it. It wasn't that she didn't believe in counseling, but that she did not see the need. I needed help, so I decided to go even if it was by myself. I hoped that if I went, she might agree to come with me. At the dinner table I announced I was going. There was no reaction on her part. I decided to see a psychologist a friend had recommended. After seeing me once, he wanted to meet with her, but I was not sure I could get her to go. After some discussion, and much to my surprise, she agreed to see him. It was now mid-September.

Each of us met with him separately and were to go for a joint session. It was scheduled for 10:30 in the morning, she was to pick me up at school after my 9-10 a.m. class. I rushed out after class to be sure I wouldn't be late since it would take 15 to 20 minutes to get to his office. I was afraid if I wasn't ready when she arrived, she might not wait, and just go back home. I waited outside for 20 minutes, and she hadn't shown. It was almost 10:30 when I called and asked why she wasn't picking me up. She said she forgot our meeting. I wondered just how accidental her forgetting this appointment was. She talked continually as we drove to his office. She pointed out facts about the various local landmarks as we passed them: "Natasha lives down that street," "Didn't we buy a rug from that store?" "That's the house where we had Keith's violin repaired." She wouldn't shut up. I asked her to stop, but she just kept talking. I was already angry at her for forgetting our appointment. Now, knowing we were late, this continual guided tour of our route was making me incensed. I wanted to scream! In the course of the session the doctor asked for an example of Lou-Ann's abnormal behavior. I described our trip to his office and related the comments she made while we were en route. He looked at her and asked, "Would this type of behavior be normal for you?"

"No, I would not normally do this," she replied.

"Did you do it?" he then asked.

"If Clint said I did, I must have."

This conversation took place less than 30 minutes after the ride in the car.

When the session ended, she drove me back to campus for my afternoon classes. We were about a mile down the road from his office when I asked,

"What did you think about what he said?"

She replied, "What did he say?"

In less than five minutes she could not recall what had just happened over the past hour. Was it because she did not care and did not pay attention to what was said, or did she really not remember? The major accomplishment of this first joint meeting was that she agreed to see a doctor. The psychologist didn't think there was any physical reason behind her behavior, but he wanted her checked anyway to eliminate that possibility. I had been trying to get her to see her doctor for months, and she had always refused. This time she made an appointment for the middle of October. As part of our counseling sessions, we took a battery of tests to determine our interests and identify our personality traits. This was to identify ways in which we were, and were not, compatible, and to help determine how we could work out our differences. One conclusion the psychologist made after a number of visits was that Lou-Ann indeed did not seem to be concerned about our relationship and was not willing to work to rectify the situation. Hence, he felt that I would be justified in leaving her, if I so decided. This was not what I wanted to hear, or why I went to counseling in the first place. I was not looking for justification to leave, but for ways to clarify and rectify our problem. During the late fall, Lou-Ann would ask the same question three or four times, even after only a few minutes. She began to call me at school during the afternoon.

"How many cups of coffee do you want for supper?"

"I'll have two cups, like I usually do."

Five to ten minutes later the phone would ring again. My secretary would buzz me, "It's Lou-Ann."

"How many cups of coffee do you want for supper?"

"I'll have two cups, like I usually do."

She would call four or five times most every day with the same question. But at least when I got home for supper, she would have prepared two cups of coffee for me.

She also started to exhibit what I now know is sometimes called the "gramophone syndrome" — to monotonously retell the same anecdotes over and over. The stories would be about the guinea pigs we had had a few years earlier, the relative ages of the entire family, including our daughter's boyfriend, and the places we had lived since our marriage. She always had a rapid speech pattern but as time went on, she lost the ability to control the speed of her speech. This was especially true as she would tell these stories. She would talk so fast it was difficult to understand what she was saying, but she would repeat the stories word-for-word each time she told them. As I later learned, stereotyped behavioral routines and rigid rituals are not uncommon in Pick's disease. One can see this repetition along with her now simplistic and awkward writing style in two letters she wrote to her parents.

> September 21, 1986 — "When Tim came over this spring, Maria showed him some of the films that Clint took when they were babies, toddlers and youngsters as well (sic) of Maria running track and Keith playing football and hockey. He has put them on a videotape now so it is much easier to watch them because you don't have to rewind each film. It's

great because you both are on it when you visited us in N. Syracuse when Maria was real young and then when you both and Grandmother Durmeyer visited us in Columbus. Pictures are great but movies are better because you can see them moving."

October 22, 1986 — "I don't know if I told you but Maria and Tim started looking at our movies of the kids when they were infants, toddlers and older. Pictures are great but movies are even better and Clint put them on videotape so now it's even better since we don't have to rewind each reel. It's also great because we have you in two of them twice, once in N. Syracuse and once in Columbus, and Grandmother Durmeyer in Columbus and also Clint's dad."

She also didn't remember major activities in other people's lives, like our son's state championship football game. She started to talk to herself, especially when looking at her pictures and yearbook. She would write notes to herself and others regarding simple, everyday activities to keep track of what she was to do: "put bra in wash," "Tylenol 6:45," "clean sink," "ask Maria about her classes." Being "pre-headachy" and having a backache became reasons for not doing things. She stopped going to church. She could not be counted on to have prepared the evening meal. I would get home from school around 6 p.m., and supper would not be started. She would be watching the news on TV in the kitchen and would get mad if Keith and I talked. She would go downstairs to watch her tapes, usually *A Man Who Loves Bears*, which she still watched two or three times each day. She would come up at 8:30, and be in bed before 9:00. The only things she seemed to react to were animals and infants or toddlers, either live or in pictures. When she entered into conversations she would, in most cases, talk about things that had nothing to do with the subject under discussion. Usually it was something about our guinea pigs or our children when they were young. She had shown no emotion or affection in months, not even a hug or a kiss. She even refused to dress or undress in front of me.

As the time for her October physical approached, the psychologist suggested that I not talk to her physician, Dr. Martenis. He felt that it would be better for the doctor to see her without any preconceived ideas about her condition. If something was physically wrong, he would be able to determine it during the exam. Hence, I did not say anything to Dr. Martenis about her behavior. When I came home from school the day of her physical, I asked how it had gone. She said she had canceled her appointment because she had some back pain, and it would have been too much for her to go. She had had some back problems before this and had been under treatment with Dr. Martenis. But was this just an excuse to not go? I was afraid she would not reschedule her physical. I felt relieved when she called and set up another appointment for the day before Thanksgiving.

Her work with the temporary employment agencies had been fairly regular during the summer and early fall. Then during the fall, if she got to work five minutes before starting time, she would leave five minutes early. This temporary employment continued until the first week in November when the agencies stopped calling her for work.

During the month between doctor appointments, I made a list of the things she did that were different and problematic. I also asked Maria to do the same. I decided not to follow the psychologist's recommendation, and five days before Lou-Ann's appointment, I spent an hour with Dr. Martenis. I gave him both lists and we discussed her behavior.

Since we didn't seem to be making any progress with the psychologist, we stopped seeing him in the middle of November.

Chapter 4

Diagnosis

The phone rang. It was 9:30 in the morning on November 26, 1986, the day before Thanksgiving. Lou-Ann's doctor appointment was scheduled for 8:30. It was Dr. Martenis.

"Clint, I just finished examining Lou-Ann. I think she has a frontal lobe brain tumor."

I knew something was wrong but this?

Dr. Martenis continued: "I've scheduled a CT scan for her on December 11th. I called because I'm not sure that she will remember and be able to tell you about the test. I decided to schedule it myself instead of going first to a neurologist, which would take more time. Lou-Ann is in the front office, just ready to leave. After she left my office she turned off all the lights in each examining room as she walked down the hall."

What does one say or do at a time like this, especially when your wife does not believe there is anything wrong? This couldn't be happening to us! It was one of those moments that a person can mark when life has irrevocably changed, and things will never be the same again. A time when all plans, and hopes, and aspirations evaporate. The future as we dreamed of it fades to nothing. Now the future only goes as far as the results of the next test. But at the same time it also put a new perspective on what had been going on over the past months. There was a possible physical cause for her actions. So it wasn't that she didn't love us anymore, or that she didn't care about us, but that she had lost the ability to show and express that love. From this point on, my life became simple, not easy, but simple. Her well-being became my ultimate priority, everything else was secondary.

Every decision I made from then on I tried to make with the view of how it would affect Lou-Ann — would it make her life easier, more comfortable, or more enjoyable. During the physical she was unable to express any indication of her condition.

"Did anyone suggest that you should have a physical?" asked Dr. Martenis

"No, I just thought that it was time to come in," she replied.

"How is your marriage?"

"It's fine. Clint and I aren't having any problems."

She had written a note to herself so she could tell him she had had some intermittent ringing in her ears, occasional head "twinges" for which she took Tylenol, without much relief, and some recurrent back pain. Dr. Martenis' notes on this visit included the following: "There is certainly a marked change in her personality as I remember her. She does indeed have a flat affect to a degree, but suddenly laughs almost inappropriately. She does talk in a forced, rapid monotone and a seemingly unrestrained fashion. I tried to get at some of the features that her husband mentioned, but she will admit very little. She denies that she has any problem with noises bothering her, and she certainly did not give any indication of lights bothering her eyes when I did a fundiscopic exam [examination with a beam of light]."

What do I say when she walks in the door?

"How did your physical go?" I asked as she entered the kitchen.

"Dr. Martenis has scheduled a CT scan in two weeks," she replied.

She said it without any concern or emotion in her voice, as if she were just relaying some unimportant detail of the weather. The possible severity of the situation did not register with her, but at least she remembered.

Two weeks until her CT scan. Dr. Martenis was reasonably sure a tumor could be the cause of her trouble. It is amazing how quickly one can become prepared for the findings of such a test. My two-week research in the medical library made that conclusion plausible. Given the other possible alternatives, a tumor was one of the better things we could hope for. As part of her studies in the physical therapy program, Maria had taken a course in abnormal psychology during the summer.I read the section on brain tumors from her text, which was followed by a discussion on dementia, and in particular Alzheimer's disease. A box at the top of a page included a short description of Pick's disease. This description jumped out at me because Lou-Ann seemed to exhibit many of the symptoms mentioned.

Pick's disease

Even rarer than Alzheimer's disease. Pick's disease (first described by Arnold Pick of Prague in papers published in 1892) is a degenerative disorder of the nervous system of unknown cause, usually having its onset in persons between 45 and 50. Women are apparently more subject to Pick's disease than men, at a ratio of about three to two. Onset is slow and insidious, involving difficulty in thinking, slight memory defects, easy fatigability, and, often, character changes with a lowering of ethical inhibitions. At first there is a rather circumscribed atrophy of the frontal and temporal lobes; as the atrophy becomes more severe, the mental deterioration becomes progressively greater and includes apathy and disorientation as well as impairment of judgment and other intellectual functions. The diseases usually runs a fatal course within two to seven years." (*Abnormal Psychology and Modern Life*, 7th edition. Coleman, James, James Butcher, Robert Carson. Scott, Foresman, Glenview, IL, 1984, p. 506.)

Lou-Ann was in that age range, she was not thinking as rationally as she had in the past, she was having problems with her memory, and she certainly had changes in her character. Her symptoms seemed to fit this brief description. Could this be the source of her problems?

December 11, the day of the CT scan. By now she was having a hard time sitting still for any length of time so I made sure we arrived just before her appointment. The lab was running behind so we had to wait. The first 15 minutes went fine. We read magazines together. Then she announced she was leaving.

"No, we can't leave. It will only be a few more minutes."

"I don't care, I'm leaving!" she responded and started to get up.

I took hold of her arm and sat her down in the chair.

Two minutes later, "I'm not waiting!" and up she got. "Honey, you can't leave now. Let's go and see how much longer it will be."

A little walk to the receptionist. "How much more time until Lou-Ann is called?"

"You will just have to wait." Not much cooperation and understanding on her part. Back to our seat.

Several more "I'm leaving," and "No, we're staying." I was ready to sit on her to keep her in her seat. By now we were becoming the entertainment of the waiting room.

"Louise-Ann Erb." At last.

We had an appointment with Dr. Martenis to discuss the findings the day after the CT scan. Lou-Ann really did not have any idea why she took the test and what the possible consequences might be.

Dr. Martenis reported, "I have some good news and some bad news. The CT scan showed no tumor, but it did show some atrophy (degeneration of the brain), which is not normal for a woman of your age." Which was the good news, and which was the bad? My hoped-for solution, that they would find a tumor, it would be removed, and by Christmas she would be well on the road to recovery, was destroyed. The atrophy was a condition of dementia, which held a more bleak outlook for her. My emotions plummeted as if they had fallen down a mine shaft. The CT scan gave no real answer so she was scheduled to see a specialist, a neurologist.

Friends were genuinely interested in the results and wanted to be encouraging when they said how good it was that there was no tumor. Their well-intentioned comments had the opposite effect. This would happen many times over the course of the next several years — people genuinely trying to be encouraging, but their remarks being demoralizing. I could accept these comments in the spirit in which they were said, but at other times, people made stupid and insensitive remarks that I could not accept in the same manner.

As Christmas approached, Lou-Ann's behavior became more and more bizarre. She would sit in a dark, or near dark, room and use a flashlight when she moved around. She would put Vaseline on her lips every 10 to 15 minutes. She would sit and chuckle to herself.

Her parents visited before Christmas, and her mother asked her about her actions. She replied, "I know I am irritating my family, but I don't know why." Her comment didn't relate to the reason for her behavior, but that she didn't know what she was doing that irritated us. Lou-Ann would say she was "dis-eased" and frustrated that she did not have a full-time job. She made no decisions regarding Christmas, purchased no presents, wrote no Christmas notes, and did no planning for the meal. She had reached a point where she seemed incapable of making these decisions. She took all statements literally.

"Hold your horses."

"That's silly, I don't have any horses."

Aphasia, the impairment or loss of the facility of using or understanding spoken or written language, is a characteristic of Pick's.

On December 22, Lou-Ann met with Dr. Gomez, a specialist with the University Health Center Associates in Neurology who performed a neurological examination. During the exam she was asked to repeat digits both forwards and backward. She repeated five digits forward, but only three backwards. She dismissed digit repetition as silly, and wouldn't do any more. After being given three items to remember, she was only able to recall one after three minutes of distraction. She was able to copy geometric designs with only one minor error. After three minutes of distraction, she was asked to redraw the copied items, but could only reproduce two. She was able to construct the face of a clock and place the hands to show twenty minutes past seven. She bisected a line, drew a daisy, and on a sketch of a map of the United States identified north and east, as well as the locations of the states of Vermont, Florida, Texas and California. The affectual changes were more drastic than the cognitive deficiencies in the examination. I asked Dr. Gomez if she might have Alzheimer's or Pick's disease, but he was inclined to believe her problem was more psychological in nature. He prescribed additional testing, which included an electroencephalogram (EEG), a neuropsychological evaluation, a full battery of blood tests, and suggested a magnetic resonance imaging (MRI) scan. These tests are given to determine if the dementia is due to treatable causes such as drug toxicity, metallic and organic poisoning, nutritional disorders, or numerous metabolic disorders.

The EEG was administered the next day and the results were completely normal.

December 31, 1986, New Year's Eve — We never did much on New Year's Eve, but Burlington started a First Night celebration a few years before, which we enjoyed. It was a nice way to end the year, milling together downtown with a group of people, but yet by ourselves. We enjoyed doing things by ourselves, just the two of us, now that our kids were older. We didn't get this opportunity very often. It was usually cold so we would bundle up, walk arm in arm, and just enjoy being together. It was like dating again. We would take in some of the activities, usually run into some friends, stop at a restaurant for a warm drink, then head home, and end the year in a most enjoyable fashion.

I bought First Night buttons, and we outlined some plans on which performances we would like to attend. We found a parking spot that was central to where we would be, then headed for the first event — a cello, clarinet, and piano trio playing a variety of classical pieces at the local Congregational Church. Everything went well for the first three or four selections. Then they played a very modern piece, which included some dissonant chords. She immediately got up and walked out. "Where are you going?" I asked.

"I don't like that music. I don't want to listen to it."

We walked around because we still had some time before the next event, a concert of Bach selections on the new pipe organ at the Catholic Church. As we walked, she seemed distant and on edge. This was not our usual relaxed and cozy time together. We arrived at the church early and got good seats near the front. The first piece was Toccata and Fugue in D minor which has a powerful beginning. Within the first few measures, Lou-Ann was out of her seat and up the aisle. I hustled after her. "What's the matter now?"

"It's too loud."

"Do you want to hear anything else, or is our evening over?" I asked.

"I don't want to listen to things that hurt my ears."

So much for a cozy evening together. In a huff, we went to the car and headed home. No enjoyable ending to this evening. Even though I longed for some moments like we had in the past, they could not be resurrected. The past was just that, the past. I didn't know it at that moment, but that intimate part of our life together was also something in the past, not to be experienced again.

By the first part of January she did no housework, claiming that the vacuum made too much noise. She started to collect icicles from outside and put them in the refrigerator with the ice cubes. Sound seemed to bother

her more and more. She tried to get away from all sounds whether it was dogs barking or trucks driving by. No radio or TV could be played on the same floor where she was. She couldn't read or look at her stack of pictures while the TV was on, even if it was in the basement. When I talked to her in a normal tone of voice she sometimes complained, "You're yelling at me. Don't do that. Talk softer."

"Let me show you yelling if you think I AM YELLING AT YOU NOW!"

I knew she was losing the ability to control her actions, yet my patience was growing short. I felt more and more ashamed for not being able to control myself better. Her actions and reactions to things around her were becoming more and more unpredictable. I could no longer count on her behaving in a consistent manner.

She began saying things that made no sense. She was sitting on the sofa reading, with the knife by her side, when I said, "Put the knife away." She replied, "I can't because it will be a waste of electricity." She would make other illogical comments, "Would you be quiet please so that I can wash my hair?" She would ask questions that seemed irrelevant and pointless, "Was David's father at the concert two years ago?" I found the following list of expressions that she had written down. I can only speculate that she was trying to keep track of what she heard, but didn't understand.

Expressions and Words

- on its last legs
- water over the dam
- pinky (5th finger)
- bull's eye
- 6 of one, ½ dozen of another
- thank goodness
- thank heavens
- over the horizon
- waste not, want not
- go over with a fine toothed comb

Every day while our daughter was home on her mid-year break from college, Lou-Ann would beg and plead, in a baby's voice, to see Maria's calendar by the artist Sandra Boynton which consisted of humorous drawings of animals. She had a fantasy about a place where animals could talk, and kept a list of which animals she wanted in her fantasy land.

She saved everything, chewed the same piece of gum all day, saving it on a piece of paper during meals. She used the same piece of dental floss over and over again. After brushing her teeth and rinsing her mouth, she would save the remaining water in her glass to make tea. She grocery shopped once a week, and always ate at Burger King when finished. She often approached strangers with babies to tell them one of her ritualized stories, such as how we chose Maria's name. She also carried a comb with her that she used to scratch her face, scalp and body. She claimed she was nauseous and started to carry around a small wastebasket in case she threw-up, which never happened. She now carried the wastebasket, as well as her phlegm mug, everywhere.

Her neuropsychological examination was held at the hospital on January 16, 1987. This examination was six hours long, given in two sections, with a break for lunch. She brought a paper cup for her phlegm mug, which she spit into during the testing. She would put her fingers in her ears when an ambulance approached, a plane flew overhead, or blocks were moved on a table. The results of the tests did not shed much light on her condition. Her performance on the various tests were in the normal range, e.g., IQ of 99, but were definitely below her precondition level. This time she repeated seven digits forward and five backward. She had mild to moderate impairment of verbal memory, but spatial memory was intact. Her deficits were primarily in the areas of abstract conceptualization and problem solving. The psychologist said given the results, she was surprised that a tumor was not found on the CT scan. Her report also stated, "The lack of widespread involvement strongly argues against a dementia of the Alzheimer's type. . . . The chances that Mrs. Erb's personality change could be attributed to primary psychiatric disease appear remote."

Ten days after the neuropsychological exam, she met with Dr. Pierattini, a psychiatrist, for a psychopharmacology assessment to determine if her symptoms were caused by psychological problems. When he asked why she was there she replied, "I'm irritating my family and I'm not aware of it." She denied that there was a problem. For this visit she did not bring a phlegm cup, but carried a large comb and a jar of Vaseline. Even though she did not know why she was being interviewed by a psychiatrist, she was cooperative during the session. His conclusions were that she did not exhibit any major psychiatric illness, and the evidence pointed toward an organic cause in the frontal lobe of the brain. He supported the recommendation for blood tests, a lumbar puncture (spinal tap), and the magnetic resonance imaging (MRI) scan.

Lou-Ann never liked needles and absolutely refused to have blood drawn for testing. I tried to convince her that she had to go through with it, but to no avail. Dr. Pierattini had no more luck than I when talking to her. Since she was uncooperative in doing this work-up, and because she might be in some danger if all this was caused by some unknown brain disease, he suggested I obtain medical guardianship so she could not stop any of the necessary evaluation. I would have to go to court to get this, and hence would have to obtain the services of a lawyer. This was the start of many legal considerations that I would have to deal with over the next year. It is important to face the legal and financial issues early in the course of the disease.

After three weeks of daily talking, arguing, and pleading, Lou-Ann finally agreed to the blood tests. What seemed to be the key was when I told her it could be done without pain. Dr. Pierattini did the drawing on February 2, after dulling her arm with ice. When we got to his office, she was somewhat hesitant and I was afraid she would put up a lot of resistance. I don't know whether she felt it or not, but he got the blood he needed. The results came back normal. These tests did not give any help in determining a conclusive cause for what was wrong, but they did eliminate some possible conditions.

Unfortunately, there are no definitive diagnostic studies for Alzheimer's or Pick's disease. The clinical diagnosis of probable Alzheimer's or Pick's is accomplished by eliminating other possible causes. Postmortem examination is required for confirmation of the diagnosis.

Dr. Gomez felt it was time for the magnetic resonance imaging scan, MRI, so it was scheduled for February 26. This scan gives a more precise picture of the brain than a CT scan, and we were hoping it would give a conclusive answer to her problems. We had to go to Albany, New York since no one had the equipment in the area. The test consists of having to lie very still in a large magnet, which encircles the area of the body that is being examined. In Lou-Ann's case, this was her head. The amount of room where the person lies is small, and many people who are claustrophobic have great difficulty. Lou-Ann was in the machine up to her chest. A computer image is obtained as the person is being bombarded with radio pulses. It is a painless test, although every 3½ seconds one hears a boom, boom, boom.

It took well over two hours to drive to the laboratory. She had now put herself on a very rigid schedule. We had to stop exactly at noon for lunch. Fortunately, we were driving through a town when the clock struck 12 so we could eat.

We had to wait more than half an hour at the laboratory before they could take her. She was chewing gum and started to become restless as time went on. I had a hard time getting her to throw the gum away when they called her, and she insisted on taking her comb in with her. The test was to be divided into two 15-minute segments. The first was to obtain an overall picture of her brain and this would be followed by a closer look at specific areas. Any movement by the patient would obliterate the results, even if the movement occurred during the last few seconds of the test. Lou-Ann put up some objection to lying down, but I said I would stay with her by the foot of the machine, so she lay down and was slid into place. She tried to itch herself, but I got her to lie still. The test began. Boom! Boom! Boom! She tried to scratch her nose. She lifted her leg to scratch her knee. The technicians were in communication with us through a speaker system, and were saying that she had to be still. I talked to her continually, "Don't move! Don't scratch! Lie still! Keep your leg down!" For me it was one of the longest 15 minutes of my life. For her it must have been hell. The test was stopped after the first part because there was no use in continuing. They didn't think they had any useful results. It turned out they were able to determine that she had a mild enlargement of both lateral ventricles. This meant there was some atrophy of her brain — one of the symptoms that occurs in Alzheimer's and Pick's disease. There was no evidence of any mass. This was just a confirmation of the results of the CT scan. This was going to be the test that would give us the answer. The EEG, CT scan, and blood tests didn't point to any specific cause, but this was supposed to give a detailed picture of the situation and would help determine the course of future therapy. I was extremely frustrated and angry as we left, especially thinking that her movement during the test eliminated any possible results. Lou-Ann was relieved just to be out of the place. Our emotions were going in opposite directions. As we got in the car and started up the interstate to Vermont, Lou-Ann picked up her phlegm mug and began to spit into it. That was the last straw. "Take that phlegm mug and shove it up your ass!" I screamed. In our entire married life, we never talked to each other in that way. What was this disease doing to us? The return trip to Burlington took 30 minutes less than the ride down. After that, whenever anyone would come to our door, the first thing Lou-Ann would say was, "Clint told me to take my phlegm mug and shove it up my ass." I really made an impression on her because this greeting continued for the next few months. My sins followed me, they were now public. Anger was one emotion she could recognize in someone else. Her parents visited after the MRI. I told them to be prepared for an unusual greeting, but I didn't tell them what it was. She didn't disappoint. "Clint told me to . . ." Fortunately, they saw the humor in it. As someone goes through all the ups and downs of dementia, there are a number of events that can be looked upon as extremely sad or very funny. You have to laugh and see the humor in what happens, otherwise the disease will consume you. Much of the time, the humor comes after the fact, and only as you look back upon what happened.

In the meantime, I had contacted a lawyer friend and began the process of obtaining a limited guardianship regarding medical treatment. On February 12, the request was filed in Chittenden Probate Court. Dr. Pierattini filed a report that described Lou-Ann's condition and elaborated on the necessity of this request for guardianship. Part of the process consisted of notifying all interested parties of the guardianship proceedings. I told her family what I was doing and why, but they didn't fully understand how far Lou-Ann had progressed in the disease, and how limited her life had become. Unbeknownst to me, her family had been getting together to discuss what was happening. Her brother called to talk about the guardianship.

"What would you do if the guardianship was not approved?" he asked.

"There's no question that it won't be approved," I responded.

"But what if it isn't?"

"The only thing that could stop it would be if someone stepped in, and presented a strong argument as to why it is not appropriate. And I doubt very much it would be refused even if someone objected. If that did happen, I am out of the picture. Her welfare would be in their hands. It would be their responsibility to take care of her." I knew I could never turn my back on her, but I was getting angry. As the conversation continued he said, "You are taking away her right to make her own decisions."

"You don't understand, she can no longer make decisions. What she has lost, I am giving back to her, standing in for her to make those decisions that she can no longer make. Don't you think I have her welfare in mind? I'm not going to do anything that is not in her best interest." After a two-hour conversation his questions seemed answered. He had a better understanding of her present condition and the reason for having to have the guardianship. She could stop the entire diagnosis process by refusing any more tests. The guardianship would give me authority over all her medical needs, to have tests conducted or to place her in the hospital, even over her objection. The guardianship was not challenged, but it hurt that after 24 years of marriage, my devotion to her would be questioned.

The original hearing was scheduled for April 2, but because of the gravity of the situation, and the necessity of placing her in the hospital for further testing, the court agreed to move it up to March 19. Maria, Tim, our lawyer, and I were at the hearing. The judge asked Maria for her opinion. She told of her concern for her mother and expressed support for this action. The entire hearing lasted less than 15 minutes, at which time limited medical guardianship was granted. Over the years, Lou-Ann and I had talked about wills, but we never acted upon it. On March 4, we went to our lawyer to have them written. They were basic in that both of us left everything to the other if either of us should die. She answered all the questions that were asked in regards to what the wills meant, and we signed them. I was not sure that she really understood, but she had enough right answers to make the documents legal. It had become critical that we get any legal documents taken care of before she would totally lose comprehension of what they were about.

Throughout our marriage she had an ongoing battle with weight. She had put on some extra pounds over the past months, and in the beginning of March she announced she was not going to eat desserts or between meals.

From that point on, she did not touch a dessert or have a snack. As a result, her weight came down over the summer to a point where she weighed only slightly more than she did when we were married. She really looked good.

By March her headache "twinges" had become constant. She often didn't understand simple questions Maria asked about knitting. She made animals noises and faces in front of the mirror. She played the piano more frequently in short time spans during the day. Her notes to herself were becoming more detailed, "Eat chicken and rice for lunch." One night I came home late from a meeting. She had had diarrhea and hadn't made it to the bathroom in time. She was wearing her nightgown, and had a trail of diarrhea on the living room and bathroom rugs. She had just left it, and hadn't attempted to clean it up. It happened the next day, and she left that also. She was eating Velamints, a peppermint mouth freshener, as if they were candy. They contained a small amount of magnesium, but in the amount she was eating, it was as if she were taking Milk of Magnesia. The Velamints were acting as a laxative. She became very angry and belligerent when we took them away from her. It was like taking candy from a small child. She spilled a cup of water on the living room rug while watering a plant. I asked if she was going to clean it up, and she said, "Yes." I watched for five minutes and she made no attempt to clean it. I asked a second time if she was going to clean the rug. She said she had already done so, and then went into the bedroom paying no attention to the rug. A few days later she spilled a glass of water in the bathroom, and didn't do anything to clean that up either. Water was all over the wall and the rug. I asked her why she hadn't cleaned it up, she said, "Never mind." She became more defensive in response to questions, especially questions regarding explanations about her behavior. Her responses were, "Never mind," or, "Oh, be quiet." Everything now had to be done on a strict time schedule. One morning I rolled over and put my head on her shoulder and would not let her up for a few minutes. She said, "Let me up because I'm already six minutes behind my schedule."

Dr. Pierrattini arranged for her admission to the Medical Center Hospital, and on March 31 she was admitted to the psychiatric unit for further evaluation and observation, including a lumbar puncture. She was given both mental and physical exams upon admission. Her mental exam was not significantly different from the past, although she described her mood as "yucky." "Thought processes were significant for repetitive speech with frequent use of the word 'yucky.' The patient uses inappropriate details for descriptive purposes, especially with dates and numbers" (quoted from the hospital report). The physical was completely normal although she refused to have any blood drawn or a breast examination.

"Throughout the patient's hospital course, she continued to exhibit bizarre behavior. She overall was pleasant with frequent smiling, but she was not engageable in conversation. She remained in her room most of the time, keeping the door closed and remaining quite isolated. She continued to be alert and oriented times three [person, place, and time]. She occasionally was found wandering in the hall carrying her cup and wastebasket. There was frequent inappropriate laughter, and she often asked repetitive questions. The patient refused groups. She spent much of her time in her room looking at old family picture albums. She was noted to dwell upon precise details in regard to time and dates, e.g., she would ask for Tylenol exactly every four hours for her 'head twinges.' If the nurse were a minute late, she would be at the nurses' station asking for this medication" (quoted from the hospital discharge summary).

The CT scan was repeated, but she had to be given Valium to sedate her so they could go ahead with the test. They found central and cortical atrophy within the frontal and temporal lobes. This meant there was evidence that the surface and interior of the frontal and temporal lobes of her brain were shrinking. This was a slight change from the first CT scan back in December. It was reported that, "This can be an early form of Pick's disease." Another EEG was attempted, but Lou-Ann did not cooperate, and the test could not be conducted.

An initial attempt was made to perform a lumbar puncture, with the use of Valium for sedation, but she highly resisted that. A lumbar puncture was performed on April 7 under general anesthesia. The results of this procedure proved to be normal. She had some brief vomiting after the anesthetic wore off so she was given an IV to rehydrate her. She was able to walk around the floor of the hospital wing with the IV in her arm since it was on a movable stand. When I visited I asked her why she had the IV. She said she didn't know. A nurse came in to remove the needle from the back of Lou-Ann's hand and immediately she attempted to help the nurse remove the tape. The nurse said, "Wait two seconds." I knew precisely what

Lou-Ann would do. She said, "One-thousand one, one-thousand two," and started to pull at the tape again. Earlier in the week, when Maria visited her between classes, she kept asking when I was going to be coming in. But ten minutes after I arrived she said, "You can go home now." I guess ten minutes of me met her needs or perhaps it was all she had allowed in her schedule. Lou-Ann was discharged from the hospital on April 10, 1987. The diagnosis: "Dementia, most likely Pick's disease."

Maria was living on campus at UVM at the time, so Keith and I were the only ones left at home. We could feel the release of tension in the house while she was gone. We even began to speak to each other in a civil manner. Her ten-day stay in the hospital showed just how much pressure the family was under when she was home. But what would it be like when Lou-Ann returned? The past five months we spent living in two-week increments, as she took test after test The resulting diagnosis — Pick's disease: no known cause, no known cure, two to ten 10 years life expectancy.

How is God's hand in this?

Chapter 5

Coping Alone

April, 1987

    I met with Kathy Slinker, the social worker with the University Health Center Associates in Neurology, after Lou-Ann's discharge from the hospital. This was the beginning of a good friendship. She wanted to talk about our future as we faced living with Pick's disease. The concern was not only for Lou-Ann, but what I also might face as her caregiver. It was at this time I first heard about the Alzheimer's Association and their support groups. The local support group and the Association were to play major roles in our lives over the next six years.

    We talked about many issues, but most memorable was that of support or a possible lack thereof. For many families, one consequence of dementia is abandonment. The support and encouragement expected from others does not materialize. Those most responsible for the care of the patient end up being left by themselves as other family members and friends keep their distance. As we talked, I did not think this would be a major problem for us. After all, we had been very active members of our church, and I was sure that our Christian friends, and others, would be there for us. I could see how, over the course of time, if the disease continued for eight to ten or more years, as is the case for many Alzheimer's patients, the paths of people's lives might lead in other directions. But Lou-Ann was declining at an extremely rapid rate, and I did not think she had more than a year or two to live, so in our case time didn't seem to be an issue. How wrong I was.

I called Janet, Lou-Ann's sister, to discuss the full extent of our plight so she could be prepared to help her parents accept Lou-Ann's terminal condition. I didn't want them, or anyone else, to dispute the diagnosis. I felt I had accepted the facts as well as I could and did not want to be challenged to hold out hope for a misdiagnosis or some possible miracle cure. After talking with Janet, I called the Fillions, Lou-Ann's parents, to update them on her condition. They didn't say much during our conversation.

Lou-Ann had not gone to church since the preceding fall. Going to church by myself was hard because so much of our life centered around our faith in Christ and the work we did together there. During the morning worship service, I told the congregation about Lou-Ann's condition. After the service one woman expressed a deep-felt and sincere concern for Lou-Ann and our family. Her husband followed with his expression of sympathy — with a big smile on his face he said, "Ditto for me."

Two groups of people seemed to find it easy to offer help. There were those who truly wanted to help. They knew I would take them up on their offer and were willing to assist me. The second were those who knew their offer would never be acted upon. It was easy to offer when they knew they would not have to back it up. Was their offer genuine and real? No one would ever know.

Then there was a third group. Those people who, for whatever reason, kept their distance or walked by without even a hello. Some people had legitimate reasons for not being able to help. Then there were other people who couldn't be sure whether I would call or not. Could they take the risk and hope their offer wouldn't come back to haunt them? This disease had already put us in a position where we were shunned by some people.

After church, a young woman came over and gave me a big hug without saying a word. That act meant more than a lot of what others did say. Some people knew that if they weren't sure what to say, it was best to just keep their mouths shut. There were other ways to show one's concern: a hug, a handshake, a card, or a simple, "I'm sorry." I wish more people knew and practiced that.

For the past six years, I had been helping coach the Burlington High School girl's 4x100 relay team. I started when Maria was running, and after she graduated, the coach asked if I would like to stay on to help. The mother of one of the girls on the team, Diane, was in the hospital the same time as Lou-Ann, so I stopped in to see her during one of my visits. That week at practice Diane asked how Lou-Ann was doing. This was when the team found out about her condition. Some of the girls knew Lou-Ann because she came to all of the meets when Maria was running. Gretchen, a senior on the team, came over and gave me a hug. Working with the girls was a good outlet while coping with the whole situation.

As a caregiver for a dementia patient, it is critical to realize that you cannot confront this alone. For a time you may be able to manage, but eventually you will be overwhelmed by the disease. Dementia will destroy two people if the caregiver does not have both physical and emotional assistance. There are generally four major sources of support: family, friends, the institutional church, and the medical community.

In our support group, people found that help from family ranged from full participation in providing care to denial of the illness, which many times resulted in active resistance to appropriate action. Individuals with dementia can, for brief periods of time, mask the extent of their loss of functioning capacity. During short visits they may not appear to be as incapacitated as the caregiver contends.

"There's nothing wrong with Dad except he's a little forgetful. That's to be expected of a person his age."

There are few statements from family members to the caregiver that can be as devastating as those. To the caregiver this is translated as: "Why are you exaggerating his behavior?" "What's wrong with you that you cannot cope with what he does?" "You must be doing something wrong if he behaves the way you claim because he doesn't act that way around me."

Some family members cannot face the loss of their loved one, and physically keep their distance. In our group, there were families in which some children had great difficulty even visiting their ill parent, and hence, stayed away, while other siblings took an active role in their care. When the ill person and family members don't live close to each other, it is difficult to participate directly in their care. Encouragement to the caregiver is still important and can be accomplished through frequent telephone calls or other expressions of support. A day or weekend visit to give respite is a big help to the caregiver, and a great way of showing support. Caregivers need to get away for a while, even if only for a few hours.

Joyce, a person in our support group, moved to Vermont a couple of years ago to take care of her mother who had Alzheimer's. Her mother was reaching the point where she could not be left alone during the day while Joyce was at work. Joyce called her sister, who lived out-of-state, to discuss arranging daytime care. When asked if she thought $7 an hour was appropriate compensation for staying with their mother, the sister replied, "Well, would you do it for that pay?" There was no recognition that Joyce had been providing that care to their mother for more than three years. Joyce related this story with tears in her eyes.

Over the course of time, friendships change. People move, interests change, and that which was the common denominator in a friendship ceases to exist. This is usually a gradual process, unless you are involved in a move. Caregivers have all they can do to meet the responsibilities of caregiving, so that the preservation of friendships often falls more to the other person in the relationship. If the friend is not willing to make the effort to maintain contact, the friendship often dies. The caregiver's life becomes so centered and focused on the person needing care that it is unrealistic to expect the caregiver to put the extra effort into maintaining friendships.

I found that my circle of friends changed very quickly as Lou-Ann progressed into her world of Pick's disease. Many people I had called friends in the past dropped out of my life, while others entered. The common denominator with a number of my new friends tended to be the illness of my wife. Many came from the Alzheimer's Association, others were support people from the medical community.

From my experience, and that of many members of our support group, the institutional church did not respond well. Individuals within the church stepped forward, but as an organization, the church left much to be desired. This was true regardless of whether the church was Jewish, Catholic, Protestant, liberal, conservative, or evangelical, and it did not seem to be a function of the level of involvement of the family in the life of the church.

Segments of the medical community could be very helpful. Social workers and nurses associated with day-care centers and nursing homes proved to be very supportive. But other segments of the medical community were not well equipped to be of assistance in matters of coping with the disease. Many physicians did not understand the day-to-day problems one faced living with dementia because they had not been personally exposed to it. They were knowledgeable, to varying degrees, about the physiological aspects of the disease but not necessarily to the caregiving concerns.

Just as some people will be a disappointment in that they will turn their backs, there will be others, who seemingly come from nowhere, to give support. For me, it was three students who were advisees of mine and who were also in one of my classes. I remained in contact with each of them after they graduated. At the time, Maryellen and Maribeth were sophomores, and Carolyn was a graduate student. I became their advisors in September of the '86-'87 academic year. During that fall semester, Maryellen and Maribeth were in my section of a math course for elementary teachers. All three were members of my class in the spring semester.

It was during this spring semester that most of Lou-Ann's testing was taking place. On a few occasions I had to cancel class because of a conflict with some test of Lou-Ann's, hence my class knew something was happening. Maryellen and Maribeth, seeming to sense my concern and apprehension, would stop by my office whenever they were near, and would ask how Lou-Ann was doing. It gave me a chance to share what was happening and express some of my concerns. They were sensitive in that if I didn't want to talk, they wouldn't press. For some reason, I knew their interest in both Lou-Ann and myself was genuine, and they could be trusted with sharing this personal struggle. At times, after class, they would stop in unannounced and say, "Come, let's go for coffee." It would invariably be at a time when I was down or Lou-Ann was going for another test. I doubt their timing was just coincidence. We wouldn't always talk about Lou-Ann, but their continual contact said they cared.

Carolyn would come to see me for advising, and for help in the math course. She also expressed concern as it became apparent that my family was having some medical problems. As we talked, she shared that she had entered graduate school to have a career to support herself because she was going through a divorce. As the semester progressed, we got to know one another, and were able to give each other encouragement. It meant a lot to be able to give, as well as receive, help and support. She was able to have a deeper understanding than the younger students of some of the difficulties that Lou-Ann, I, and our family were facing since she was older and going through her own personal crisis.

When talking to people about the loneliness that I was experiencing as a result of friends keeping their distance, I frequently heard, "perhaps they don't know what to do." Why do people try to make excuses for others who have turned their backs on us? It was not my fault that they were faced with having to make a decision whether they would or would not be supportive. I didn't chose to be in this circumstance either. Also, why was it that 18- and 19-year-old students, who I'd known for only a brief time, seemed to "know what to do" while my 45- and 50-year-old friends, who had known both Lou-Ann and myself for years, didn't know how to help? I could not accept this as a reason for so-called friends severing their relationship with us in our time of need. They made a decision, either by a conscious act or by putting our plight out of their minds. They were not unaware of their choice.

"How are things going?" became a devastating question. How should I answer? Were people being polite when they asked or did they really want to know? I felt if I answered truthfully, it would sound as if I was looking for sympathy.

While sitting in church, I was struck by the thought that Lou-Ann would probably only be coming to this building one more time. Because of our faith, death was not something to be feared. Throughout our life together, we were always a couple, sharing and participating in the events in each of our lives. Now, as we were beginning to confront the most important event either one of us had ever faced, we would not be able to do it together. She would not have the opportunity to prepare for her own death. This disease would eradicate any possibility of her understanding what was happening. She wouldn't be able to finalize aspects of her life or to say goodbye to those she loved and cherished. I would have to do this for her. In many ways, I would have to live for both of us.

Lou-Ann was a woman of dignity, who had always maintained a proper demeanor. As she lost her ability to sustain these characteristics, it became my responsibility to make sure she was always viewed and treated with dignity and respect. This became a major priority of mine the moment I received that first telephone call from Dr. Martenis. Hence, as she gradually lost the ability to care for her personal needs and appearance, I took them on for her. Over the course of her illness, there was nothing that she had ever done for herself that I did not have to do for her.

We were a couple and would remain a couple until her death. Even as she passed into a state of total helpless, if someone wanted to know me, they would also have to know Lou-Ann—we were one, together. Her existence would be continually affirmed. We would avoid isolation as well as we could. She would be given the opportunity to participate in activities that were appropriate for her abilities. We would accept the level that she was at and delight in the things she did. We would not waste time, energy, and effort wishing for what we would never have again, and likewise, would not spend time bemoaning what the future held. There would be plenty of time after her death to do those things. We would enjoy, as fully as we could, the fullness of the moment, and take pleasure in what we had.

This was also an opportunity for others to share in the last days of Lou-Ann's life, to take satisfaction in knowing her, and be a help to her as she had been a help to them in times past. It was an opportunity to learn more deeply about life and death, physical and spiritual existence, and to sort out what was truly important and lasting in life in a way that did not present itself very often. Individuals who chose not to be a part of our lives at this time lost an opportunity to grow in ways that they might never have again. In this, I was sad for them.

"The word 'care' finds its roots in the Gothic 'Kara' which means lament. The basic meaning of care is: to grieve, to experience sorrow, to cry out with. I am very much struck by this background of the word care because we tend to look at caring as an attitude of the strong toward the weak, of the powerful toward the powerless, of the haves toward the have-nots. And, in fact, we feel quite uncomfortable with an invitation to enter into someone's pain before doing something about it.

"Still, when we honestly ask ourselves which persons in our lives mean the most to us, we often find that it is those who, instead of giving much advice, solutions, or cures, have chosen rather to share our pain and touch our wounds with a gentle and tender hand. The friend who can be silent with us in a moment of despair or confusion, who can stay with us in an hour of grief and bereavement, who can tolerate not-knowing, not-curing, not-healing and face with us the reality of our powerlessness, that is the friend who cares." (From *Out of Solitude* by Henri J. M. Nouwen, Ave Maria Press, Notre Dame, Indiana, 1974, p. 34)

April 17th — Maria turned 20. Our family went to a nice restaurant to celebrate. Lou-Ann remained home because her behavior had become too erratic to chance being out in public for a big occasion like this. After, we came home and had a Ben and Jerry's birthday cake so Lou-Ann could be a part of the festivities. She came out of the bedroom to sing "Happy Birthday," but immediately went back and refused to join us while Maria opened her presents.

April 19 (Easter Sunday) — Lou-Ann's 46th birthday. It was a good day — sunrise service, church breakfast, and a small afternoon birthday party. Lou-Ann stayed involved with the small party for about a half an hour. Besides our family and Peg Devlyn, a friend of Lou-Ann's, I invited two couples, Harry and Susan Alexander, and Roger and Grace Thompson, who had been friends of ours for a number of years. I was hoping to be able to count on these people for the long haul and wanted them to share in our little celebration. Who knew how many more birthday parties we would have? The possibility that each event we celebrated might be the last of its kind always lurked in the back of my mind.

It was time to take her car keys. By now, the only time she drove was when she went grocery shopping. Fortunately, she never became lost while out by herself, but the possibility was becoming greater all the time. Some people put up a lot of resistance when they have to give up driving, since they are losing a certain degree of independence. I knew of situations where the car had to be disabled in order to keep them from driving, but Lou-Ann never reacted that way. When I asked for her keys, she gave them to me without hesitation. Thursday was her day to grocery shop so Thursday mornings became our time when we would do the shopping together. She always ate at Burger King after shopping, so that was also included in our routine.

The first time we went shopping was the Thursday after her birthday. I was not fully prepared for this experience. She shopped entirely by coupons. If she had a coupon, she bought the item, if not, forget it. There was no walking up and down the aisles, selecting items we needed, no waiting for me to find something, just hurry to get each coupon purchase. There was one place in the store she always went even though she had no coupons for a purchase, the pet food aisle. She looked at all the dog and cat food bags even though we never owned a dog or cat. She went there to look at the pictures of the animals on the food bags. Every time we went shopping she had to go to this section to look at the pictures. She also carried her wastebasket with her into the grocery store, as well as Burger King. Thankfully, the phlegm mug stayed in the car. Shopping together was going to take effort. I had to keep reminding myself that this was as good as it would ever be, to enjoy this time together because it would not be long until we could not go out like this.

If that first day of shopping hadn't been draining enough, when we arrived home we discovered that our house had been burglarized. A window in the side door had been smashed, and all our video and stereo equipment had been taken, along with some money. Keith had left for work shortly before we arrived so the thieves did not have much time to break in and take what they did. What a way to initiate this phase of caregiving. It felt as if everything was going wrong in my life. If something bad could happen, it would.

Trying to meet my outside responsibilities as well as Lou-Ann's increasing needs was taking its toll. At school, besides my teaching, writing, and committee work, I was responsible for the development of a new program for people who had already graduated and wanted to become certified to teach. At church I was chairperson of the governing board and, as such, directed the morning worship service each Sunday since we were without a minister at this time. I was also chair of the pulpit committee, which was responsible for the search for a new pastor. All this plus trying to be both a father and mother to our children, who had the usual problems of growing up, but now also had to deal with the decline and imminent death of their mother, was taking every bit of energy I had.

The disease was taking its toll on our children as well. It was harder on Keith than Maria because he was living at home and had to confront Lou-Ann's behavior every day. Maria, on the other hand, was living at school and did not have the day-to-day pressure of interacting with her, and seeing her mother decline. Keith was an average student, but now his work was declining and graduation in June was in jeopardy. This became a very touchy issue between us.

Since he had an interest in cooking, he applied to and was accepted for admission at the New England Culinary Institute. Their school year did not begin until after Thanksgiving, so he would have to figure out what to do for the few months after graduation from high school.

About this time a new nursing home, the Starr Farm Nursing Center, which was less than a half-mile from our house, opened. I went to their open house and it seemed perfect for us — close, a skilled staff, and a new facility. Only the level one, (skilled) wing was opening at this time. The level two (intermediate) wing would not open because they had yet to hire and train personnel to staff that section. This was where I wanted Lou-Ann when the time came to place her in such a facility. I decided that I would do all I could so they would get to know the family, including Lou-Ann, on a personal basis. If she was to be turned down for admission, they would have to say no to our face, to an individual and family with whom they were well acquainted. I planned to visit the home every month to keep our name and face before them.

May, 1987

A couple of weeks after the open house, I visited Starr Farm to introduce myself and tell them about Lou-Ann and my desire to have her placed there. I met with Judy, Starr Farm's social worker, and had Lou-Ann's name added to the list of potential residents. This first meeting went well. Judy seemed like a very supportive person.

Tim called and wanted to have lunch with me. I suspected what was behind this meeting. We started with some small talk, and briefly discussed Lou-Ann. Then he asked the big question, my permission to give Maria a ring. I was very touched by his action. Me a father-in-law? I certainly didn't feel like I fit that description. I didn't ask Lou-Ann's father for her hand. I didn't want to give him a chance to say no. Tim had chosen the ring and in two weeks wanted to surprise her with it. When I was a senior at Clarkson I picked out and surprised Lou-Ann with an engagement ring on her birthday. Déjà vu.

The realization that Lou-Ann would not be able to join in the excitement of the engagement and wedding of her daughter hit hard. This was just the first of many important family events that she would not be able to experience. She would be physically present, but in terms of being able to participate and share in the excitement, she would not be there.

May 13, 1987 — Lou-Ann signed the power of attorney, which gave me the authority to do legal transactions on her behalf. I don't think she had any idea what she was signing. At the time, I thought this was the last legal detail we would have to contend with. I was wrong. There were legal concerns throughout the duration of this whole experience.

She was getting worse. She now talked most of the time and drummed her fingers a lot. She was also becoming more forgetful. Peg stopped by, after not seeing her for two weeks, and noticed the change. A big question I had was, just how fast were things going? The doctors didn't seem to be able to give me any answers, but I felt that if I had an idea of what to expect, I could better prepare for it.

If things were not bad enough, the hot water tank sprang a leak. Fortunately, I found it before it caused any damage to the basement. The plumbers who replaced the tank were very careful to keep the rug dry. The only problem was they used the washing machine drain to empty the remaining water from the tank and forgot to reattach the washer to the drain when they left. That night, Keith did a load of laundry. The washer drain was left hooked over the dryer so when the washing machine went through its cycle, all the water poured through the dryer, and soaked everything on the floor, including the rug. Half of the rug had to be pulled up, and the pad replaced. Things like this happen in every household, but when everyone is living under the pressure of dementia, something like this could be the event that pushes the level of stress beyond that which the caregiver can endure. Life goes on. Life's everyday crises don't stop just because you're living under the pressure of dementia.

At the end of May, Keith, Maria, and I met with Dr. Pierattini to talk about their mother and to try to initiate dialogue to bring out their questions and feelings. I thought a meeting with the psychiatrist would be helpful in answering any medical questions they might have. This meeting didn't prove too fruitful. Maria asked some questions, but Keith was detached and didn't participate. Maria mentioned that Lou-Ann was beginning to play with matches. Dr. Pierattini felt we should seriously think about getting someone to stay with her. It was less than six months since her first doctor's appointment, and she was already reaching the point where she could not be left by herself. Things were moving so fast it was hard to keep pace and accept how far along she was with this disease.

The pulpit committee approved a candidate for pastor of our church. He was to come preach in June and be voted upon by the congregation. It would be good not to have to lead the church services anymore. It had taken a lot of effort that could now be focused on Lou-Ann. I had only so much energy, both physical and emotional, and under circumstances like this I had to be careful how I spent that energy.

June, 1987

Maria came with me when I visited the Starr Farm Nursing Center this month. We dropped in under the pretext that I wanted to show her the facility. I also wanted Judy to meet Maria and begin to get to know the family. Starr Farm's plan was to open the intermediate wing sometime in September and have it filled by December. This time frame didn't seem to fit Lou-Ann's decline in that it would be filled before she needed to be placed, but I would cross that bridge when I came to it.

Lou-Ann's condition was declining rapidly, and I knew that it might not be long before she wouldn't recognize people. I decided to write some of our out-of-town friends to tell them what was happening so if they wanted, they could visit her over the summer. Her condition would come as a surprise because my last contact with them was last year's Christmas letter. In that, I just mentioned she had been to the doctors to determine the source of headaches.

Since the meeting with Dr. Pierattini wasn't successful, I decided to see if family counseling would help. We met with a husband-and-wife counseling team and seemed to have some success at our first session. Their questions were phrased in such a way that they were asking how each of us perceived how other family members felt about what was happening. Some issues came out, and they got Keith to participate. At this time, he didn't seem to be taking an interest in anything that was happening in his life. He couldn't even tell them when he was to graduate.

At times, even before she became ill, Lou-Ann and Keith had some strained relations. Her behavior, since she became ill, seemed to accentuate those feelings, and it was becoming extremely difficult to try to meet both of their needs. I was hoping that one outcome of these counseling sessions would be that we would become better informed about how each of us was

thinking. We could then better help each other cope, and be more understanding of each other's feelings. I left this first session with some hope that
this could be accomplished.

Keith's Graduation

Our relay team had a successful season and qualified for the New
England meet, which was to be held at Boston College. The New England
meet was the day after Keith's graduation so I had to leave for Boston with
the track team right after his party. Lou-Ann's family from Boston, as well
as my mother, Peg, and some of Keith's friends were at the party. I would
be gone for a day and a half.

Before I left, I tried to talk to Lou-Ann's parents about the probability
of needing to place her in a nursing home. I knew it was not a decision as
to whether, but when, Lou-Ann would have to go to a home. Besides the
level of health care she would require, I would not be able to get the financial
help I would need from Medicaid unless she was in a nursing home. I
wanted her parents to begin to face some of the future decisions I would
have to make. They didn't want to hear about nursing homes. Obviously
this would take time for them to accept. Unfortunately, they had heard a
number of negative stories about care at nursing facilities.

While I was gone, the house became a battleground. Keith and Lou-
Ann got into a fight over the loudness of his music and her record playing.
She also walked in on him just as he was getting out of the shower. My
mother got into an argument with Maria about her talking on the phone for
over an hour. When I returned, I then got into an argument with my mother.
Everyone was on edge when we went to church, but things calmed down
some after that.

How could I meet all of Lou-Ann's needs and at the same time deal
with others — friends as well as family — who could not, or would not,
accept what was happening and, as a result, were not only not a source of
support, but in some ways becoming another burden. I did not have the
energy or time to do this. Ownership of problems was an important issue
that needed to be resolved if I was to remain focused on the care of my wife.
I had to go back to the decision I made at the time of Dr. Martenis' first
telephone call. Lou-Ann and her needs would take precedence over everything. Everyone had to be responsible for their own actions and feelings.

This didn't mean I would not help others as I could, but I would not do it to the detriment of Lou-Ann.

Our second family counseling session was not very successful. It was raining, and Keith did not show up. After waiting a few minutes, I called to find out where he was. He said he was not coming because he would get wet, and besides, he had to be at work in one hour. I insisted he come, but when he did he was still mad and mumbled most of the time he talked. I left the office very frustrated. It didn't seem as if this was going to work. Keith was not spending much time at home anymore. His relationship with the family was almost nonexistent.

Medicare, Medicaid, disability, wills, power of attorney, assets, and debts are issues that need to be dealt with when managing the care of another adult. I had to consider the financial obligations we would face when Lou-Ann could no longer be by herself. Financial planning is something that needs to be contemplated as soon as the disease is diagnosed, especially if the financial circumstances are somewhat complicated. We did not have a lot of assets besides our house and automobile. We had a small joint savings account and some stock. As I investigated Medicaid, it became apparent that we would lose her IRA, which amounted to a little over $4000, but that could be applied toward a prepaid funeral. I had applied for Social Security disability, but no decision had yet been made. Dementia was not a condition they always approved for disability. I did not know how much day care would cost, or how I would pay for it if the Social Security disability was denied. The prospect of having to pay for the nursing home was well beyond our means. Often one needs the advice of a lawyer to sort through all the laws and regulations, but not all lawyers are up-to-date with the changing regulations regarding Medicare and Medicaid. So people have to be sure their lawyer can give accurate advice. Alzheimer's support groups are places where one can get information regarding lawyers who are most helpful.

June 26 — Lou-Ann had her first appointment with Dr. Gomez, her neurologist, since being discharged from the hospital. He said she had deteriorated since her last visit. This wasn't news to me. I asked about a possible time frame as she declined, but all he would say is that her regression was "moderately rapid." "Speech is monotonic, delivered with no pauses, except to breathe, prayer-like with no emotional toning, utterances are a series of facts. One example is a narration of her curriculum vitae" (from Dr. Gomez's notes). At the end of the appointment, while I was talking to Dr. Gomez, Lou-Ann walked out to the reception room and was touching a little baby. I had to go and get her because she was making the parents very nervous.

Even though Dr. Gomez wouldn't give me a time frame for her decline, I figured she would probably need 24-hour care by August and would have to be placed in the nursing home next March. I thought that at this rate she would probably die during the winter of '88 or spring '89. I could not get the medical profession to speculate on the course of the disease.

In the elevator on the way to the doctor's office, we met the person Lou-Ann worked for at St. Michael's College. Lou-Ann did not recognize her, even after she introduced herself.

Our next door neighbor had just had a little boy. Lou-Ann went over to see him everyday. After what happened in the doctor's office, I went with her to see what she did. She made a tour through the entire house, counted their older daughter's stuffed animals and other toys, then looked at all the knickknacks in the house. It was great that they let her do this. It was a time of pleasure for her, and who knew how much of that was left in her life. She had started counting anything and everything. Numbers seemed to be something she could remember.

Lou-Ann had been walking in on Keith and Maria, in their bedrooms as well as the bathroom, no matter how much they protested. The bathroom door could be locked from the inside, but it was easily unlocked from the outside. She knew how to unlock the door, and did so even when someone complained. She kept walking in on them, and there was no way to stop her. I put key locks on their rooms, as well as the bathroom, to give them some privacy. She stopped trying to enter after a few unsuccessful attempts.

July, 1987

It was 1:30 a.m. Lou-Ann got out of bed.

"What are you doing? I asked.

"I'm going to take a shower."

"You just took one before you went to bed."

She came back to bed when I showed her the wet towel. This didn't always work, and sometimes she took another shower. Luckily, she would then return to bed, and not try to get dressed until the morning.

Our 25th wedding anniversary party. On Sunday, two days before our actual anniversary, I invited neighbors and friends to an open house to mark the occasion. About 45 people came. It was an opportunity for people to see Lou-Ann in a situation where they did not have to be one-on-one with her. Talking with her would be less awkward for them. It had become obvious that many people were avoiding her when she was outside, so this was a chance for them to realize that she was not someone who needed to be feared. It was also a chance for her to interact with people she knew.

We dressed her for the occasion and she looked nice. As people came she began to tell her stories, turning from one person to another. This went on, without stopping, for about two hours, until she became tired. She had enough. She went to our bedroom, changed into jeans, then went down-stairs and watched her *A Man Who Loved Bears* tape. It was good to see her be able to interact, at her level, with others. People listened and were polite. Since she no longer showed emotion, it was impossible to tell whether she enjoyed the party, but I could not help but think that, to the extent that she could, it was a fun time for her.

July 7 — One does not plan to celebrate their 25th wedding anniversary under these conditions. Lou-Ann claimed she knew it was our anniversary, but it didn't seem to mean much to her. She went downstairs to watch *Sesame Street*. At 4:20 p.m., the exact time we said our vows, I went down to see her.

"Come here and give me a hug. It's exactly 25 years since we said our vows."

"Be quiet, I can't hear the Cookie Monster."

This month's visit to Starr Farm was with Lou-Ann. Her physical appearance was so normal that at first glance no one would ever suspect something was wrong. I took Lou-Ann on a tour of the facility and stopped in to see Judy. Lou-Ann had no reaction to our visit. They didn't know when they would be opening the intermediate wing. Lou-Ann, an attractive person, who looks younger than her 46 years, elicited a certain amount of sympathy when one met her. I didn't like to play on people's sympathy, but in this case getting her into Starr Farm outweighed my ethical concern.

People could not help but react when they met Lou-Ann. Her case brought home the tragedy of Pick's disease, the slow loss of mental capacity of someone in the prime of life.

Now that I was more involved with preparing for the nursing home, I realized that because of the way my will was written, if something happened to me before Lou-Ann died, she would receive all my resources, and they would be used up. The expense of the nursing home would take everything. I knew I should remove her from my will, leave everything to Maria and Keith, but I could not bring myself to do that. As a result, I split everything three ways, leaving her with one-third of my inheritance. Three weeks later, I finally came to the point where I could, and did, remove her completely from my will. Sometimes knowing what the appropriate action should be was not enough to be able to carry it out. Knowing what to do and doing it were two different things. This was only the first of many times that I would be faced with the dilemma of carrying out difficult decisions.

The time was coming when I would have to have someone stay with her during the day. The neighbors across the street had a dog that was tied, and only their family could come near it. Lou-Ann tried to go over and pet the dog. Their daughter heard barking and came outside just in time to put the dog in the garage as Lou-Ann approached.

She seemed to continually be washing her fingertips. If she did anything she had to wash. The problem was if she didn't have water poured for something, she washed them in the toilet. At least it was always flushed.

As a result of the letter to friends, two couples from Syracuse came for a visit. It was nice they took the effort to see her one last time, but one friend could not accept Lou-Ann's condition. She tried to offer a variety of possible causes for Lou-Ann's actions. I was irritated that she argued with me about the diagnosis. Why was it that people who knew basically nothing about the disease suddenly had insights that six months of diagnosis didn't uncover? I knew she was just having a hard time accepting Lou-Ann's condition, but it was as if she was telling me that I hadn't done enough to take care of her. She claimed that "we had to have hope." For me hope didn't rest in wishing she would get well, or that perhaps the doctors had made a misdiagnosis. Hope for me rested in the promises that our faith in Christ held: the promise of the strength to meet the demands that would face us and the promise of the future resurrection of those with faith in the risen

Lord.

Carolyn was taking a summer course and stopped in to see me. We went for a milkshake and talked for more than two hours. Being able to establish a friendship that was mutually supportive was helpful to me. It was nice to be able to share and have a certain degree of intimacy with another person, just being able to talk openly, be yourself, and know you will be accepted without any judgment on the other person's part.

Intimacy with Lou-Ann was perhaps the biggest thing I missed. The mutual sharing of our lives, the everyday happenings that were only of interest because they happened to each other. Coming home and knowing that no matter what happened during the day, I would be unconditionally loved, cherished, and accepted, being able to be open to the point of vulnerability, and knowing that I was safe. Knowing that someone was looking forward to my presence as much as I looked forward to being with her. I guess that was a facet of love. Now my love for her would have to be sufficient for both of us.

Relationships now held the potential to be different than before. We had been married for 25 years. Everyone knew we were faithful to each other and would do nothing to violate the commitment to our marriage. But now I was married, but at the same time, in some ways, not in a married situation. Interactions I had with other women, which before would be in one context, could now have the potential to have a different meaning, both for myself and the other person.

Lou-Ann and I both had personal friends of the opposite sex who were not close friends of the other. This was never a problem because of our commitment to each other, but now, what kind of meaning would be placed on my having dinner with a woman friend? Relations with the opposite sex become more muddled when faced with long-term illness such as dementia. At the same time, caregivers need to have relationships with others to be able to face the trials of the disease. Strength, perseverance, and compassion did not come solely from within, they also came from others who gave encouragement, support, and love.

July 21 — Today Maria, Lorri (Tim's sister), Denise (Maria's maid of honor), and I went shopping for Maria's wedding dress. As she tried on one dress, I leaned over to Lorri and said, "That is the dress she will be married in." After another week of looking at dresses, Maria decided on the one I had mentioned to Lorri. While Maria was trying on dresses, the sales-woman mentioned that it was unusual for fathers to help their daughters choose their wedding dresses. I viewed myself as a stand-in for Lou-Ann.

Tim and Maria were not getting married until July 9, 1988. Since we were not sure what Lou-Ann's condition would be then, I asked whether I could bring her to the store to take some pictures with Maria in her wedding dress. They were more than willing to do that. They had a nice yard with many trees so they suggested we take the pictures there. Maria wore the model dress, and we brought the veil. It was made by Lou-Ann's grand-mother and was worn by Lou-Ann at our wedding. It was one of many things Maria would have at their wedding in honor of her mother. When we took the pictures, Lou-Ann refused to stop chewing her gum and remove her coat. So the pictures have Lou-Ann wearing an orange raincoat and chewing gum while Maria is dressed in her wedding dress. What we had was what we got.

We finally received word that Lou-Ann's Social Security disability claim was approved, effective last December. This was going to be a big help in paying for the day-care services.

Our bedroom had never been painted since we moved into our house. I felt Lou-Ann deserved the right to have at least some time in a nice looking room so I decided to paint it. As I tried to clean the walls and prepare for painting, Lou-Ann stayed by my side, telling her stories, repeating one after another, starting over again when she finished them all. The guinea pigs, how old certain people would be in the year 2000, descriptions of all the apartments where we had lived, the names of Maria's old boyfriends, repeated over and over again. I was ready to scream. I would open the window, she would close it — open, close, open, close, open, close. She couldn't have done a better job annoying me if she had planned the whole thing.

Fortunately for my sanity, my friend Harry Alexander called, and that evening we went to the movies. Afterwards we had a chance to talk, and I was able to vent my frustrations with him.

The next day I painted the room. Once again she went through her stories as she drummed her fingers. On top of that, the windows were now wet with paint. I had to keep them open for ventilation, as well as letting them dry, so they wouldn't stick to the sill. Everytime she closed them she would get paint on her hands. I'd have to wash her hands before she touched anything, then repaint the portion of the window she touched. I'd go back to painting the wall, then she would shut the window again. Patience, patience, patience.

She was unable to set the time on our clock radio, and her speech was becoming more and more limited. She was starting to even have trouble saying some of the words in her stories. Her decline did not seem to be slowing up.

When she cooked, she tended to make the same dish over and over again, usually with, as she called them, "frozen boiled peas." We ate tuna casserole five days in a row. Her repertoire of recipes was now limited to four or five simple dishes. Once she made chicken and rice, and those were the only ingredients she included — no celery, no onion, no spices, no bouillon — just chicken and rice.

We had a small garden next to our garage that had a trap for Japanese beetles. She would go to some of the neighbors, bring their beetle traps back to the house, and empty the bugs into our compost pile. I had to take the traps back because she just left them next to our garage. I could not get her to stop doing this. I just hoped all those bugs were dead by the time she brought them to our yard, otherwise we would have the largest colony of Japanese beetles in New England.

We had been shopping and eating at Burger King every week for more than three months. Every visit was the same. She took the wastebasket with her, but left the phlegm mug in the car. Her order was the same every time. As we were going through the line, an elderly gentleman who worked there filling orders stopped me. "I've noticed you come in every week, and your wife brings along a waste basket. Why does she do that?" he asked.

I didn't want to embarrass him, or make him feel bad for asking, so I tried to respond in a way that would soften the answer.

"That is a good question, and it's okay that you asked. My wife has Alzheimer's disease and does some strange things without any particular reason," I replied.

"I'm sorry," he said.

We continued to eat there for months after that, but I never saw that gentleman again. I never knew what happened to him.

The first time we ate there, I made sure we sat in a corner booth, so she would have a degree of privacy. Everything went fine until she finished her meal. She then opened her purse, pulled out some dental floss, and flossed her teeth while sitting in the booth. What could I do? She was like a child, but a child had the capacity to learn. With a child you could look to the future, and know they would mature and learn that certain behaviors were not socially acceptable. Society also accepted particular behaviors from children because they were children. But Lou-Ann could no longer learn. It did no good to try to correct her with the hope she would learn to stop a particular behavior. Those days were long gone. I just made sure that everytime we ate, she was in a position where she could not be seen by most other customers. Because her appearance was normal, she would not be given the latitude of a child, even though mentally she was a child. Her behavior was not disturbing enough to others to deprive her of the pleasure she received from these times in public. I also enjoyed doing this with her. These few moments of being together, sharing an activity we had done in better times, even if it was only sharing french fries, was so hard to get anymore.

This behavior of flossing in public was normal for her. This was who she was now. We just had to accept her idiosyncrasies. There would come a time when her behavior became too bizarre, but until that time came, we were going out together.

Keith was an asthmatic. We had taken him to a specialist when his allergies first became problematic at the age of three. As he grew, he had to contend with medications and ways to control his allergies. The doctor did not want this to become an issue that would set him apart from others his age. His race already did enough of that. The doctor told him that this was just the way his body worked, and for him this was normal. This was the way he was, and we all had to accept it. I never forgot this description of his situation, and now it was a perfect way to describe Lou-Ann. For her these actions were normal, no matter how much we would like them to be different, they wouldn't change. We had to accept and love her as she was. She had lost a lot, but I was sure she hadn't lost the ability to know when she was loved and accepted.

She also described things as she perceived them, but she no longer had what one could call a "socially acceptable" filter to pass her comments through. She described what she saw, and in almost all cases, she was accurate. One day, while we were waiting for our order to be filled at Burger King, she went up to the man standing next to her, gently poked him in the stomach with her finger and said, "You have a fat tummy." Yes, Burger King was an interesting place to be when we were there. He smiled and said, "Yes, I do." He understood that something was amiss with her, and that was okay with him. He interacted with her in a kind and gentle manner that did not take away any of her dignity. I appreciated that, and it gave me assurance that others, even strangers, could be sensitive to her needs and help her through awkward times.

August, 1987

I had a long talk with Kathy Slinker, the social worker from the Health Center. Lou-Ann was to become a part of a study under the direction of the director of neurology, and Kathy was helping to coordinate this work. I knew Lou-Ann would have wanted to contribute in any way possible. Hopefully her participation would benefit others. I wanted to take advantage of any positive outcomes that could come from our hardship. I knew this would have pleased Lou-Ann. Kathy also gave me the name and telephone number of Audrey Campbell, the person in charge of the Alzheimer's support group, and suggested I call her.

The next day I called Audrey to find the time and place of their next meeting. We talked for more than an hour. I had been struggling with the issue of when to place Lou-Ann at Starr Farm. I knew her best chance of getting a bed was when they were first filling the wing. Once all beds were taken, I didn't think one would become available for quite awhile. The question became, do I put Lou-Ann in the home, say by Christmas, even though she wouldn't have to go until March? In March there might not be a bed available, and she would have to be placed in another home that didn't have all the benefits that Starr Farm held for us. Talking with Audrey helped me sort out all the ramifications. I decided that if the opportunity came for Lou-Ann to go to Starr Farm, I would take it. The benefits far outweighed the few months she would have to be there when she could still be at home.

Earlier in the summer, Keith had been selected for the Vermont-New Hampshire Shrine All-Star football game to be played August 8 at Dartmouth College. The Fillions were coming for the weekend, but decided to stay with Lou-Ann rather than go to the game. That evening after the game, Lou-Ann's mother mentioned that she thought Lou-Ann was getting better. She was looking for things that just did not exist. Do I point out Lou-Ann's decline or not say anything? I kept my mouth shut.

It had been months since Lou-Ann had eaten any snacks or desserts. Lou-Ann's mother made a peach cobbler for our dinner after the Shrine game. As she served dessert, Lou-Ann asked if she could have a piece. After she ate one, she asked for another. This was the beginning of a craving for any and all kinds of food, especially sweets.

The Fillions stayed beyond the weekend so we were able to visit a couple of local nursing homes, including Starr Farm. I asked a neighbor, who was the administrator at one of the homes, if she would talk with Lou-Ann's parents. She was a big help. She was able to answer their questions and give them accurate information. They liked Starr Farm and had a nice visit with Judy. With this visit with the Fillions, Starr Farm had now met the entire family.

Our neighbor no longer let Lou-Ann visit their home. She had gone into their house and tried to pick up their baby boy. They felt bad about having to stop her from coming in but could not take the risk this presented. I didn't blame them.

With school starting in less than a month, I needed to find someone to stay with Lou-Ann during the day. I could see from her decline over the summer that she would no longer be safe by herself. I talked with an organization in Burlington that helped to bring people together who needed home assistance with those who were willing to do that type of work. The following week they gave me the name of a woman who was interested in staying with Lou-Ann. We scheduled a time to get together on the 17th of the month.

In the meantime, I decided to have Starr Farm do a preliminary evaluation of Lou-Ann so I would have a better idea if they would be willing to accept her. Judy and the Director of Nursing, who had never met Lou-Ann, came to our home to see her. After an hour we were told she would not be accepted if she had to be admitted at this time. They said everything was fine, except for a concern about wandering. She was so physically able she could walk off before anyone could get her. I had a hard time accepting their conclusion because she did not have a history of aimless wandering. I was sure they would have some residents who presented more of a wandering problem. If they couldn't handle a person like Lou-Ann, I thought they had problems. I didn't think they were telling me the entire reason, but arguing with them at this time would not be helpful for Lou-Ann's future placement, so I decided to say nothing and just continue to keep in contact. I had Dr. Gomez talk with them to put in a word for her.

Lou-Ann liked to walk but always followed the same route. She left the house, went to our next door neighbor's backyard where there was a swing set for their two little girls, and swung exactly 20 times. She then walked to the next neighbor's house and rang a wind chime in their backyard three times. Around the front of the next house, she read a sign in the driveway, then she was off to the backyard of the next house to count the number of trees. She crossed the street to count the clothespins on the clothesline of that house, and began the loop back home, visiting other yards along the way. This continued for 20 minutes until she returned home. Everyday it was the same, no variation. I wouldn't be surprised if she stepped in the same footprints every time. Every night we went for a long walk around the neighborhood too. I enjoyed these walks because it was a time to be together, when life seemed to take on a certain degree of normalcy.

I opened a checking account in Lou-Ann's name because Probate Court (the guardianship), Social Security, and Medicaid all required an annual accounting of Lou-Ann's finances. The only income she had was from her disability checks. Both of us signed the signature card even though she would never write a check. Any expense attributable to her would come from this account. The canceled·checks would be an official record of what I spent on her behalf.

I had been dyeing her hair for a number of years. On Sunday, before I left for church, I put dye on her hair and she was to wash it out 45 minutes later at 9:15. When I returned at 11:15, she greeted me just as I left her, in her bathrobe, the plastic cape around her neck, and the dye still in her hair. I was afraid the dye might have burned her scalp. I could not get her to wash her hair so I had to force her head under the faucet to get it wet. Once it was wet, she let me finish washing it. Her scalp was okay.

Lloyd, Lou-Ann's brother who was a contractor in Boston, offered Keith a job for the three months before he had to start culinary school. It was going to be good for both of us not to be around each other. We hardly saw each other anymore. He left for Boston the day before he said he was going, without even saying good-bye.

The last time we had gone shopping, Lou-Ann had tried to put cookies and pies in the cart. As we walked by the open candy bins she reached in, took a handful, and ate them. I bought a 24 ounce bottle of chocolate syrup, and in three days she drank the entire bottle. She had begun to eat and drink everything in the kitchen. She ate coconut, sugar, and baking chocolate and drank vanilla, honey, and maple syrup. I had to take everything from the kitchen and lock it in Maria's room. Our cupboards were bare. It was the easiest way to keep her out of the food. Another solution would have been to put child locks on each cabinet door, but removing the food was easier for us.

Her finger drumming had become incessant. She rattled the can of coffee beans, tapped glasses together, and drummed her fingers on anything. She stood in one place and bounced up and down to the beat of music. Half the time, instead of walking, she marched.

I met with the woman who was interested in staying with Lou-Ann. This meeting went well, and we set up a time for her to come to meet Lou-Ann. A couple of days later, I had to call to change the time of her visit, and during the conversation she told me that she wanted to be paid in cash. I could not do that because I needed a record of what I paid for the Probate Court for the guardianship and for Social Security. She said she could not do it unless she received cash. So now, with classes starting in two days, I had no one to stay with Lou-Ann.

Chapter 6

Daycare

The first week of classes started with no one to stay with Lou-Ann. This worried me. As I shared my predicament with a colleague, a work-study student in our office told me of a woman, Lisa, who lived in her apartment house who had done home care. She would see if Lisa would be interested in staying with Lou-Ann.

Thank you God! Lisa, a single mother with an eight-year-old daughter, Mindy, was interested. She visited later in the week, and we finalized the arrangements for her to begin the Tuesday after Labor Day. Lou-Ann would only be by herself for the first week of classes. Lisa didn't have a car so she would have to take the bus to get to our house, and I would drive her home. Mindy would take the bus to our house in the afternoon when she got out of school.

Lou-Ann had started some new behaviors. She ate jam by the spoonful. Since it had to be stored in the refrigerator and I couldn't move it to Maria's room, I wouldn't be able to have any around until she no longer lived with me. The other day she got up at 6 a.m., fixed cereal for her breakfast, then returned to bed. She didn't eat until we got up awhile later.

Her cereal was more than a little soggy.

It was time to cut her fingernails, but she refused to let me do it. Every time we went shopping, I let her get a candy bar. I told her I wouldn't get her a Milky Way until we cut her nails. It worked.

I had to take Lou-Ann to the beauty parlor when she needed her hair cut. We scheduled her appointment for early in the morning so she wouldn't disturb too many customers. She talked incessantly to her hairdresser, Hope. Hope told me that when Lou-Ann still came by herself, she would sit in the hall because she claimed she did not like the music being played in the shop. Hope had to come out and get her when ready. Hope had cut Lou-Ann and Maria's hair for 16 years, ever since we moved to Vermont.

Hope was one of the people who stayed by us throughout the duration of this disease. Once it became necessary to bring Lou-Ann to get her hair cut, Hope refused to accept any compensation for her time. Then when Lou-Ann went into the nursing home, Hope would come on her day off to cut Lou-Ann's hair. She did that right up to Lou-Ann's death. She didn't ask if I would like her to do it, she just said she would be there to cut Lou-Ann's hair. She came every six weeks for the almost five years Lou-Ann was in Starr Farm.

We would reminisce about times past while she was cutting Lou-Ann's hair. I obtained a glimpse of Lou-Ann I never would have known. It was exciting hearing all the stories Hope had about Lou-Ann and Maria. These times of sharing memories, and knowing that Hope cared deeply about our family, was a big comfort to me.

I was going to dye her hair after we returned from her haircut, but she wouldn't let me do it because her "hair was too cold." We ate and then went shopping.

This shopping trip proved that one could be assaulted in a grocery store and noone would intervene. One side of the first aisle was lined with produce, with open bins of candy and other sweets on the opposite side. As soon as we started down the aisle she headed for the candy. I had to physically pull her away as she protested, "Let me go! You're hurting me!" Next to the candy were the baked goods. She tried to open the display and take a doughnut. Sample pieces of doughnuts were by the display, I gave her one so we could move on. She finished it by the time we reached the end of the aisle. She wanted to find a restroom so she could rinse her mouth.

She started to go through the "Employees Only" door of the stockroom to find it. As I went after her, she again protested in a much louder voice, "Let me go! Let me go!" As I restrained her with a bear hug, I started to sing, "Oh let me go, let me go, let me go lover." She sang along with me, and forgot that she had wanted to rinse her mouth. We were quite a sight standing in the middle of the aisle singing together as I held her in a big hug. I had to keep holding on to her as we began shopping again since she tried to go her own way.

I could not put up with trying to chase her through the store, so with only four items, we headed for the under ten items checkout lane. I had to let go of her in order to get my wallet, and pay for our purchases. The moment I let her go, she rushed for the candy. She moved quickly, I gave the cashier a $10 bill, and went running after her. By now, some people were in line behind us so I had to squeeze by their carts to chase her. It was an interesting sight as I ran after her. I caught her just as she rounded the corner and was about to grab some caramels. Back to the line, but this time I blocked her escape by angling the cart in the checkout aisle in front of the cashier, so she was caught between the cart and myself. The cashier gave us the strangest look as she handed me our change, but she didn't say anything. I was sure we were the topic of conversation at many dinner tables that night. This was the last time we went shopping by ourselves.

Lou-Ann seemed to enjoy Lisa's company. Mindy was sick the second day Lisa stayed with Lou-Ann, so Mindy came to the house instead of going to school. During the day, she threw-up on our sofa. Having the two of them here was like having another family move in with us.

Our new minister stopped by to meet Lou-Ann. I had had lunch with him prior to this so we could get to know each other, and so I could apprise him of Lou-Ann's condition. During his visit, she told him that he had a big nose, was going bald, and had a pot belly. He seemed to take it all in stride.

During the summer Janet, Lou-Ann's sister, started to visit once a month to help with Lou-Ann and give me some respite. Her visit this month was the first time she had come since Keith had left for Boston. He traveled to Burlington with her, but didn't contact me. He stayed with some friends. This would not be the only time he returned to Burlington without contacting me. I wrote him every couple of weeks, describing things I thought he would have an interest in, such as last week's football game, and updating him on the condition of his mother. I also wrote about our relationship, his new place in the family since he had graduated, and the expanded responsibility he now had for himself and the family. I had to view him in a new light, let him have more room to make his own decisions. He had to be aware that this was also a two-way street in that he had to accept the responsibility and consequences of his actions.

Lou-Ann couldn't be left alone anymore. Our next door neighbor left his motorcycle sitting on the sidewalk in front of his house, and when Lou-Ann was out for a walk, she tried to sit on it and knocked it over. The bill came to over $750. Fortunately, she didn't hurt herself.

She still counted a lot, but now she was not as consistent as in the past. She had to start 3 or 4 times before she could get going, "1, 2, 3, 1, 2, 3, 4, 1, 2, 3, 1, 2, 3, 4, 5, 6, . . ."

The library in the town where we went to church had a bake sale, and some people from church were helping with the sale. Homemade pies were not a common occurrence in our house anymore, so I decided it would be a nice ride and a chance to get Lou-Ann out among people she knew. For the ten minutes we were there, no one came to say hello to her. A number of people who knew us were there helping with the sale, but for whatever reason, they chose to keep their distance.

I had to restrict her freedom to walk out of the house whenever she wanted since she needed to be watched more closely as she went about her activities. To do that, I installed deadbolt locks to the outside doors. Since she could open them from inside, I had put them on backward, that is, with the key opening inside and latch on the outside. The keys had to be near the doors in case of an emergency, and so other people could come and go as they pleased. The purpose of these locks was to keep Lou-Ann in the house, not others out. This way we could leave her for a moment without the possibility that she could walk out. A burglar would think we were nuts if they came and saw those locks.

Wandering is a major problem with individuals with dementia, and the potential of this happening to her was increasing. A demented person can become lost in their own neighborhood, and some have even traveled great distances from where they started. A friend's wife who had Alzheimer's lost her way when driving alone from her sister's in New Jersey to Burlington. She was missing for more than half a day. It was determined that she went to Buffalo, over 250 miles out of her way, before she got turned around. Somehow, she was found in White River Junction, on the eastern side of Vermont, not on the way between New Jersey and Burlington. Another person who used to perform on Broadway left his home in Burlington and, with a credit card, took a bus to New York City. He was found by the police wandering on Broadway late at night.

Lou-Ann always had a great fear of bees, wasps, or anything that could sting. She had taught fifth grade in an old building with large windows, and each spring wasps would join the class. She had kept a bottle of RAID next to her desk at all times to defend herself. When she sprayed a wasp, I think she drowned it in the spray before the spray itself killed it. One day, while taking her routine walk around the neighborhood, she saw a bee on a flower. Picking it up in her fingers, she killed it so she could "put it in our compost pile." It stung her on her finger, but she did not react. In the past she would have avoided that bee at all costs. She had seemingly lost the capacity to experience fear.

The nursing home required that all arrangements with a funeral home be completed before placement could be made. After talking to people who had used the services of some of the local funeral directors, I decided on one that had a good reputation and was near. I met with the funeral director to discuss the arrangements. I asked Maria if she wanted to come along to help with the decisions, but she declined. She was not having an easy time with these details. I chose the casket and vault. The cemetery plot was my responsibility, so I had to make those arrangements myself. I used Lou-Ann's IRA funds to purchase a prepaid funeral. Since the reason we had to cash in the IRA early was medical, we did not have to pay a penalty. It was good to make these decisions then, without the emotion of her imminent death, because I could be more rational about what I decided. It also allowed time to change my mind regarding some of the choices, if I so desired. I found the funeral home to be most helpful, and not pushy, during this entire process.

All our accounts, checking and savings, along with some stock were in both our names. I had to remove her name from these so she would meet the eligibility requirements for Medicaid. Once she moved to the nursing home, Medicaid considered what was in her name hers, and what was in my name mine. While we lived together, they considered half of everything to be hers. Hence, I could not apply for Medicaid until she was physically in the nursing home. Even though the house was exempt from the financial considerations of Medicaid, I decided to transfer this to my name also.

September 25 — Lou-Ann had her regular appointment with Dr. Gomez, along with a meeting with Dr. Bradley, the head of neurology and the director of the research project she was to be a part of. She had not changed on some of the tests Dr. Gomez administered, like drawing geometric designs, repeating number sequences forward and backward, and counting backward from 100 by seven, but her memory had deteriorated. She could not remember three words she was given or facts, such as who was president before Ronald Reagan. While I was talking to Dr. Gomez, she disappeared. I found her by the first floor elevator, three floors down from the doctor's office.

I brought her back to Dr. Bradley's office, and we waited there to talk about the research project. He wanted to draw blood for his study, but she refused, which didn't surprise me. He outlined his research project and what he was hoping to find. I asked for his prognosis of how long Lou-Ann had left since I had not been able to get anyone else to give me an idea of the length of the progression of the disease. I knew no one could say for sure, but I wanted a professional opinion to add to my own intuition. This kind of information was important to me because it would give a time frame in which to make decisions regarding her welfare. After the usual "each person is different" disclaimer, he said, "If her decline remains as it has been, she definitely does not have two years, and it is probably closer to one." This was similar, even a little longer, than what I had hypothesized.

Maria called after we returned home from the doctors. She was all excited about finding a wedding band she liked for Tim. I had to shift gears and come back to the world of the living, going from contemplating the death of my wife one moment, to sharing the excitement of my daughter in planning for the biggest moment of her life. Throughout the remainder of the course of the disease, I would find myself living in two different worlds, the world of Pick's and the world of normal living. My feelings, sometimes from moment to moment, rose and fell as I moved from the world of the living and the excitement due to the anticipation of Maria's wedding, to the world of dementia and Lou-Ann's impending death. My emotions were yanked back and forth as I tried to exist in both worlds.

Maria wanted to show me the ring, so we took a ride downtown. On the way home, we stopped by the cemetery so she could see the choices for burial of plots. It was hard for her. She didn't say much. Harry Alexander had come to stay with Lou-Ann while we were gone. I could not leave Lou-Ann now without getting someone to stay with her. No longer could I hop into the car for a quick trip, even for the most mundane reason, like getting a carton of milk. The simplest of activities now took a lot of planning.

My monthly visit to Starr Farm was uneventful. The intermediate wing was still closed. The longer they waited, the better for us.

October, 1987

Lou-Ann was having trouble with her sense of time. She was becoming confused as to what day it was. She said that a visit with the Thibaults occurred a few weeks ago, when in fact it was at the beginning of the summer.

The Fillions came for a visit. After picking them up at the bus station, we had to stop at the Grand Union in the local plaza. Her father was to stay in the car with her while we went grocery shopping. After ten minutes, he came into the store saying she had left to come into the Grand Union. I looked all over the store, but couldn't find her. After ten minutes she walked into Grand Union. She had gone to the gift shop, two stores down, and had just looked around. Luckily, she didn't touch anything there.

A few days after the Fillions left, I bought two pieces of carrot cake, my favorite dessert. She put them on two plates, sat them on the table, and didn't pay any attention to them until I went downstairs ten minutes before we were to eat. When she came down to say that dinner was ready, she told me she ate my cake. In fact, she had eaten both pieces.

When she sat at the kitchen table, she repeated a couple of ditties she had made up.

"Jug, bowl, jug, cup, . . ."

"Space, space, no-space, space, . . ."

It took a week to discover the origin of the first little saying. The wallpaper in our kitchen had a pattern of many vases, bottles, jugs, and glasses. She was naming the order of a pattern in the wallpaper, but she was going in a circle, not in a straight line. The second saying took longer to decipher because we couldn't interpret what she meant by the "space" and "no-space." In the design some bottles and jugs had tops. Some had a space between the top and the bottle, hence "space," while for others there was no such space, the "no-space." She was following this pattern in the wall-paper. She was limited in so many ways, yet she could see patterns that the rest of the family had a hard time distinguishing. It was good to see her use her mind, even if it was only in this simple way.

Janet and Richard, her husband, came for the weekend. While we sat around the table, Lou-Ann wanted something and said, "Give it to me!"

I responded, "You have to say the magic word."

"Give it to me!"

"You have to say the magic word. It's a 'p' word."

She thought for a moment and said, "Pimple."

"No, that's not it."

She pondered the idea again then responded, "Pumpkin."

Janet replied, " It's a 'lease' word."

After another moment of thought, Lou-Ann said, "Please."

I wanted to show Janet and Richard the burial plots so the four of us took a ride to the cemetery. As we entered and drove down the lane, Lou-Ann commented, "There's a lot of tombstones here."

Her language continued to deteriorate. When talking, she would become fixated on a word and say it over and over. She often sounded like a stuck record. She couldn't seem to remain focused anymore. She asked what I was going to fix for supper. If I recommended something for her to make, she would say okay. She needed a lot of assistance in preparing the meal.

I was starting to feel so lonesome. Even though we hugged, she felt so far away. It felt like everything I had ever hoped for and wanted in a relationship was being torn from me, and there was no one to turn to for that closeness I longed for.

I made blueberry pancakes for our Sunday breakfast for a couple of months, a little special something for the two of us. We had been using a commercial brand of syrup which came in a plastic bottle instead of Vermont pure maple because it was too expensive. As we finished eating, I noticed there was enough left in the bottom of the bottle for one more breakfast so I didn't have to get anymore until the next week. My back was to Lou-Ann as I started to wash the dishes while she sat at the table.

She said, "We need more syrup."

I started to turn toward her and began to say that we had enough for another week when I realized what had happened. She had drunk what was left in the bottle.

It was like a trigger that set me off. I blew up, took the bottle from her, and threw it across the room. It bounced off the refrigerator, but that did nothing to ease my anger. I picked it up from the floor, grabbed it by the neck, and started to pound the table.

"Why," BANG!

"do you," BANG!

"continue to," BANG!

"do things," BANG!

"like this?" BANG!

On the fourth hit, the end of the bottle broke off, but I was not aware of that. On the fifth swing the remaining syrup came flying out. There I stood with syrup all down the front of me, on the ceiling, wall, floor, table, and stove. Lou-Ann, who was sitting at the table across from me, was fortunate to be out of the line of fire. As a result of my outburst, she started to cry.

I stood there full of embarrassment, ashamed of myself. I knew she couldn't help herself.

Part of my anger was directed at myself because I left the syrup in a place that gave her the opportunity to drink it. I should have realized what she would do. It was my responsibility to keep her from such situations, and I didn't do it.

Having a special time together, like this breakfast, gave a moment of normalcy in our lives. It was as if, for a few moments, we were able to overcome this disease and return to our life as it was before. Lou-Ann's drinking the syrup yanked me back to the painful reality of our situation.

I led her out of the kitchen before she could walk in the syrup and track it on living room the rug. Her memory lasted only for a minute or two, so I knew if she went into the living room she would stop crying because she wouldn't remember what I had just done. In just a couple of minutes, she was off doing something else, completely oblivious to my efforts to clean up the kitchen. It took me 45 minutes to clean up the mess. Our ceiling had never been painted because there was a design in the plaster. As a result, the syrup was immediately absorbed into the plaster when it hit the ceiling. The spots of syrup could not be wiped off. They remained.

Anger is a natural consequence of the disease, and it will show itself in many ways. You have to be able to release that anger, otherwise it can destroy you. There are better ways than the above to dissipate that emotion, but rest assured, anger will be present. A friend of mine, whose husband had Alzheimer's, would take her dog for a walk when she felt over-whelmed. She claimed her dog was in the best shape of its life. I have heard of instances in which the caregiver's anger became focused on the ill person, which could lead to abuse. My experiences have made me more sympa-thetic toward people who have struck out against the ill, but innocent person. There, but for the grace of God, go I.

A couple of nights later when we went to bed she lay down facing me. "Can I lay on your shoulder?" she asked. It had been over a year since she had said she couldn't do that because my heart made too much noise. For more than ten minutes she lay in my arms with her head on my shoulder. The tears trickled down my cheeks as we lay there together. I hadn't known if I would ever experience closeness with her again, and now she was in my arms. It was the most wonderful feeling I had had in a long, long time.

Two weeks after the maple syrup incident, Tim and Maria were to come over for dinner after church. I made a special meal of chicken and rice with all the side dishes. Just as the meat was coming out of the oven, they called to say they would be an hour or so late. We could not delay dinner for them because Lou-Ann could not wait that long.

I began to clean up the dishes after we had finished eating when I saw Lou-Ann reach in the half-filled can of cranberry sauce and eat some of what was left with her fingers. That was supposed to be for Tim and Maria. Again I let my anger get the best of me. I grabbed the can from her, but this time I was going to be smart. I threw the can in the sink so any mess this caused would be readily cleaned up. I led her out of the kitchen because I was still angry with her, and I didn't want to see her face. I was surprised by the little amount of cranberry sauce I had to wipe up as I cleaned the sink. She must have eaten more than I had originally thought.

A half-hour later, Tim and Maria arrived. As Maria walked into the kitchen she said, "What's that on the ceiling?" I looked up and saw the rest of my cranberry sauce, spotted on the ceiling above the sink. Our sink is stainless steel and has a bottom that rounds up to the sides. As the cranberry sauce hit the sink, it must have slid across the bottom and up the sides. I evidently threw it hard enough so that some of it flew all the way to the ceiling. Our ceiling was beginning to take on a unique design. I finally learned my lesson. That was the last time I threw something in anger.

November, 1987

Suddenly Lou-Ann became more affectionate than in the past. Since she was now mentally at about the level of a three-year-old, her actions were also at that level. She wanted to put her arm around me or sit on my lap when we were together on the sofa. She didn't pull away when I went to hold her hand, and when I hugged her, she hugged back. One had to accept and enjoy these actions at the level she could give them. These were not the behaviors of a 46-year-old wife, but those of a 3-year-old child. It was important to take pleasure in what one had at the moment and not look back at what was or ahead at what might be. To do that would be to lose the opportunity of the moment.

She seemed to be more relaxed than in the past. I always thought that deep down, she had known that something was wrong, even though she could never verbally express it. I wondered, if now, even that understanding was gone?

This was the beginning of a three-month period where she became affectionate, when she seemed to enjoy life more than she had in the recent past. I thought of it as an eye of a hurricane. There was a peace and calm surrounded by all this fury, and for a little time, one had a brief reprieve from the destruction. We were in the eye of the hurricane called Pick's disease, and for a little while, we had a relatively tranquil period, but that too would soon pass and be lost.

I was on a state review team for a local college and a meeting there kept me out late one night. I asked the Thompsons to stay with her, but they had to leave at 9 p.m. I got home 10 minutes after they had left. Lou-Ann didn't remember that they had been with her.

In order to go to church every Sunday, I had to arrange for someone to come and spend the morning with her. People had been very helpful when I called, but I was getting tired of always asking. I wished the church would have helped arrange for people to come, since they knew my need to have someone stay so I could attend the Sunday morning worship service. During the week, Lisa had to leave at 5 p.m. so anytime I had something that kept me away from the house after that, I had to get someone to stay with her. I felt like I was begging for help when I asked people to stay with Lou-Ann. Basically, the only time I got out of the house was when I was at school or church. Once a month, Janet visited from Boston, which gave me one Saturday that I could do some things for myself. Those times were so important for my well-being.

This was preregistration time for the next semester at school, which added to my stress level. I was having a harder time dealing with stress than in the past. There was no time to unwind. There were no outside activities that gave me enjoyment. My emotions felt so blunted that things that used to be enjoyable now seemed empty.

Keith was coming home from Boston to start school. I hadn't seen or talked to him since he left in September. He would be home a week before he left for culinary school. When he arrived, he went to his mother and gave her a hug. It was as if he wanted to give some sign of reconciliation. We went to the nursing home so he could see it. He was not enthusiastic about going but seemed to be making an effort to give support. We had a good week together. It was good to have him home.

Lou-Ann had been practicing the piano on a regular basis as she had done her entire life, but she was now having trouble completing her piano pieces as well as her stories, stopping in the middle of both of them. It also took her three or four starts to get into her stories.

People become less inhibited as the disease takes its toll. Lou-Ann had begun to hold her breast and crotch. She had, on occasion, reached over and grabbed the person sitting next to her. One night she did that to Tim. What do you do when your future mother-in-law reaches over and grabs hold of your crotch? Welcome to our family!

A few days later, as I passed the end table in our living room, I saw quite a sight. When she chewed gum, she used only half a stick at a time. I bought her some the last time I went shopping. On the end table were 36 open wrappers, and on each wrapper was a partially chewed piece of gum. She had taken each piece, torn it in half, chewed it, and placed it on its individual wrapper. I guess she wanted her gum broken in before she chewed it for any length of time.

One Sunday morning Cheryl, one of the girls from our youth group, was staying with Lou-Ann. Peg's daughter called the house to let us know Peg had just been rushed to the hospital in serious condition with internal bleeding. Cheryl called her brother at her home to tell him about Peg, and he came to the church to tell their mother. The message got confused by the time it was translated at church. I was told Lou-Ann was having heart trouble. Cheryl's brother and I left right away. When we arrived home, we got everything straightened out.

The next Sunday, I couldn't get anyone to stay with Lou-Ann so I had to pay Lisa to be with her. When we took Lisa and Mindy back to their apartment, I decided to stop at the hospital to visit Peg. Lou-Ann behaved herself while we were there, but she told three people, two of whom were visiting Peg's roommate, they were fat. They didn't say anything to Lou-Ann, so I didn't respond either.

We invited the Thibaults for Thanksgiving. Lou-Ann became very excited with a house full of people. As soon as she sat down at the table, she put food on her plate and began to eat before anyone else was ready.

December, 1987

Lou-Ann now cooked very little. I had to prepare all the meals. The other night she turned off the oven on my macaroni and cheese so when the timer went off it was hardly warm.

Counting continued to be a consistent activity for her. She counted buttons on her dress or a person's shirt, the shelves in our basement, anything that was convenient to count. She counted the street lights on the way back from driving Lisa and Mindy home. There were 346 street lights between where they lived and our house. She had not been getting dressed when she got up. Some days she didn't get dressed until the middle of the afternoon. Once I took her pajamas off, she dressed herself. Our evening walks were becoming shorter. We only got to the next street when she wanted to return. Even the Christmas lights didn't seem to hold an interest for her. We went for a ride to see the lights, but were hardly gone when she wanted to come back home.

Lou-Ann had her doctor's appointment. They wanted a blood sample, and she gave no resistance to having it drawn. He asked for a writing sample, but she wouldn't write much. The appointment got her excited. She was really wound up by the time it was over. Dr. Gomez asked if I wanted medication to calm her. Her excited behavior was unusual, so I told him no.

A woman who was studying language patterns of Pick's patients was present during Lou-Ann's appointment. She asked if she could come to the house to talk more with Lou-Ann for her study. I was glad somebody was taking an interest in the disease and using this opportunity to gather information that might be helpful to someone else. I was becoming frustrated with the medical community because nobody was following her case. Lou-Ann would have been pleased if she could add to the body of knowledge about this disease. The woman who was with us was going to call to set up a time to visit. I never heard from her again.

I had to come home early from school because Lisa had to leave for a doctor's appointment. I decided that Lou-Ann and I could get our Christmas tree after we dropped Lisa off. The weather was lousy. It was snowing and blowing hard. Driving was becoming treacherous.

We stopped at Elm Hill Farm, which sold trees and maple syrup. I decided to get some pure Vermont maple syrup for her Christmas present. I knew that was something she could enjoy. I bought a gallon in a decorative plastic jug that had a screw top and was sealed with foil. I put it in a bag behind the driver's seat in our car so she wouldn't see it. I parked the car so she could see me as I looked for a tree. The trees were lined up on each side of the driveway.

"You stay right here while I look for a tree. You can watch me. I'll be right back." I got out, walked a few feet in front of the car, and waved at her. She sat there watching me. I had only looked at two trees when all of a sudden — HONK, HONK. She started to blow the car horn. I ran back to the car, "Honey, don't blow the horn. I'm not leaving. I'll be right in front of you. I'll come right back as soon as I find a tree." She looked right at me as I said this.

Two or three more trees — HONK, HONK, HONK. Back to the car again. "Please don't blow the horn. I've got to get a tree. I'll stay where you can see me."

A couple of more trees and HONK, HONK, HONK. "Lou-Ann! Don't do that! I can't pick out a tree if you continue to do this. Sit there and don't move!"

I started to look again. If this continued, I was going to forget about a tree. Where was the fun we used to have as we picked out a tree together? I would never see those days again. At least she could still come with me. All of a sudden it dawned on me that I had been looking for five minutes and there was no sound from the car. I looked back and shuddered at what I saw.

She found the jug from the back seat and was sitting there very content, drinking the syrup. She had unscrewed the cap, and without taking off her woolen mittens, stuck her thumb through the foil seal, and was drinking as if her life depended on it. Syrup was running down the sides of her mouth, all over her mittens, and down the front of her jacket. She was a mess. I got so mad I slapped her hands. We left without a Christmas tree.

I got her home, cleaned her up, made supper, did two loads of laundry, changed the guinea pigs, collected and took out the garbage, and swept the kitchen floor. These days were getting me so tired. I got her dressed in her pajamas so she could go to bed. After a few minutes, she got up, stood in her pj's in front of the door, and wanted me to unlock it so she could go outside to see the Christmas lights on the street. The need for a nursing home was getting closer and closer.

Since this could be her last Christmas, or at least the last one where she could interact to some degree, I invited all our family to come. This would be the first time we had both sides of the family together here at one time. It would be a big squeeze because our house was small.

Even though Keith had only been in culinary school for a month, he said he would make Christmas dinner for all of us. He worked hard on a meal of chicken in wine sauce with cream of broccoli soup. He simmered the chicken parts for four hours to make the stock he would use for the meal. Maria was making the dessert. She looked for a bowl in which to mix the frosting for the cake, but they had all been used. She found one in the sink that contained greasy water, so she emptied it and made her frosting. As we got closer to the meal, Keith couldn't find his stock. His stock was the greasy water that Maria had thrown out. He was crushed. He improvised a stock in an hour, but it wasn't the same as what he had previously made. Even with that the meal was delicious.

While we opened our presents, Lou-Ann got up, wandered about, and then returned. She was not as excited as I thought she would be, especially considering the amount of candy she had eaten.

Peg, who had recovered from her crisis of internal bleeding, came over Christmas evening to spend some time with us. She received a call from her son-in-law in Texas that her daughter has just delivered their first child, a little girl. It was an exciting way to cap off a delightful day.

January, 1988

Everything seemed to be going at a relatively steady pace. There hadn't been any major ups or downs, although Lou-Ann was still slipping.

Our love for each other seemed so pure right then. Anything Lou-Ann did for me, or any affection she gave, was simply because she wanted to do it. She could no longer realize a causal relationship between actions. "If I do this for him, he may do that for me" was no longer within her reasoning capacity or thought process. Likewise, I knew that anything I did for her would not result in some form of reciprocal action. I showed my love for her simply because I loved her. Our interactions were not encumbered with possible ulterior motives. Our demonstrations of love were simply that, demonstrations of love.

She seldom looked at pictures anymore. She just walked around the house and lay on the bed. She still played the piano, although all pieces were at one tempo — fast — and she continued to count everything. She also dried the silverware, made coffee, helped to make the bed and change our guinea pigs, and did a wash once in a while. Her last wash was one bra in a full load of water and detergent.

She continued to put her head on my shoulder at night, but now she went on and on with her stories as she lay there. On top of that, she tapped out her stories on my chest as she said them. I couldn't get her to stop, be quiet, and lie still. One night she went on and on and wouldn't leave me alone. Out of desperation, I got up and slept on the sofa. In the morning, she was completely quiet and refused to get up from bed until Lisa arrived. I didn't know if my leaving during the night had anything to do with it. How could something I so longed for become an annoyance?

I had two evening classes every spring semester. This was another time that I would have to impose on people to stay with Lou-Ann. Including church, this meant I would need someone three times a week. It seemed that all I did was ask people to stay with her. How much could a few individuals take? There was not a large number of people left to ask. Peg heard me mention this predicament to Maria so she called and said she would be at the house by 5 p.m. every Tuesday and Wednesday to stay with Lou-Ann after Lisa left. She didn't ask if she could help, she knew my need and said she would be here. This alleviated a big worry. Peg epitomized the slogan of the Alzheimer's Association, "Someone to stand by you."

Mindy came down with the chicken pox so she was at the house all week. Lisa had never had them so I was sure she would get them also. I suggested they move in if she got sick. That would be a lot of fun.

Lou-Ann sat down as I was writing a letter to her parents. I asked her if she wanted to write anything to them. She wrote, "Thanks for helping me get to Columbus, Ohio." I had no idea where that came from. It had been 15 years since we left Columbus when I graduated from Ohio State University. I told her to write about Christmas. She wrote, "Merry Christmas to you!!!!!!!!!" "Tell them about Keith making dinner." She responded by writing, "Keith is making Christmas dinner!!!" "Tell them about the Thibaults coming for Thanksgiving." She wrote, "The Thibaults came for Thanksgiving."

She liked to count the shelves in the basement, and she knew there were 19 of them. She counted, "1, 2, 3, 4, 5, 6, 7, 8, 9, 19." The task of counting to 19 must have taken too long for her because she just skipped the middle numbers and went right to 19.

I couldn't get anyone to stay with her so I could go to our annual church meeting on a Friday night. Keith said he would come home that weekend and stay with his mother just so I could go to the meeting. It was starting to feel like Keith and I were pulling in the same direction. It sure was a big help, and was one less source of concern.

February, 1988

We started the month with chicken pox week. Lisa came down with it on Monday, so Tuesday she and Mindy moved in with us. The electric blanket, the downstairs space heaters, and the TV were on all day. Our electric bill had doubled since Lisa had been taking care of Lou-Ann.

I had a sense Lou-Ann was moving into the next stage. She did not get as excited as she used to and was starting to get names mixed up. Peg said that Lou-Ann called her Lisa a few times.

Sometimes it was hard to realize that this was really happening. There were times when she did something that was so tender and touching. After putting her to bed, she got up to go to the bathroom. When she came out, I took her back to the bedroom and tucked her in bed. She peeked out from under the covers and gave me a big smile. I kissed her on her forehead and asked, "Who am I?"

"You're my lover," she replied. I wasn't sure whether she was being affectionate, or whether she couldn't remember my name.

She received a letter from her mother, I asked her to read it to me. She started and immediately began to laugh. She completed one line, it was difficult to understand what she was saying, and handed me the letter. "Do you want me to read it to you?" I asked.

"Yes."

While holding the letter in both hands, I put one arm around her neck so we could both see it. After one sentence, she ducked under my arm, and went to the living room. When I asked her who she was, she said her name and continued on to mention her teaching job in Mattydale, New York. She stopped, and went into her "jug, bowl, jug" routine.

"Did you work for St. Michael's College?" "No." Wrong.

"Did you work for UVM?" "No." Wrong.

"Did you work at the Champlain Valley Office of Economic Opportunity?" "Yes, and my boss was Don Goff." This was correct.

"Did you work for the Governor's Task Force on Hunger?" "No" Wrong.

The chicken pox finally ended. It had been a long week and a half having everyone around 24 hours a day. It seemed as if I was taking care of two sick children during this time.

Lou-Ann seemed to have almost no level of concentration anymore. She would get up from the table at least a couple of times during dinner. I had to go after her to get her to return and eat.

One morning she came into the kitchen and said, "So you're Clint. We ate together."

While taking Lisa and Mindy back to their apartment one night, I asked Mindy what she did in school that day. She described a game they played where her teacher said a letter of the alphabet, and she had to give a word that began with that letter. I started to play the game with Mindy.

She gave an immediate response to all the letters until we came to J. Silence, until a voice from the passenger's seat said, "Jerk."

On the way home, after dropping Lisa and Mindy off, I played the game with Lou-Ann.

"A" "Apple"

"B" "Banana"

"C" "Cat"

"D" "Dog"

"E" "Elephant"

"F" "Fuck you." She said it in a very matter-of-fact way.

I nearly drove off the road. I had never heard her say those words in the 29 years that I had known her. She didn't say it for shock value, she simply said it because it was the first f-word that came to her mind.

Keith was home at the time, so I tried it again when we got back. She was consistent in that she replied to each letter with the same response. After the "F" response, both Keith and I start laughing and she joined in. She usually laughed when other people did, but I was sure it wasn't for the same reason as everyone else.

The Fillions and Janet came for a weekend visit. Lou-Ann's mother was having a hard time accepting Lou-Ann's decline. Lou-Ann was getting in her way as she was cooking, and I heard her say, "Lou-Ann, don't be so childish!"

March, 1988

Lou-Ann was having a hard time concentrating on a single task. She was now getting up four or five times at every meal.

She had become affectionate to everyone. She wanted to hug and kiss anyone who came in the house.

Lou-Ann really made preparing a meal a challenge. She tried to eat raw rice as I was making chicken and rice. As I trimmed the ends of the asparagus, I tossed them into an empty milk carton so I could put them into our compost pile. She ate them from the carton, but when we sat down for dinner, she left most of her meal.

Maria came home on a Saturday afternoon to bake some goodies. She opened two packages of yeast, mixed them in a cup with a little water, and sat it on the counter. The yeast began to activate as Lou-Ann came in the kitchen. Before we could move, she picked up the tablespoon in the cup which was full of yeast, and licked it clean. After three hours, she got sick and threw up.

It was time to start to address the wedding invitations. It was four months until Tim and Maria's marriage, and I was going to address all the invitations and announcements in calligraphy. It was difficult to realize that Lou-Ann wouldn't be sharing in this event.

Her appointment with Dr. Gomez was on the 25th. There were no surprise findings. He thought the deterioration would become faster as the disease progressed. She became excited in his office again. He asked where Maria and Keith were. She responded that Maria was in college, but Keith "isn't anywhere." She seemed to be at the level of an 18- to 24-month-old child now. She continued to spit in her phlegm mug and put Vaseline on her lips every ten minutes.

I had not contacted the nursing home for a couple of months. I had waited to call until after this appointment in the event there was some development that would help her case. When I called and asked to speak to Judy, the social worker, I heard, "I'm sorry, but Judy doesn't work here anymore."

"Has there been a date set for when you will be opening the intermediate wing?" I asked. "We started to place residents in that wing a month ago." Now what do I do? All my work at making sure they knew us had evaporated. Judy was my main contact and now she was gone. On top of that, they had been accepting residents for the intermediate wing for a month.

"Would you like to talk to Anne Johnson, our new Director of Nursing?" I might as well talk to her so I could begin the process of introducing ourselves to them all over again. "Hi Anne, I'm Clint Erb, and I have an application on file for my wife, Lou-Ann."

It was pretty obvious my name did not trigger any kind of recognition. So I started at the beginning and told her about Lou-Ann. We talked for about 15 minutes, and at the end of the conversation she said she would like to schedule a meeting with Lou-Ann to reevaluate her. As the conversation ended, she came as close as one could to saying that Lou-Ann had a bed without actually saying it. I was completely dumbfounded when I put down the receiver. I was not sure what had just happened.

I finalized the arrangements for our burial plots the last day of the month. They were under a big tree in a city cemetery that overlooked Lake Champlain.

April, 1988

The time for the nursing home seemed to be rapidly approaching. I was starting to have to feed her to get her to eat all her meal. Her memory was also deteriorating. She didn't know what Easter was and hadn't gotten my age correct since my birthday last month. She could not remember if she had eaten or not.

Church was becoming so depressing. Going by myself increased my feeling of loneliness since our belief had been the glue of our marriage. Hardly anyone asked about Lou-Ann anymore, and it had been a long time since she was prayed for during the service when the sick were mentioned. Lately, the only interaction I had with our minister was at the door when he asked, "How is Lou-Ann?" I responded, "okay" because I believed if he really wanted to know, he would visit her at our house. I felt like the person who was beaten and robbed in the parable of the good Samaritan. The priest and religious man walked past him without giving any assistance.

Anne Johnson and a social worker from the managing organization of Starr Farm came to see Lou-Ann. I met them as they walked up the driveway. They were going tell Lou-Ann why they were here. They wanted to be open and truthful with her, which I liked. As they got to the door, Lou-Ann came to see who was visiting. "Honey, this is Anne Johnson from the nursing home. She has come to talk with you."

Lou-Ann reached out with both hands and placed them on Anne's breasts and replied, "Women have breasts and vaginas, and men have penises." What a way to welcome a visitor. This certainly didn't leave much doubt that something was amiss.

The interview went well, and Lou-Ann was accepted as a resident. She would be placed at the end of May, but the exact date remained to be established. It was necessary, and the best thing for both of us, but the realization that we were this close to actually placing her left me numb. Intellectually, I knew this was the right thing to do, now I just had to convince my emotional side.

Since Maria's birthday was two days before Lou-Ann's, the Fillions came to help us celebrate both days. They seemed to take the news of the nursing home without much reaction. Her mother looked pained at first, but after a minute it passed. After her parents left for Boston, Lou-Ann could not remember they had visited nor that she had just had a birthday.

May, 1988

This was the last month we would be living together. It would be a month of preparing for the separation. There was nothing that could be done to help Lou-Ann get ready. I wondered how she would react.

Such a beautiful day. Spring was in the air, the sun was bright and birds were singing. It was such a good day for Lou-Ann. I took down the storm windows and put up the screens. It was so nice out, I left the doors open. Lou-Ann went in and out all day. She walked in the backyard, composted leaves, and counted the slats on the fence and the boards on our picnic table. I washed the car, she wanted to do the spraying. She sprayed the side of the car as I was washing it, getting me wet. If I hadn't known better, I would have thought she was doing it on purpose. As I washed the grill of the car, she got in and tooted the horn. She had a great day outside. I don't think she got out much when Lisa was with her. She recognized the neighbor across the street, but called another woman by her six-year-old daughter's name.

I had to go to the funeral home to finalize the arrangements. They needed to be completed when she entered the nursing home at the end of the month.

I stopped by Starr Farm on the way to school to make the final plans with Anne Johnson. There sure were a number of forms to be filled out. The date was set: Monday, May 30, 10:30 a.m., Memorial Day. As I drove to school, tears started to roll down my cheeks. This was going to be harder than I thought.

The big event for the day was when Lou-Ann walked out of the house when both Lisa and Mindy were preoccupied. She tried to go to the neighbor's dog, which was tied up. Fortunately, the neighbors were outside and got the dog in before she got close. At least these worries would be gone when she was in Starr Farm.

The spring semester at the University of Vermont ended, and Maria moved back home. We needed two cars to bring all her things home. As we unloaded the cars, Lou-Ann got into the passenger's seat of Maria's Toyota and sat there for 15 minutes. She loved to go for rides.

A few days later, as I walked to my car after school, I ran into an acquaintance who I had not seen for a couple of years. She asked how Lou-Ann was doing, so I gave her a quick rundown of her condition. Her response was, "I know just how you feel." I smiled and said nothing, although I really wanted to say, "How dare you make such a self-serving, egotistical statement? I don't even know how I feel so how can you know? You have no idea what it is like to live with someone who is slipping away each day. What makes you think you have the ability to enter my head and heart, and feel what I feel? You don't have the slightest idea of what it takes to get through each day with dementia. If you really think you know how I feel, put it into action, not words. Platitudes don't help, actions do."

"I know just how you feel," is one of the worse things that can be said to anyone going through a traumatic experience like this. Never had anyone made this statement in our support group, and the people there had the best understanding of what each of us was experiencing. But none of us truly knew what the other was experiencing. We could empathize with each other, and try to relate to what was happening, but we would never "know just how you feel."

Maria and I spent the entire day shopping. We looked for a wedding gift for Tim, a going away dress for her, and clothes for Lou-Ann for the nursing home. In a way, I was substituting for Lou-Ann since much of this shopping would normally be done with one's mother.

We bought Lou-Ann a robe, three gowns, one pair of sweatpants, and two tops. She was in bed, taking a rest, when we got home. She got up as soon as she heard we had clothes for her. Stripping down to her bra and panties, she tried them all on in the living room. She wore a sweatshirt and the sweatpants the rest of the day. Maria and I went out again while Peg stayed with her. Peg could not get her to take off these clothes when she went to bed. When Maria and I returned, we got her to put on one of her new gowns. She seemed so sweet and innocent. There was still something very attractive about her. The fact that she would shortly be in the nursing home had me looking at her in a little different light. I could feel some release of tension, just knowing others would soon be looking after her day-to-day needs.

The next morning Lisa washed Lou-Ann's hair. It was still quite wet and messed up. Maria told her to come in the bedroom and shake her head at me. She came in and asked me to shake her hand.

Peg invited us over for dinner with her family. This would be the last time Lou-Ann would have the opportunity to eat out. They knew she might be difficult, and in spite of that, were willing to open their home to us. This was a genuine offer, so I decided to accept it. How much of our immediate future would be spent doing things for the last time?

Lou-Ann wanted to get up from the table all the time, so I sat next to her with my leg over her lap. That kept her seated. She ate much of her meal with her hands. She didn't drink out of her glass, but reached over to Peg's son-in-law's glass and drank from it. She ate from the large salad bowl. She finished the meal on my lap, helping me eat my ice cream. She laughed, giggled, and counted all the while we were there.

One friend from the support group had to sit to the right of her husband when they went anywhere to eat because he reached over and ate off the plate to his right. One had to make allowances to take someone like this out to eat. I knew of others who refused to take their loved one out because "they will embarrass themselves." In many of these cases, the reality of the situation was that the well person was the one who felt embarrassed. Maintaining the dignity of the sick individual is important and should be a major consideration when making the decision as to whether such activities are possible. There does come a time when it is impossible to do such things, but sometimes the person is removed from circulation sooner than necessary.

We invited the Thibaults over for dinner before Lou-Ann went into the nursing home. As we were sitting around the kitchen table before dinner, she got up and went into the bathroom. A few minutes later I saw her out of the corner of my eye entering the kitchen from the living room. The only problem was that she was totally naked. She undressed when she was in the bathroom. Fortunately, I was able to catch her before she came into the kitchen.

A week before Memorial Day, I went to Montpelier to pick up Keith's belongings from school. The culinary school's year consisted of six months of classes followed by six months of co-op work. Keith would be in the kitchen of a nearby summer resort, the Basin Harbor Club, for his work experience. As I drove into Burlington, someone pulled out in front of me. Both cars were totaled, but thankfully, no one was injured. I was sore for a couple of days, but it went away. Lou-Ann would be driven to the nursing home in a new car.

Chapter 7

Acclimating to the Nursing Home

Memorial Day, May 30, 1988

Maria and I packed Lou-Ann's things the night before. I don't think any of us slept very well.

I called to Lou-Ann, "Come honey, we have to go."

She got in the car as if we were going on our usual ride. Tim and Maria were in the back seat. As I glanced at her, she was looking straight ahead, waiting for the car to move with all the innocence of a child.

I put the key in the ignition, but I couldn't turn it. I rested my forehead against the steering wheel. How could I drive her to the nursing home knowing she would never permanently return to her own house? She trusted me like a child trusts his or her parents, and in some ways I felt I was betraying that trust. I wished she could know what we were doing, and understand why we were doing it.

Maria asked, "Do you want me to drive?"

"No, I will take her to the nursing home."

I turned the key, and we backed out of the driveway. Since this would be the last time she would go for a trip in the car, in the immediate future, I drove past the nursing home and we went for a ride before coming back to Starr Farm. We arrived a little before 11 a.m.

I pulled up to the front door, got out, and opened the trunk to get her things. "Do you want to help carry something in?" I asked. She grabbed the large jar of Vaseline then walked in the front door without waiting for the rest of us.

We entered her room, 19B, and began to unpack. It was a double room, but she wouldn't have a roommate because the facility wasn't full. She wanted to leave the room, but I kept her with us. Since this would be her home from now on, why shouldn't she be able to come and go as she pleased? So after 15 minutes, I let her leave. Two minutes later, the door alarms sounded, and everyone rushed to look for her, she had disappeared. I went to our car and there she was, sitting in the passenger's seat, with her seat belt on, ready to leave.

I stayed until she had lunch and left around 1 p.m. She was in unfamiliar territory. It was as if she had been placed on Mars, she knew noone, and the physical environment was completely foreign. There was nothing about her surroundings that was familiar except for a couple of stuffed animals we brought, a lamb and Sammy the skunk. The Director of Nursing felt I should not visit for a week to let Lou-Ann become acclimated to her new surroundings. Big mistake!

We returned home, and Tim and Maria cleaned out the refrigerator. I cleaned our bedroom closet, removed her clothes, then vacuumed and rearranged the bedroom furniture. Late in the afternoon Keith, Maria, Tim, and I went out to eat. Directly after dinner, Maria left for the VA Hospital in White River Junction to begin her first six-week physical therapy affiliation.

Meanwhile, the nursing home staff had their hands full. Lou-Ann walked out the emergency exits and wandered into other resident's rooms. Someone had to be with her at all times "because she tends to sneak out exit doors if not monitored" (nurse's notes). They tried to orient her to the facility, but she could not understand what it was all about. She had to be fed because she could not sit still long enough to eat. She went in other resident's rooms, took food, and became aggressive when the staff tried to take it away from her. She went to bed at 9 p.m., and asked to see me. Later she got up, and tried to go out the side door that was near her room. By 10:30 p.m., she fell asleep and slept through the night.

She was up by 6 a.m., walked into other rooms and out the front door. She walked constantly, at a very fast pace, except for brief two- to three-minute periods of rest, always accompanied by a staff member. They had to take shifts walking with her in order to get the rest of their work done. Dr. Gomez was called to see if he would prescribe something to settle her down. He wouldn't prescribe a sedative without my approval. The doctors were very good about not prescribing any major medication without my authorization throughout her stay at the nursing home. After speaking to me, he prescribed 10 mg of mellaril for a week.

The first thing the next morning, I went to the Medicaid office to turn in the application for benefits.

June, 1988

Every Thursday a person came to play the piano for the sing-along with the residents. It was something they all looked forward to. The first Thursday Lou-Ann was there, that person did not show up. The staff knew she could play so they took her to the piano, she sat down, and proceeded to sight read all the music for the sing-along. She sang with them as she played. The head nurse said it almost brought tears to her eyes because she seemed so happy and enthusiastic. They had a brief glimpse of what she used to be like.

On Sunday, Maria and I visited for the first time. Not seeing her for a week did tricks on my memory. I had already started to forget just how limited she was. Seeing her again, after just one week apart, brought me up short.

When we walked in, she was sitting in a geri-chair. This was a cardiac recliner with a lap tray that acted as a mild restraint since she couldn't get out without help. Her first words to me were, "Let's go now." The halls of the nursing home formed a square that surrounded an outside patio. We went for a walk around and around and around the facility. After, we went to her room and she lay on her bed. I lay down beside her, and we stayed like that for over an hour. She got up, collected some of her things — a comb, Vaseline, books, pictures, hair brush — and left the room with the idea of going home.

Monday, one week after her arrival, she became incontinent for the first time. She was in the geri-chair for longer than usual and didn't say anything to indicate that she had to go or that she was wet. Three days later she became totally incontinent.

That week I was measured for my tux for Tim and Maria's wedding. It was hard to realize that after almost a year of planning, this day was almost here.

She seemed so matter of fact when I came to see her. She knew me, but reacted like I never left. A month ago she would say, "You're home!" when I arrived from school. A number of times during each visit she asked to go home.

If the geri-chair was in the upright position and her feet were on the floor, she would slip out under the lap tray. She went to the front door and asked to go home. She continued to count many things: lights in the hallway, tiles in the ceiling. She sang to herself, chuckled frequently, especially when she was nervous, and did not respond to simple questions such as, "How are you today?" The verbalizations she now made were short and usually requests, "Take me for a walk now," "Give me something to drink."

Her behavior increased in intensity after the one-week prescription for mellaril expired. An additional 30-day dosage was prescribed to keep her more calm. She was eating well, but needed assistance.

I had to get some more sweatpants because she was going through them faster now that she was incontinent. I took her outside for the first time since she arrived 20 days ago. We sat on the porch for vie to ten minutes then went back to her room and lay down together.

I had lunch with our new minister. Part of our conversation centered on my feeling that we had been abandoned. Upon leaving he said people were telling him they would like to help, but just didn't know what to do. "If people are really sincere about wanting to help, I'll give you a specific thing they can do. They can visit and walk Lou-Ann in the nursing home. She only gets out of her geri-chair once, or at most twice, during the day, in addition to when I come. She would enjoy it, and it would sure make me feel better if she was getting more exercise." Whether people asked, and he said anything to them, I would never know, but no one ever came to walk her.

The void in my life seemed to be growing. I wondered just how big it would get? It was becoming a real weight to carry, and one that I longed to lift and fill. The pain of having that emptiness was real, and I didn't know the cure. I longed for an affectionate touch and glance that had some real meaning. What did God have in store for me? Was there anyone in my future? I really wanted to know, now. But I guess I couldn't serve Lou-Ann to the fullest if I knew those answers. What did the future hold for both of us? How long would we live in this state of suspended animation? Only time held the answer.

I bought three more cemetery plots so we could have a small family site. We might not use them, but if we didn't act now, we would lose the chance to have them together. I was required to get corner markers for the plots. I stopped at a local monument dealer, and while talking to the woman there, I discovered she was related to Audrey Campbell, the head of our support group. "Audrey's mother went into the fetal position before she died. Is Lou-Ann in that position yet?" she asked. The insensitivity of some people amazed me.

Two weeks before Tim and Maria's wedding, my mother came to make the wedding cake. Lou-Ann recognized her when she visited.

Lou-Ann had her first doctor's appointment since she had been at Starr Farm. This would be the first time she had left the facility. They dressed her for the trip, and she was ready when I arrived. She was so excited to leave she came down the hall without her shoes.

I took two bed pads for the car in case she wet one, an extra pair of sweats, and an extra diaper. This was how we prepared for a car ride when our children were toddlers. She was dry all the way. She now had her period and continued to put her hand inside her pants. It was hard to keep her from doing this.

While we were in Dr. Gomez's office she said, "I want to go home."

"Where is home?" I asked.

"28 Tudor Lane," she replied. This was the address where she had grown up. She hadn't lived there for more than thirty years.

She loved the ride. It was like old times in that she counted all the way to the doctor's office, but not on the way back. She walked right into the nursing home when we returned.

July, 1988

On our second ride I drove past our house, but she didn't say anything or give any indication that she recognized where she was. The third time out, I drove by slowly and asked, "Who lives here?" "We do," she replied. I asked her a second time, but she started to count. She still counted as we traveled, but not as enthusiastically as before.

July 4 — Today we stopped by the Alexander's for ten minutes. She did not know Susan.

We started to deal with the idiosyncrasies of nursing home living. Her high school yearbook, which she looked at daily, disappeared. They found it in the bookcase along with her jar of Vaseline. I think another resident must have taken them.

One of the aides put polish on her fingernails and toenails. It made her hands look good because it was becoming hard to keep them nice. Since she kept her hands down her sweat pants a lot, she had a tendency to get feces on them, then spread it over herself and anything she happened to have on the lap tray of her geri-chair.

Her piano playing was getting worse. When she first arrived she would play Grieg's Holberg Suite, Op. 40 through twice. Now, most of the time, she didn't even finish one section. She stopped, and I had to say, "Here's where you are, play some more," while pointing to the particular measure of the music. She usually picked it up at that point, and played a little more before stopping again.

Hope came to cut her hair before the wedding. We had an appointment for a haircut on May 31, which had to be canceled since it was the day after she entered Starr Farm. Her hair was beginning to look very shaggy. She didn't recognize Hope.

We celebrated our 26th wedding anniversary on the 7th. We didn't do anything special because of all the preparations for Tim and Maria's wedding.

July 9 — Tim and Maria's wedding day. It was the hottest day of the year, 97°. It had to be well over 100° in the church. It was amazing that no one fainted during the ceremony. I used three handkerchiefs just wiping my forehead, even before the ceremony began. Maria was so nervous at first that she was shaking before we walked down the aisle. I held her tight for the first few steps. We were pulled up short a few feet from the end of the aisle when someone stepped on her train as we went by.

"Who gives this woman to be married to this man?" the minister asked. I responded, "Lou-Ann and I do." I wanted her name mentioned. She couldn't attend so I wanted everyone to be aware that she was as much a part of this event as any of us who were physically present.

The reception was held at the church, immediately after the wedding. We had also planned another reception at the nursing home for family and some close friends, especially those who were not local and had not seen Lou-Ann for a number of years. Tim, Maria, and I traveled from the church to Starr Farm in an air-conditioned limousine. It was rented for an hour, and since the ride was only 20 minutes from the church to the home, we picked up Lou-Ann, and the four of us went for a half-hour ride. It was a nice way to be together, with some privacy, and to cool off in the air-conditioning.

By the time we got back everyone had arrived. The wedding party, still dressed in their finest, walked around the home to greet the residents. Many asked if this was for real. Someone asked if Tim and Maria were actors in a play. The entire nursing home got into the atmosphere of the celebration. We took pictures with Lou-Ann and the family. I brought a special dress for Lou-Ann, and the staff had her all dressed, including make-up and panty hose when we arrived.

One lasting image of the day was when Tim and Maria were ready to leave on their honeymoon. They were saying good-bye while standing on the sidewalk next to the circular driveway. Lou-Ann started to wander around the driveway, looking at the flowers and bushes along the way. She was in her own world and did not have a clue as to what was happening. One of Maria's friends, who was a nurse, was walking with her. She had no comprehension of the significance of this moment. Instead of standing arm in arm, as one, watching our daughter take the biggest step of her life, I was by myself as she wandered aimlessly about by herself. For the first time in a while I was feeling weak, lonely, and vulnerable. The realization of the loss of the ability to share came crashing down on me. I was standing in a group of 30 friends and family, yet I've never felt so alone.

It was a relief to have the wedding over. I didn't realize how draining the whole event was. But living by myself gave me some quiet I hadn't had in a long time. My days were still very full since I was teaching summer school.

Tim and Maria knew a family who was being transferred to Florida for nine months by IBM, and needed someone to house sit while they were gone. The timing couldn't have been better because they left for Florida one week after the wedding, while Tim and Maria were gone, and would be returning one week after school finished. The Thibaults and I moved their things into the house so everything would be ready when they returned from their honeymoon.

During this time, Lou-Ann would sing a few ditties from *Sesame Street* in a high squeaky voice, "In and out, in and out, first they go in, and then they come out." When a staff member walked by while she was in the geri-chair, she stuck out her leg to nudge them and asked for a hug. She usually sat at the nurse's station by the door to a little kitchen. She asked for juice whenever someone entered the kitchen. It was a very active location so she had a lot to look at. The nurses believed she had become less verbal than when she first entered a month and a half earlier. She had started to gain weight and was up to 160 pounds. This was probably since she was eating well and lacked exercise because she was in the geri-chair.

Sixteen laps to the mile was what I counted as we walked around the halls of Starr Farm. It was good exercise for me as well as Lou-Ann. It usually took three to four minutes to walk once around. One day a nurse, new to the facility, stopped us as we were walking and asked, "May I help you? Who are you looking for?" She didn't say much when I told her Lou-Ann was a resident.

There was an outdoor Mozart concert series every summer in the Burlington area. Lou-Ann and I always went to three or four concerts every year. I bought tickets for three concerts. I was going with Carolyn, Peg and her family, and Harry and Susan Alexander. Maria started to tease me about going on a date as I was getting ready to go with Carolyn. This disease caused all kinds of role reversals. When Maria was younger and starting to go out with a few friends, I would tease her about being on a date. She would claim that it wasn't a date, she was just going out with a friend. "We're not a 'thing' Dad," she would exclaim. A "thing" was a couple who were going together. Now it was her turn to get back at me. "We're not a 'thing' Maria."

July 21, Friday — I brought Lou-Ann home for the first time since she went into Starr Farm. When I pulled into the driveway, I asked, "Who lives here?" "We do," she replied. She walked to the bedroom and climbed in bed. She stayed there for almost half an hour before she got up and went to the bathroom. This was something she never did in the nursing home. She saw a piece of gum on my dresser, took half a stick, and chewed it until dinner.

The next day at Starr Farm when we went for a walk outside, I let her go unrestricted. She headed down the driveway and walked the quarter mile to our house. She went right to the bedroom and lay down. When we were about to leave, she saw an advertising insert from the paper, sat down, and looked through it.

July 30, Two Months Since Entering Starr Farm — The summer had been hot. Keith came home to spend the night in the basement because his room at Basin Harbor was so hot. Since he would be coming and going, I left the side door unlocked. I left Lou-Ann around 9:30 p.m. as she was about to go to bed. Around midnight I began to get ready for bed. Since Keith was home, I had the bedroom door partially closed for some privacy. As I got undressed, out of the corner of my eye I saw the door begin to swing open. I started to turn to tell Keith I would appreciate it if he would knock before entering, when I heard a very familiar voice say, "Let's go to bed now." It was Lou-Ann. It was as if she had been sitting in the living room and just came in to go to bed. She was dressed in a hospital gown and had on a pair of Attends (adult diapers) and her docksides. She had gotten out of bed, put on her docksides and walked out of the door. She went by the nurse's station when the nurses and aides were in other resident's rooms doing rounds. Luckily, I had left the outside door unlocked otherwise she wouldn't have been able to enter the house. She stood there with a little smile on her face. How I wished she could tell me what was in her mind, what she was thinking.

I took her back to Starr Farm. We had to buzz the intercom to get someone to open the locked door. Their mouths fell open when they saw us standing there. She went right to her room, and I tucked her in bed. A few minutes later she was up so we walked around the corridors, then watched some television together. After half an hour we took one more lap around the facility, she went to her room, and around 1:30 a.m., I tucked her in bed again. The nurses were very apologetic over the whole incident, but I viewed it as Lou-Ann's victory. She still had a mind of her own.

The Mozart concert helped me relax. A picnic, a warm summer night, and good music — that was hard to beat. Harry, Susan, and I had tickets to the concert at the South Porch at Shelburne Farms. The swallows swooped low as the sun went down and a few bats flew overhead as the stars came out. Lying on the grass, listening to the music on a moonlit night also brought back memories of times past with Lou-Ann. After the concert ended, as we parted, Harry said, "I'll call you next week." For some unknown reason he didn't call. I never heard from them again. I remembered my thoughts in response to Kathy Slinker's comments when Lou-Ann left the hospital, "Abandonment, it will never happen to us."

Two years later I called, Harry apologized for not staying in touch, and we set a time to get together. The next day there was a message on my answering machine saying he couldn't make it but would call to arrange another time. This was the last time we ever spoke to each other.

August, 1988

I had my first run-in with the staff at the nursing home. When I arrived around 3:45 p.m., Lou-Ann, as usual, was in the geri-chair. As I leaned over to give her a hug, she dug her fingers into my shoulder when she reached up to hug me. I released the chair and removed the lap tray so she would be in an upright position. She immediately began to repeatedly slap the top of each knee while counting fast, "1, 2, 3, 4, 1, 2, 3, 4, 1, 2, 3, 4." The chair had malfunctioned when it was pulled back to the reclining position and her knees were jammed against the bottom of the tray. Both knees had deep red spots the size of a quarter. She had obviously lost the ability to verbalize pain.

I got her up to walk to her room, but after a few steps she started to collapse in my arms. The heat of the day and the pain in her legs caused her to faint. They checked her pulse — 150, a little while later, it came down to 112.

I picked up the wedding pictures from the photographer and brought them to show Lou-Ann. When I asked her to name the people in the pictures, she named individuals who were in our wedding party. She couldn't recognize that these were from Tim and Maria's wedding, not ours.

She identified one of the ushers as my cousin, who was an usher at our wedding, whose name hadn't come up in conversation in years. She also said Tim and Maria were engaged, not married.

She didn't say much to anyone anymore, including me. Dr. Gomez said she would probably lose the ability to talk. It seemed so improbable that someone who was so articulate could lose something that was so much a part of her.

Since she had been in the nursing home, I tried to do activities with her to keep her active and hopefully give her some pleasure. Old Maid was one game she enjoyed, but we had to make our own variation so she could play. She could deal the cards, but had forgotten how to hold them so she lay them on her lap tray in front of her, face up. I didn't match any of the cards I was dealt and held them all in my hand. She drew one card at a time, and checked to see if she had the match in front of her. If there was no match, she placed the card face up with the others and drew another. She played the entire deck. Most of the time she couldn't remember where in front of her she put a card, even if she had just laid it down the play before.

I brought her home Friday with the idea of keeping her until dinner. She climbed in and out of bed a few times, lay on the sofa, then we took a little walk outside. When we came back, we went downstairs to look at the video of the wedding. She saw about half of it, didn't always pay attention, but didn't keep getting up. She then wanted to go for a ride and back to Starr Farm for dinner.

Having her home was not always a delightful experience. Tim and Maria picked her up from Starr Farm after church and brought her home. We changed her once while they were here because she was wet. Just after they left, she had a bowel movement. Her sweat pants got messed as I took them off. I cleaned them as best I could, but didn't have any paper towels upstairs to wash her off. I told her to sit on the toilet while I went for some. I ran downstairs, but by the time I got back, she had climbed into bed. So much for the clean sheets I put on the day before. I washed and dried her sweat pants so she could go back to the nursing home.

There were times when I was aware a significant event had happened, I didn't have to think in retrospect about the importance of the incident. On August 22, such an event happened. She wanted to lie down, and as she was standing by her bed, I asked for a hug. She hugged me then, said, "I love you very much." It was the first time she had said something like that on her own volition in a long time. Something told me I would never hear her say those words on her own again. I never did. This was the last time she would tell me that she loved me. That moment has been burned in my memory as if it happened yesterday.

September, 1988

September meant the start of school, and with it the question of how to balance the responsibilities of my work with Lou-Ann's needs. Since she was taking more time to eat, I wanted to help feed her. The aides couldn't take the time I could because they had so many other residents who needed their assistance. I would try to be to Starr Farm by 5 o'clock each evening. No one at school questioned the fact I would not be available after 4:30 p.m. Nursing home at 5-5:30, stay until 9-9:30, home to make dinner around 10, a time to unwind, then to bed, alarm set for 6:30 a.m. I found it difficult to get to bed before 1 a.m. It wasn't that I was not tired, but for some reason I found it hard to call an end to the day. The possibility of getting any school work accomplished after I left my office was out of the question. I needed to be especially efficient when I was at work, and for me that was no small task. Except for some slight variations in time, this would be my daily schedule for the next 4½ years.

Some people encouraged me not to spend every day with Lou-Ann. Each individual has to make their own decision regarding how often they visit, but for me, I wanted to be with her. It was not a duty, but a pleasure. Starr Farm was like our second home, this was where I felt the most relaxed, the most complete. I had the huge benefit of having the nursing home within a few minutes of our house. Others have situations, due to family responsibilities or location, that make it impossible for them to visit as often.

I firmly believe it is very important for the well-being of the resident that the caregiver have a visible presence at the nursing home. In my experience, when families cared, the staff seemed to take on an additional level of interest in that person. Families got to know the staff, and vice versa, on a personal basis. The staff became more familiar with what made the resident more comfortable and how the family would like things done. Families were able to maintain more control over the care of their loved one. They could be on top of what was developing, and what changes might be necessary in the management of the resident's care.

On the other hand, one has to realize that a nursing home is an institution. Each individual does not have a private nurse so there are times when things don't get accomplished in the exact manner one would like. I saw families become so demanding that they became a detriment, rather than a help. It is important that one's presence add to the atmosphere of the home, rather than detract from it. Family members need to be firm in how they want their loved one looked after, but they also need to be reasonable in their demands. I never came across a person working at Starr Farm who was not concerned about the welfare of the people they were responsible for, but some families didn't seem to realize one catches more flies with honey than vinegar.

There were some great people at Starr Farm. The residents, their families, and the staff took on the role of an extended family. The same families kept crossing paths since many people tended to come at about the same time for each visit. For the most part, families looked after one another and took an interest in how each resident was doing. There were some residents who were there because of some physical problem, who had their full mental capacities, who took a liking to Lou-Ann, and looked out for her welfare. For this I was glad. Since Lou-Ann no longer had the capacity to express her needs, these individuals became her advocates with the staff. It became a positive relationship for everyone, Lou-Ann was looked after, and they had another purpose in life. I let them know how much I appreciated their interest. I also knew I would get another opinion of how Lou-Ann's day had gone.

As I entered the door each night, I ran into residents who were walking the halls. I tried to learn their names so I could give them a personal hello as we passed. As I walked Lou-Ann, we passed others in the corridors who weren't as mobile. For those who had few or no visitors, it was a time to know someone cared. For a brief moment their existence was confirmed. I felt I was giving something back, adding my contribution to making Starr Farm a better place to be.

It amazed me how residents could be a comfort and support. Bell, a wonderful older woman with Alzheimer's came over to say hello to Lou-Ann as she sat in her geri-chair. Lou-Ann had been reaching out to people who passed by so when Bell got in arm's length of Lou-Ann, she reached out and placed her hand on Bell's breast. Poor Bell was mortified.

"Don't do that!" she exclaimed.

I apologized, "I'm sorry she did that to you. Lou-Ann has a mental illness that makes her do such things. She would never have done that if she were well."

"How sad. It's too bad she has to be that way," she replied.

Her indignation turned immediately to compassion. I was touched that a person, who herself was demented, could understand the sadness in Lou-Ann's condition and relate to it. After that, Bell always had a special place in my heart. As Bell continued to decline over the years, I never once heard her say anything negative about any person. Nursing homes are filled with very special people.

Lou-Ann had quieted down the past few weeks, so I asked Dr. Gomez to take her off of mellaril. I didn't want her on medication that was not necessary.

She had been given Dixie cups to act as her phlegm mug, but she chewed and swallowed the edge. She was now starting to spit on the floor. How could we stop that?

I brought in a small toy football to see if she would play catch. I took the lap tray off her geri-chair so she could move. She sat in one corner and threw the ball to me across the nurse's station. She did well and sometimes even caught it with one hand. This was a nightly activity. Occasionally she threw it to a nurse or an aide as they walked by. We both enjoyed this. She never had much interest in playing catch before she was ill.

There we were, spending three or so hours every night, doing things together with no outside distractions. What would happen to marriages, ours included, if couples would take that amount of time to be and do things together?

I brought Lou-Ann home to have dinner with Tim and Maria. This was the first meal she had eaten home since she entered Starr Farm. I let her get up and down as she pleased. After dinner, the four of us sat on the sofa and looked at Tim and Maria's wedding pictures. She went outside a couple of times, the first to just walk around the house. She picked up some leaves and put them into our compost pile.

I got a call from the nursing home asking my permission to move a specific resident in with Lou-Ann. Winn, this woman's present roommate, could not stand her outbursts and yelling. Lou-Ann didn't need a roommate like that. I suggested Lou-Ann and this woman interchange rooms. It wouldn't be long until the wing was full, and Lou-Ann would have a roommate, so this way I had some choice as to whom she was with. Winn was a quiet and personable individual with a nice family. She had running shoes and jogged around the facility every day. She also had dementia but could communicate. Lou-Ann moved up the hall to room 15B. She still had the window side so she could look out when she was lying down.

I had a confrontation with our minister at Deacon's meeting. I disagreed with something he had included in the bulletin, and one thing led to another. I lost my cool, and let everyone know how I felt about the church's lack of support. He called me at home after the meeting, which helped some, but people still didn't get it. I was told, "I'm praying for you." What are they praying for? They didn't know our specific needs. Their prayers must have been like those of a child when they pray, "God bless the missionaries," general with no direction. They had done nothing to find out what our needs were, but if they did that, they might feel they would have an obligation to do something about them.

One thing that hurt in all this was that Lou-Ann had always been one to try to minister to others in their need, but now that she had needs, very few people were there for her. She called one friend every week for over a year, after this friend's husband died, but that person had only called once since Lou-Ann became ill.

My outburst at the meeting had some effect. Four days later, the church sent flowers, one couple had me over for dinner, Lou-Ann received cards from two other deacons, and was even prayed for during the next worship service. The show of sympathy was encouraging, but short-lived.

Apple picking is a big activity in the fall in Vermont. I picked Lou-Ann up at 2:30 p.m. Tim and Maria came with us. The weather was perfect and we had a great time. To get back to the orchard we rode a wagon, pulled by a tractor. She couldn't figure out how to get on the wagon so I had to lift her up. She sat on the edge of the wagon with her legs dangling off the side, and swung them back and forth. She didn't know how to get off when we stopped so I gave her a big hug and lifted her down. She wandered throughout the orchard as we picked apples. I gave her a Macintosh, she took one bite, then threw it away.

We had dinner at home and didn't get back to Starr Farm until 8:30 p.m. It was nice to have times like these. It was important for her to get out and have some freedom to roam.

October, 1988

Two aides planned to conduct an in-service session on dementia for the staff at Starr Farm. They asked if I could help them with it. I had learned so much over the course of the last few years that could be of some help to others. They talked about the basic care of the patient once they were in the nursing home while I shared what it was like to care for such a person at home. Our support group had shown me how important it was to share these experiences. Some good could come from all this.

I had been concerned about Lou-Ann's lack of physical activity during the day. The problem was that she was quickly out the door when they left her on her own. To give her more mobility, but also keep her within bounds, they put her in a wheelchair. She was restrained around her waist to the extent that she could not get out of the chair. She seemed to be happier since she could get around more, but it was hard to assess because she couldn't verbally express her feelings. In addition, she had lost the ability to show any facial expression, no smiles, no frowns, just a blank appearance.

Keith's co-op experience ended, and he decided not to go back for his second and last year of culinary school. The chef at the Basin Harbor Club worked at a resort in Florida for the winter and asked Keith if he would like to go down and work for him. Keith stayed here, but at first did little to find work. His lack of direction started to get on my nerves.

I had been active with the support group so when a place opened on the Board of Directors for the state Alzheimer's Association, I was asked to fill it. The Alzheimer's Association was interested in all forms of dementia, and not just Alzheimer's disease. I accepted because I could learn more about dementia, make important contacts throughout the state, and contribute to helping others in a similar situation. At the first board meeting, I was also elected to the Executive Committee. I hoped I hadn't taken on more than I should.

Saturday a neighbor was driving by the entrance to Starr Farm when he spied Lou-Ann in her wheelchair, near the end of the driveway approaching the road. He quickly called and someone rushed out to get her.

She had more mobility in that chair than people thought. In some ways she still seemed to have a mind of her own. They were not going to put her in the wheelchair on weekends because the reduced staff had a harder time keeping track of her. This wouldn't be too bad because I brought her home every Saturday and Sunday afternoon and didn't take her back until bedtime. She spent a lot of this time in bed, which gave me a chance to prepare dinner, and get other jobs done around the house.

Being at home for this extended amount of time meant that I had to change her at least once, if not twice. I remembered a conversation with a friend in Syracuse when Maria was just born about changing diapers. I was told we would find out what changing was all about when Maria became a toddler, and we had to change her diaper as she was trying to crawl away. That didn't compare to changing a 160-pound adult, whose hands were going everywhere, and was trying to walk away. These were exasperating times. I think it was because this was such an overpowering symbol of her condition.

While out for a ride, we dropped in on Tim and Maria. She seemed lost in their apartment. Tim's parents were there, but Lou-Ann didn't recognize them. One could tell she was uncomfortable because she was more restless than usual. It was sad to see her distressed in her own daughter's home.

I heard that a colleague at the university left his wife. I thought they had a good marriage. Why was it that people didn't always want to make the commitment to each other to make a marriage work? I realized that there are circumstances where divorce is appropriate, but I also knew of couples where that was not the case. I wanted to keep my wife, but I couldn't. My marriage was ending, and I had no say in the matter. Where was the justice?

November, 1988

Lou-Ann's language continued to deteriorate. When someone said something to her, she would repeat the last word or two over and over.

"How are you today?"

"Today, today, today."

The Fillions visited and her mother made a dessert. It was sitting on the kitchen table waiting to go in the oven. Lou-Ann put it in, set the oven correctly, and turned it on. She hadn't done anything like that in a long, long time. When she got in her parent's car to go for a ride, she tried to put on her seat belt, but couldn't figure out how to do it. When she got into our car to return to the nursing home, she was able to buckle her belt with no trouble.

I had to go to Cincinnati for two days for a meeting. As I was in the airport waiting to come home, I was struck with the remembrance of times past. When I was away for a few days, the arrival home was always something to be looked forward to. Lou-Ann and the kids, when they were young, would meet me at the airport. It was always exciting being together again. Even if we'd had an argument before I left, it was special to be back together. Being apart for a few days seemed to make us appreciate each other more. This time there would be no such excitement upon my arrival. I would be coming to an empty airport, no arms to greet me. I left the airplane and the airport as quickly as I could after I landed.

While I was gone, Lou-Ann wheeled herself into another resident's room and found four one-pound boxes of fine chocolate on the dresser. She took one and ate the entire box. The resident was in the room at the time and just watched her eat it. When asked why she didn't stop Lou-Ann, she replied, "She looked so happy eating them, I couldn't bear to stop her."

A sophomore from my math course approached after class and asked if I had a place to go for Thanksgiving. She invited me to be with her family if I was going to have to eat alone. No adult questioned how I would be spending Thanksgiving.

I spent Thanksgiving at the nursing home with Lou-Ann. We ate in the dining room for the first time. People who didn't need help, except for possibly having their food cut, ate there while others who needed more assistance ate in the activity room. Four people to a table, table cloths, candied mints, wine, and turkey with all the trimmings made for a very good meal. Lou-Ann was belted to the chair so she wouldn't be jumping up during the meal. She sat contentedly through the whole meal. The mints were at each place in a small paper cup. By the time the meal was over, she had eaten hers, mine, and one other woman's who was at the table with us. I had to cut all her food, but she ate everything by herself, albeit very slowly.

I dyed Lou-Ann's hair every six weeks. It really should have been done more often, but it was not an easy task so I stretched it out to six weeks. We had dyed her hair for so long I could not stop doing it just because she was at Starr Farm. I had to restrain her in a chair in her room to put on the dye, which had to stay on for 45 minutes. I brought in a small black and white TV set for her room so I turned it on while we waited. She couldn't follow any story line, but the action on the screen usually kept her entertained. Trying to keep her hands out of her hair while we waited was always a challenge. I gave her a shower to remove the dye. That was always fun because she grabbed anything that came in arm's length of her, including the hand-held shower sprayer. By the time we finished I was usually as wet as she was. She seemed to enjoy her shower. I weighed her once I dried her off. This way, as time passed, I could keep track of her weight and know that changes weren't a result of having different amounts of clothes on.

I usually sang and talked to her as we walked around Starr Farm. In the past, she would join in singing some songs she could remember. Now she only occasionally sang a phrase and usually walked in silence.

She began to have a sniffle so I asked that she be given something to help with her drippy nose. She was incapable of blowing it. Putting a tissue to her nose and asking her to blow resulted in nothing. The best we could do was wipe it. Did she have any sensation that her nose should be blown? Was she in a constant state of wanting to blow her nose but couldn't? Was the feeling like the sensation you have when you have to sneeze, but no sneeze comes for a couple of moments? At the same time she started her period. She had usually had a problem with cramps at this time before she got Pick's. Was she still getting them? How could we tell? Sometimes she seemed very restless, which I attributed to cramps. She used to take Anaprox for cramps before she was sick so I asked the nurses if she could have some. Nothing could be done until the doctor approved it, so she had to wait for the nurses to call and the doctor to respond. There was sometimes a time delay between request and administration. Finally, she was given the Anaprox and something for her runny nose.

December, 1988

I had to go to a mathematics education convention in Boston for five days on the first of the month. While I was gone Keith, quit his job. Our relationship had deteriorated to the point where I was ready to ask him to leave. I think he knew we had to live separately because he called the chef in Florida to see if the offer of work still held. Fortunately for both of us, the offer stood and he could start work there on the 24th. The future for our relationship seemed bleak.

Over the past few days, I asked Lou-Ann who she was and she said, "Louise-Ann Fillion," her maiden name. She still got my name right. She talked very softly, mostly under her breath.

Before Keith left, he and Maria went with us to get our Christmas tree. This year someone could stay with her in the car. I didn't get any maple syrup this time. This would probably be the last time the four of us would ever do anything like this again. It felt good to do something as a family.

Tim, Maria, Keith, and I went out to eat before Keith left for Florida. Lou-Ann was home in the afternoon so we dropped her off at Starr Farm on our way to the restaurant. It was sad to have to leave her behind when we were going out as a family.

Lou-Ann was finishing her lunch in the TV room on a Sunday when we got to the nursing home. Her meat hadn't been cut so it was just sitting there. As I cut it I noticed her lips were bright red. At first, I thought someone had put lipstick on her, even though the color was quite bright. As she began eating I noticed her tongue was also bright red. Maybe she had eaten some hard candy? She had something clenched in her hand so I asked her to give it to me. It was a leaf and some wire from a holiday decoration. As I looked up, I saw an apple core on the top of the TV. She had eaten an entire Styrofoam apple, leaving a core, from one of the Christmas arrangements in the room. She had taken at least ten bites from the apple. Three months earlier, she only ate one bite from a real apple before throwing it away. She was in a geri-chair so noone could figure how she got the apple. She had no ill effects from it. I wondered if she had any taste left since she ate the entire thing?

Lou-Ann signed the Christmas cards to our parents. On one she wrote "Louise-Ann Fillion" and on the other "Louise-Ann Erb."

I was going to keep her home overnight on Christmas Eve. There was a risk involved, but it was worth it. This was the first time she would have slept in her bed since May. On Christmas Eve, Lou-Ann always had a buffet after church for some friends, a family tradition, and Maria wanted to be sure we continued this, so she organized it and invited some of her and Tim's friends over. We didn't eat until 9:30 p.m. Lou-Ann must have been starving because she ate heartily. I put her to bed right after that.

She woke at 7 o'clock in the morning. She was wet, but no major problem. Tim and Maria had slept at the house overnight. We had our traditional breakfast of kutchen (similar to coffee cake) and opened our presents. Lou-Ann behaved like a child in that when she opened a box with clothes, she looked at them, then put the top back on. When she opened a puzzle, she took it out of the box. I got her a small stuffed raccoon. She took it out and squeezed its stomach to see if it would make a sound. It didn't, so she put it back. I bought her four puzzles of varying difficulty. Three seemed to be about right, but one was too difficult for her.

Keith called to wish us a Merry Christmas so I put Lou-Ann on the phone with him, but she didn't say anything. Maria gave me a picture of the two of us taken at the rehearsal dinner for their wedding. I asked Lou-Ann who was in the picture and she identified Maria as herself. She had not identified the children, by name, in two to three months.

Tim, Maria, Peg, and I went to see *Rain Man*. The movie touched so many of the emotions I had been living with. After the first 20 minutes of the film, I leaned over to Maria and said, "It is weird seeing yourself as one of the main characters of a movie."

Tim and Maria wanted me to go with them to First Night on New Year's Eve. I didn't want to be a drag, but they seemed to want me to come. Lou-Ann and I had been to every one except last year when we stayed home.

Chapter 8

The Fourth Year

January, 1989

A new year. Some people say they want to see the future and know what the year holds for them. I had no desire to know exactly what the future held. In many ways I already knew more about our future than I cared to know. I had enough to face each day that I didn't need to add what tomorrow held on top of that. Our lives had become narrowed to focus on one day at a time. It was hard enough to get through each day by itself, so I tried to not let my mind wonder about tomorrow.

It was interesting to see Lou-Ann play with the puzzles I got her for Christmas. They included a 20-piece Beatrix Potter puzzle (ages 4 and up), a 10-piece wooden Fisher-Price number puzzle (ages 3-5), and an 11-piece wooden animal puzzle where the animal pieces were just placed in the appropriate cut-out spaces. She could orient many of the pieces by shape and/or pattern. The Fisher-Price puzzle dealt with the numbers 1 to 5. There were ten pieces, five number pieces plus five more with pictures representing the numbers: 1 duck, 2 airplanes, etc. She placed the "1" piece in the lower left hand corner, then placed the "2" piece next to that, then the "3" next to the "2" and so on, but they didn't fit together since they were not in the correct locations. It was enjoyable to see her use her mind to try figure out even these simple tasks. After three or four days, she started to get the position of at least three of the numbers every time she did the puzzle. This seemed to bring her a lot of delight.

After playing with them for almost a month, I was amazed how much of each puzzle she could do. She could complete a lot of the 20-piece puzzle by herself. She certainly had an idea of where many of the pieces went. She recognized the corner pieces and put them in their place. Her thinking was more focused than when I first gave them to her. When given the Beatrix Potter puzzle, she would take a piece, and put it in its approximate position, even if there were no other pieces around it.

Her high school yearbook was also a major source of enjoyment. She spent a lot of time looking through it every day. I had to tape pages back in since the binding broke because she looked at it so much. I also had to clean up many of the pages since she kept reaching down her pants.

In the middle of the month, I was helping her eat in the TV room when she drank the last third of a cup of coffee and appeared to have swallowed it. She had a forkful of food left on her plate so I fed it to her. As I raised the fork, she opened her mouth to eat, and all the coffee poured down the front of her. She had held the coffee in her mouth without swallowing.

When I had her home for the next weekend, she tried to eat coffee beans. She also unwrapped the frozen London broil I was defrosting for the next day and put the meat in the oven — no pan.

At school I did something I had never done before, I forgot one of my classes. I had been working at my computer since lunch and completely forgot about the class. It met from 4-7 p.m. and at 4:50 a student came to my office to get me. I was amazed that: 1) the students had not left, and 2) it took them 50 minutes to come to the office to see if I was there.

Lou-Ann was now walking a lot slower. The nursing home was letting her walk unattended for about an hour at a time. They just told everyone to keep an eye on her as she went around. She would occasionally stop, go into someone's room, look around, and then move on.

I stopped at Starr Farm on my way to school to spend a little time with her in the morning before classes. I walked up to her and said, "I love you." She looked at me and responded, "I love you, I love you, I love you." She hadn't said that since last fall. It was so good to hear her speak those words again. Did she know what she was saying, or was she merely repeating the last words she heard?

February, 1989

February was always a hard month in Vermont. Winter dragged on, and people couldn't wait for some sunny weather.

I sometimes stayed with her after she was put to bed. I liked to look at her when she was sleeping. She seemed so relaxed, comfortable, and peaceful. It was the same feeling I had had when watching our children sleep when they were babies. I was sitting in a chair in the corner of the room by the end of her bed trying to relax when an aide stuck her head in to check on Lou-Ann and Winn. It was somewhat dark because only the night-light was on.

"You look like you have lost your best friend," she said.

"I have," I answered.

Spitting had become a more serious problem. She spit on the floor rather than her cup. She started to get spit all over her chin and clothes. She also started to eat the paper cups she used as her phlegm mug, so they were taken from her.

She still fed herself but had to be given foods one at a time and cued to eat. Dr. Gomez said that eating could become a serious problem, and in the end she might even forget to swallow.

She was becoming more difficult to take care of when at home. When wiping her off while changing her, she would try to grab the washcloth to spit into or just hold onto it. Her hands were into everything, and she also tried to walk away. My patience ran out after having her home for only 2½ hours, so I took her back to Starr Farm.

March, 1989

This month started with the death of a friend's mother at Starr Farm. Their family had become a part of my life, and all of a sudden they weren't around anymore. Death and mortality were always in front of me at the nursing home.

Lou-Ann now spit constantly. Tim, Maria, Peg, and Russ, a colleague from the university, came over to watch a University of Vermont hockey game on TV. I also brought Lou-Ann home to be with us. She was sitting on the sofa, and I sat between her legs on the floor in front of her. She leaned over to spit in my hair, but fortunately Maria saw it and was able to stop her. At the nursing home, she had been spitting on the lap tray and rubbing it with her fingers. To try to discourage her from doing that, we covered the lap tray with a towel to absorb the saliva.

It was getting hard to remember Lou-Ann as she was when she was well. It seemed as if life had always been like this. This was what normal was in our life.

She told me she loved me again. She was in her geri-chair when I came in and gave her a kiss. She looked up and said, "I love you, I love you." In years past, I took statements like this for granted, but now they were precious.

A week off for spring break and I spent five days of it in bed with bronchitis. I had hoped to spend more time with Lou-Ann and get caught up on some school work. I was really looking forward to these few days. Even small respite breaks like this seemed to be taken from me.

She saw Dr. Gomez for the first time in six months. He was surprised at how much she had slipped during that time. She didn't know who he was, and I was not too sure if she really knew where she was. She sat quietly, looked out the window, and didn't respond to his questions, but when he asked her to reach up and touch his hand, she did so. She didn't say anything out loud throughout the exam, but at times she counted or said something under her breath. The lack of speech seemed to be a sign that the disease was advancing. He thought she would become more and more withdrawn, less mobile, and could become ill due to her lack of movement. He now wanted to see her every three months instead of every six months.

I finished reading another book written by someone who had lived through the experience of dementia. From the few books I had read, it seemed other caregivers at times tried hard to get the demented person to do something normal that they could no longer accomplish, like saying a name. How much did this frustrate the person who was ill? These books gave me an awareness as to what I needed to consider for the future. It was going to be hard when she became so unresponsive. At least now she reached out and wanted to walk hand in hand.

We went for a ride after Hope cut her hair. The day was so nice, and we hadn't been together for five days, so we drove for over more than two hours. She didn't say anything, but looked out the window the entire time. We got back in time for lunch. I was with her for almost five hours and it went by so fast. The awareness of her presence next to me in the car and the ability to reach out and touch her while we sat together was so incredible. The realization that there would come a time when we could no longer do this added to the intensity of the moment.

That night I had dessert at a local restaurant with Peg. I talked about how much Lou-Ann and I had done things together over the course of our lives, and how I was going to miss her. Peg described us as team players. It was hard to be successful when your team was no longer on the field with you. Could I really make it by myself without her?

April, 1989

She had started to do a strange thing. She raised both hands in the air, about head high, and held them there. Some nurses hypothesized Lou-Ann thought she was playing the piano, but I was not too sure of that.

Her hand in her pants had become a serious problem because of her period and incontinence. I purchased some one-piece clothes, including pajamas and leotards, so when she reached down her sweatpants she wouldn't be able to place her hands inside her diapers. This seemed to solve that problem, but it sure made changing her more difficult. She grabbed the straps of the leotards as we tried to take them off her shoulders. She wouldn't let go, so we had to pry her hands open to undress her. We gained in one area and lost in another.

Judy, the first social worker at Starr Farm, was in my evening statistics class. After class, we had a long talk about the time prior to Lou-Ann's acceptance into the nursing home. It turned out that after Judy left Starr Farm, she worked with Anne Johnson, the Director of Nursing, on a few of the pending cases, including Lou-Ann's. So when I first called and spoke to Anne, she didn't recognize my name, but knew the case as I described Lou-Ann to her. At first, two things were against Lou-Ann, her age and the fact she was going to be on Medicaid. Money always seems to be an issue in long-term care. Anne was sympathetic to our case because of the work Judy had done after she officially left Starr Farm.

Dr. Bradley and Kathy Slinker came to draw blood for their research project. Lou-Ann did not resist.

One of my favorite nurses was leaving Starr Farm. I was going to hate to see her go. When Lou-Ann first went there, I felt really supported, like being a part of a family. There didn't seem to be quite the same connection between us and the staff as new people replaced the old. The recent workers hadn't gone through the in-service about Lou-Ann, and hadn't been there for those first few weeks of adjustment. Those experiences built a bond. When she died, would any of the people who were with her for those first few days still be there?

Mary Val, a nurse at UVM and a fellow board member of the Alzheimer's Association, and I gave a workshop at Starr Farm on Alzheimer's disease and related disorders. Mary Val spoke about the technical aspects of care, and I talked about the family's perspective. This was the first of a number of workshops we would do together. It was good to be given the opportunity to use my experience to help others.

April 19, Lou-Ann's 48th Birthday — Peg brought a cake to the nursing home so we could have a little celebration. Tim, Maria, and Keith were there, as well as Peg and Janet. Janet was on her, monthly visit, which made the party a little more special.

Keith returned from Florida and would be working at Basin Harbor again this summer. He was only home for a few weeks before he started work.

A colleague at school made the suggestion that I write friends from the past who knew Lou-Ann and ask for their recollections of her. A person who lived nearby called the day she received my request. It was good to hear from her. She said she almost called a number of times before but didn't. Why couldn't someone call a friend who was in need? It had been over four years, since before Lou-Ann became ill, that we had last seen each other.

I wasn't able to see Lou-Ann until after supper on Saturday because I was at an all-day retreat in Stowe for the Deacons from church. She was saying something after I kissed her hello, so I leaned over to hear what it was. She was singing, "I love you a bushel and a peck." This was a little song we had sung together since before we were engaged. I had been singing it to her every day while we walked.

Just before I left, I lay my head on her chest and she began to kiss my forehead. She then said, "Kiss my husband, kiss my husband." Whenever

I thought there was nothing much there, things like this came out. What did she know but couldn't express? How I would have liked to get into her head to know just what she knew and understood.

As we walked around Starr Farm, I noticed Lou-Ann would walk in step with me. This led to a little game where I would skip and she would then adjust her gait to get back in step. She was able to do it fairly quickly even when I would skip two or three times in a row.

May, 1989

Her weight was now up to 170 pounds. During the next year, her weight would fluctuate very little.

I sometimes lagged behind her when we walked so she could go her own way and set her own pace. It wasn't long before she would stop and hold her hand out for me to walk with her. Now that the weather was changing, she would have more fun walking because we would be able to go outside. One of the residents told me they saw Lou-Ann sitting on the patio for a while. The fresh air and sun in her face had to be refreshing.

A child's college graduation usually marks a major change in the lives of the child and their parents. Maria's graduation would have been the time we would have begun to plan for the future, when there would just have been the two of us. There didn't seem to be much in my future except to watch Lou-Ann slip away. It was as if she had fallen over a cliff, I had a hold of her by one arm, but her hand was slowly slipping out of mine until she would lose her grip. All I had to look forward to was the moment of separation and the inevitable fall. I only asked for three things when she reached that point: that she go quickly, that she go peacefully, and that I would be with her when she died.

I felt I had a much better understanding and appreciation for Jesus' prayer the night before the crucifixion when he prayed, "My Father, if it is possible, may this cup be taken from me. Yet not as I will, but as you will" (Matt. 26:39).

We hadn't played Old Maid in a while so I got out the cards, but she didn't know what to do with them. When I handed them to her she wanted to put them back in the box. I shuffled the deck and dealt them because she wouldn't do it. She held hers in her hand so I lay mine out like she used to. She picked all the cards up and put them back in the box. She was continuing to slip physically. When we went home or finished a ride, she just sat there. I had to encourage her to get out of the car. She needed help to swing her legs out from under the dashboard.

Mother's Day — We called both our parents and let them talk to Lou-Ann. She didn't react in any way. As Keith walked into the kitchen after dinner, she reached out and took his hand. He looked at her with the warmest smile, leaned over, and kissed her on the lips. It was a very tender and touching moment.

Maria's graduation — Being a member of the faculty allowed me the opportunity to personally hand Maria her diploma. It was something I had been looking forward to doing since she was a freshman. It was over in an instant, four years of anticipation for a 2-second event. I really missed Lou-Ann not being able to be there to enjoy the moment. She deserved to see the fruit of her work of raising Maria. Not being able to share the day with her left a big void.

The rest of the family was able to be here for the celebration. Lloyd, Lou-Ann's brother, rented a large car so their father would be more comfortable on the trip. The prostrate cancer he had for the past few years had really weakened him. I was shocked when I first saw him, he was so drawn and thin. He needed assistance in everything he did. The weather was beautiful so we spent the afternoon outside. Lou-Ann sat in a lounge chair for a couple of hours. The good-bye between Lou-Ann and her father was poignant because, even though no one said anything, everyone thought this would be the last time they would see each other.

I stopped by the office while we were out for a ride. As we walked by the blackboard by my door, she picked up the chalk and made some vertical marks in a small area. "Write your name."

She wrote, "Lou-Ann Fillion," her maiden name.

"Write my name."

"Clinton Allen Erb"

I guess she still knew who I was.

Tim and Maria moved out of the house they have been living in because the people had returned from Florida. They hadn't been able to find an apartment so they temporally moved in with me. One benefit of this arrangement was that I would be eating better than before. I found it difficult to take the time to prepare a good meal since I didn't get home from

Starr Farm until after 9 in the evening.

June, 1989

I dyed Lou-Ann's hair and she sat through it quietly, watching cartoons. An aide gave me a vest restrainer to keep her in the chair, but I decided to just wrap it about her waist. When I went to wrap it around her, she took it, and tried to put it on correctly. She knew how it was supposed to be worn. I had to put her arms through it and tie it the way it was intended to go on.

The only trouble I had was when I washed her hair in the shower. She grabbed the shower head and would not let go. She started to rinse her hair as I was putting on the shampoo.

Lou-Ann was eating when I arrived from the state track meet so I helped her finish. I changed her and we went for a walk. As we came by the nurses' station, she stopped and picked up a pen but there wasn't any paper there so she started to put it back. I found a scrap piece for her. "What do you want to write Lou-Ann?" I asked.

She wrote, "Trite Lou-Ann"

"Write some more."

"Trite Lou-Ann"

"Write my name."

"Trite Clint"

I got sunburned at the track meet and some people at the nursing home said I would be hurting that night. Sunburn wasn't pain. Pain was watching your wife die.

The next day Tim, Maria, Lou-Ann, and I went to the hot air balloon festival at the fairgrounds. We walked around the grounds as the balloons were being inflated. It was a colorful sight with all shapes and colors of the various balloons. We decided to sit on the grass where it would be more comfortable, but Lou-Ann couldn't figure out how to sit down. She would bend at the knees, like she was sitting in a chair, but couldn't get any farther. When she tried a second time I grabbed her, and pulled her over on top of me. We had to slide her over because she ended up on my lap. When we went to get up, she was totally lost as to what to do. We told her to bend her knees, take our hands, then we pulled her up.

She seemed to enjoy the sights and activity and being around so many people. We met a couple she hadn't seen in a long time, but she had no idea who they were.

A dear friend from Starr Farm who always kept an eye out for Lou-Ann died. We had become good friends over the course of the year we had known each other. This woman spent most of her day in the TV room with another resident, who would feel her loss more than anyone.

I took Lou-Ann to the grocery store for the first time since our great adventure two years ago. The only thing she tried to do was take something from a man's hand as he walked by. I held her hands as we stood by the candy display while we were waiting to check out.

After we came home, I made an interesting discovery. As she walked by the desk in the living room, she stopped and went through our pile of booklets on tropical fish. She was saying something under her breath so I put my ear to her mouth to hear her. She was saying, "Fancy Platties," which was the title of one of the books. So in at least some instances it seemed she could still read.

I had to go to a two-day meeting in Kansas City. When I returned, Tim and Maria met me at the airport with Lou-Ann. I wasn't expecting to see her, so what a thrill it was when I saw her looking through the glass separating the passenger area from the general public. It was just like old times seeing her there. She seemed to respond when I arrived.

Lou-Ann's roommate, Winn, who had been unconscious for two weeks, due to a stroke, died. Lou-Ann was asleep when she passed away. The night before an aide said she found Lou-Ann sitting up in bed, looking at Winn. I never expected Lou-Ann to outlive her.

I brought Lou-Ann to our Sunday School class picnic at Peg's. She drank a lot of water, which was good because she hadn't been drinking much lately. We paid a price for that because she went through four changes of clothes and all the diapers I had at home.

When she was lying down at home I got her to smile. She hadn't done that in a long time. She didn't seem to be able to get comfortable when she was lying down. She kept moving around and changing positions. She now needed some help when she stood. She had to use her arms to help herself up.

Keith stopped in to ask my help in finding a counselor. He finally came to the end of his rope and realized his need for help. This turned out to be the beginning of a change in direction in his life that would be lasting, but at the time I didn't know that. It was not an abrupt change, but it was the start.

Kathy Slinker met us at Dr. Gomez's office for Lou-Ann's appointment. It was good having her with us because she asked some questions I would not have thought of.

Lou-Ann's grasping reflex was like that of a newborn baby. It was a result of an immature frontal lobe of the brain. As her frontal lobe degenerated, the grasping reflex would become more pronounced.

While visiting Peg, Lou-Ann would pet her dog, starting at its head, but when her hand got to its tail she would grasp it and not let go. I had to pull the tail from her hand. She didn't squeeze or pull it, she just held on. Luckily, the dog didn't get upset.

She was getting to the point where she could repeat some actions but needed help in starting other activities, like getting out of the car. She was not sure how to begin, but once someone started the action for her, like getting one leg out of the car, she could continue the process. Dr. Gomez thought she was becoming more apathetic.

July, 1989

I felt so frustrated and depressed. Lou-Ann was becoming so unresponsive. She was slipping farther and farther away. I hated to take her back to Starr Farm after having her home, so we went for a ride downtown. There was something about the activity of the city, the people coming and going, that gave a feeling of normal living.

Tim and Maria were still looking for an apartment. Even though we got along well, I was getting anxious for them to leave. The places I had to myself in the house were shrinking. They needed their privacy so there were some rooms I tried to leave to them. I guess I had become used to having the house by myself. It had been nice, living by myself, to come home to a quiet house, where things were exactly as I left them, no surprises upon entering the door because of some problem someone in the family was facing. I was forgetting what it was like to live with someone else.

Another woman moved in with Lou-Ann. I met her when I walked in, she was sitting in her chair watching TV. I introduced myself and she said, "Hello, I'm not staying here tonight." Every day when I saw her, she said she was not staying. She seemed like a good roommate for Lou-Ann, quiet and not aggressive. She hardly left the room except to eat. She spent most of her day watching TV.

Karen, a college student who worked as an aide last summer, returned to work again this year. It was good to see her. She was a connection with those first few months of Lou-Ann's adjustment. She seemed to brighten up the place, was cheerful, and always had a smile and a kind word for each resident.

Tim, Maria, Lou-Ann, and I went grocery shopping again. She enjoyed pushing the cart with me. We kept it moving while Tim and Maria stopped for things. At one point a woman asked us if she could help us, we must have looked lost.

July 7 - Our 27th Wedding Anniversary

Peg had us over for dinner with her sister. This was the celebration of one of the most important events of our lives, and she had no idea what this day was all about.

I got the mail on this day and Tim and Maria received about six cards for their anniversary, which was in two days. Lou-Ann and I had none. I wanted to scream, "She's not dead yet! This is our anniversary, a day to remember, don't forget her."

Someone gave me a copy of *How to Survive the Loss of a Love* by Colgrove, Bloomfield, and McWilliams. Two small entries seem to describe how I felt.

But this,
this slow erosion from below
— or within — It's me falling down around my life
because you're still in that life
— but not really,
and you're out of that life
— but not quite. (p. 4)

I do alright alone and better together
but I do very poorly when semi-together. (p. 5)

I was feeling depressed. It must have been evident because Maria asked if I had thought about seeing a counselor. I first said "No," but then decided it would probably be a good idea.

School was becoming a hassle. A power struggle was taking place and some faculty were taking sides for not always the best reasons. I tried to keep myself out of it, but that took a lot of effort.

Two friends of Maria and Tim's were married on Sunday the 9th. The bride was also a student of mine. It was also Tim and Maria's first anniversary. Maria was in Boston taking the board exams for her athletic trainer certification, so Tim was there by himself, not really by himself because I was invited also, but I think I was a poor substitute for his wife. I doubted he really wanted to celebrate his first wedding anniversary with his father-in-law.

Lou-Ann had begun a strange habit while walking. The sun cast shadows on the floor as it shined through the full-length windows along the length of the corridors, overlooking the patio. She would only walk on the shadows, making sure she didn't step on the sunlight.

She was spitting less and less. This was something she had been doing for more than three years. The aides told me they had seen some real changes in her lately: more quiet, less spitting, more withdrawn. I took the lap tray off her geri-chair and she did not try to get up, she remained seated. To eat, she now placed food on her fork with her fingers, then used the fork to put the food in her mouth.

I had a conversation about baseball with one of my students during my summer course. It turned out that he was the head coach of a local high school team and was playing in a newly formed Northern Vermont Senior Baseball League for people 35 and older, an old timer's league. It was similar, except in age, to the town team leagues I played in while growing up in western New York. I had played ball in college, and he asked if I wanted to join the team he played with.

I hadn't played hardball in 28 years, but it didn't take long to decide to join them. It was a God-send. Running around on a sunny Sunday afternoon, pretending to be young again, did something for my soul. It was also encouraging to see men in their 60s, and in a few cases 70s, having fun doing something they loved. The physical exercise also helped release some of the tension I had been living with.

John and Janet, a local middle school principal and his wife, invited me over for dinner. In the course of our conversation, they made an observation about one possible cause of my depression, loss of control over my life. The one part of my life I felt I still had some control over was work, but even that seemed to have deserted me. God knows, one has no control over the direction of Pick's disease.

This disease runs its own course, and we were just along for the ride. It was like riding a runaway toboggan that went down a long, steep, bumpy hill. There was nothing we could do to steer, but knowing where the bumps were could help us prepare for the sudden changes in direction, so we could hold on tight and not fall off. This was about as much control as we had over what was happening. This was why I tried to find out as much as I could about the course of Pick's disease, and what I could expect as we approached the next bump in our journey down that hill. To be reactive to every situation was to let the hill dictate how hard one hit each bump. The time to decide how to hold on and lean was not when I was being catapulted into the air. However, having some idea of what was ahead gave an opportunity to lean into the hill and make the ride off each bump less jarring. I couldn't control the bumps I hit, but I could have some affect on how smooth the ride over them was.

Tim and Maria found an apartment. It was very small, but one that could generate stories about their early married life — the kind of stories one recounts to their children, "You think you have it bad, when we were married our first apartment . . ."

I had been invited to spend a week in Pasadena with a friend of ours who moved there a few years ago. Tim and Maria stayed at the house until I returned.

August, 1989

The trip to California was the first vacation I had had since Lou-Ann became ill. All my other trips away from home were business-related. In many ways this vacation was a big step for me because I had never done anything like this on my own. A couple of trips to Dodger Stadium, a day alone at Universal Studios, a trip to Disneyland, and a walk on the grass of the Rose Bowl, a must for a graduate of a Big 10 university, let me get a little distance from the world of Pick's disease.

It was amazing how much my memory was blunted during the week I was gone. I tended to remember Lou-Ann when she was more responsive. It was a small jolt when I first saw her in the airport. She seemed more quiet, saying only, "2, 4, 2, 4, 2, 4," almost inaudibly. During one of our walks around Starr Farm, I took her to play the piano. All she played was chords, she wouldn't play any music. The playing of her music, the Grieg piece, had diminished from the whole piece to stopping in the middle, to only a page, to a line, to a few measures, and finally now, to almost nothing.

Everytime Lou-Ann left the nursing home, we had to sign out so they would know who she was with and where she was going. When I took her home after returning from California, I told her to write her name in the appropriate column, which she did without hesitation.

"Write my name here," I said, pointing to the appropriate space on the sign-out sheet. At first she did nothing, then after a few seconds she wrote, "Clinton Allen Erb." She could still put a name to my face.

One week later I asked her, on both Saturday and Sunday, to write my name on the sign-out sheet. Saturday she wrote nothing. Sunday she wrote something that made no sense.

We hadn't tried the puzzles in a while so I got them out, she couldn't do any of them. She just looked at even the simplest one, where animals where placed in a shaped cutout. I put one piece in for her, then she started and finished the rest. She completed the three simplest puzzles, but it took quite a bit of time to put the last one together.

The next Sunday I tried having her sign out again. She wrote "Kingman" twice. I didn't know where that name had come from. I thought she had lost the knowledge of exactly who I was, but I was sure she knew I was a familiar person, even though she couldn't totally place me.

She took a long time to eat on the weekend. She took the last bit of milk, filled her mouth, then spit it out on the table. She did that twice.

She continued to reach out and grab at people as they went by. When she got hold of something, she didn't let go. I gave her a plastic grocery bag to carry from the car, but couldn't get her to let go of it. I had to literally pry it out of her hand.

She was having trouble keeping the order of things straight. She tried to put on her diaper over her tights. Then as soon as we got her diaper on, she tried to take it off. I discovered her pants were wet after I changed her and tried to get her to step out of them. The only way I could accomplish that was to hold her hands in one of mine, and with my other hand, lift her legs out.

School was to start in about one week. I was starting to feel uptight again, like I always did at the beginning of a semester. This just added to the emptiness I was feeling. It was hard not knowing whether she knew who I was. Sometimes I wished I had just one day, or one evening, or even one hour with her as she had been. Not being able to ever talk with her again or have any kind of intimacy was hard to accept.

As I got her dinner tray, the minister of our church walked in. This was the first time he had visited since she entered the nursing home. It was exactly 16 months to the day since she had come to Starr Farm. "It has taken him 16 months to come to see her," I thought. I was glad to see him, but I wished it hadn't taken him so long to get around to stopping by. He stayed for over an hour, and she would occasionally reach over and hold his hand as we walked after she ate. He visited almost every week for the next three months, then he stopped coming.

Classes started and as director of one of our programs, I already had to arbitrate an issue between a student and a professor. Both acted at about the level of ten-year-olds. Both were convinced they were absolutely right, when in fact, I think they were both wrong. Why was it that most of my time was taken up by the problems generated by just a few people?

September, 1989

Last year, one week after Tim and Maria returned from their honeymoon, Maria was maid-of-honor at the wedding of Pam and Scott, friends from college. Pam had also been in Maria's wedding party. Scott had had cancer as a teenager but had recovered. There were some potential problems from the medication he had taken, but they thought those were in the distant future. However, not too long after their wedding in August of '88, he began to have some problems. They escalated until now, he was in the hospital, on life support systems, in serious condition. Pam had to make the decision of whether to remove him from the respirator that was keeping him breathing. She decided to, and he died shortly thereafter. They had been married for 13 months and had a 3-month-old little boy.

I had resolved to be composed at the wake, but when I gave Pam a hug, I couldn't stop the tears. The last time I had seen Scott was at the Christmas Eve buffet at our house. I felt so sorry for them, their marriage had only lasted such a short time. Pam was giving more comfort to those who came to pay their respects than people were giving her. I couldn't help but think to the future and wonder what it would be like when I would be in her place.

As we walked around Starr Farm, Lou-Ann reached out and shook the hand of other residents as we passed in the hall. She first grasped their arm as they walked by.

With this disease things come and go, and come back again. She signed my full name on the sign-out sheet when I took her home on the weekend. It had been almost a month since she last did that. The next weekend she couldn't write my name and wrote "Durmeyer" for hers. This was her grandmother's maiden name.

When my father was in the hospital unable to move the lower half of his body because of the cancer that was taking his life, he used to reach over his head as he lay on his back to see how far he could reach up the wall behind his bed. When asked what he was doing he would say, "Nothing." I was sure he was using that as a way to measure the speed and degree of his decline. I think I was using Lou-Ann's ability to write names in the same way. How fast was she losing the ability to understand and follow a direction, and did she also know who I was?

She had to be reminded to swallow. She had started to put food into her mouth, but not swallow. She was like a chipmunk, hoarding her food in her mouth.

Tim and Maria came, we picked up Lou-Ann and went apple picking. She didn't wander around the orchard, but stayed by us. She picked and ate an apple, actually two apples. She held out one apple a number of times to give me a bite. She might not know my name, but she surely knew that I was someone special to her. She wanted to stay close, hold my hand, and would reach out for a kiss.

Rick, the 42-year-old brother of the administrative assistant in our department, died. He had had MS and been a resident at Starr Farm since it first opened. He was the third close relative of a friend who had died in the last four weeks. Death seemed to be more and more a part of our lives.

School was becoming more problematic. I had a student come to my office and complain that I wasn't giving him enough attention in class. He felt I was slighting him. I was facing the death of my wife and he didn't think he was getting enough attention! This burned me up. I felt as if I was getting blind-sided at every turn. There didn't seem to be any place I could go for refuge.

Lou-Ann and I were walking around Starr Farm with our arms around each other when John, another resident, asked a nurse if we were going to get married. "Do you think we would make a good couple?" I asked him.

"No, you won't last past your first fight," he replied.

"Why do you say that?"

"You are too infatuated with each other to make a go of it."

"What if I told you we have two grown children and been married for 27 years?"

"In that case you should write a book about how you did it."

I guess our love for each other still showed.

October, 1989

Last month was difficult. It seemed like I was always feeling down. I found I was happiest when with Lou-Ann.

The Fillions visited for a weekend. I never expected her father to visit again. He had had an operation that improved his condition. When her mother saw her she said, "I could see in her face that she recognized me." I wasn't sure Lou-Ann knew who I was, let alone others. My mother said the same thing the previous week when she visited. How much of this was wishful thinking?

The last time Lou-Ann was home we went downstairs to watch TV and she got on the exercise bike we had in the basement. I loosened the tension and she began to peddle. She rode for 35 minutes and traveled 6½ miles before I stopped her. She would have kept going, but I didn't want her to become sore.

The Stasiors, old friends from Syracuse, were spending the weekend in Vermont and stopped by to visit. They were here two years ago, before Lou-Ann went into the nursing home. They had been sending little notes and cards to her every couple of months since she had been at Starr Farm. It was nice to get them, to know we were being remembered and prayed for. It was just a little thing they did to encourage us, but one that had an immense effect.

Basin Harbor closed and Keith headed to Utah for the winter with another fellow he worked with. When he left, he gave me a hug and said he loved me. That was something he hadn't said many times lately.

When I got to the nursing home, Lou-Ann was eating a sloppy joe on a hamburger roll. None of the residents were doing too well with it. I leaned over to kiss her, she opened her mouth wide as if someone was going to feed her. I kissed her open mouth, she then realized what I was doing and kissed me as she usually does, closed mouth, no pucker.

She started to have trouble going up and down stairs. When she got to a step, she couldn't figure out how to negotiate it. If I reached down and put her foot on the first step, she could continue the process and go up the remaining steps.

We played catch, but she would only throw the ball a couple of times before she became disinterested. After that she would only hand it to me instead of throwing it. Since that didn't last too long, I got the Old Maid cards out. I shuffled them and handed them to her. She tried to put them back in the box. I took them back, dealt them, but she didn't touch her hand. I lay mine out in front of her, like we had done in the past, turned her pile over, and handed them to her. She picked up my cards, put them with hers, and put them in the box. Old Maid was now finished.

Another visit with Dr. Gomez. I packed Lou-Ann's traveling bag, as I did on every doctor's visit, but I hadn't had to use it. She was content looking at a magazine in the waiting room, but seemed distressed while in his office. Dr. Gomez said that it is harder to swallow liquids than solids, so that could be why she had been having trouble with her milk. He laid a major question before me which I perhaps would have to face in the future. What would I do if Lou-Ann stopped swallowing? It would not be due to a physical impairment, but that her brain couldn't tell her throat muscles what to do. This would be the biggest decision of my life. Would I go to forced feeding with a feeding tube? For what purpose? The question could be simplified to whether I let my wife starve to death or keep her alive so she could become a vegetable. It might happen in one year, two years, four months, or possibly never. A decision needed to be made before the circumstance arose, but how did one make it? I didn't think Lou-Ann would want to be kept alive in such a situation, but I needed to look into it further, both medically and ethically.

Lately she had been clinging and wouldn't let go. While downstairs watching TV, she would hold my hand and lean against me. She got on the exercise bike again for 45 minutes — 9.4 miles.

When I took her back to Starr Farm around 9:30 p.m., she didn't want me to leave. The nurse was going to put her to bed so I kissed her good-bye and said, "I love you." She said, "love you, love you, love you." These were the first words I heard her say in quite awhile. As I started to walk away she reached out for me. I took one of her hands, the nurse took the other, and we walked her to her room. As she entered the door, I slipped my hand out of hers and left.

November, 1989

I had lunch with Mary Val, the nurse from UVM, to talk about the use of a feeding tube. It didn't seem to be a viable option for us. The decision to not use something like this was not very hard to make, but the strength to carry it out, if that time should ever come, was another matter. I prayed I would never be placed in that position. This disease just didn't let up. Every step seemed to get harder and harder. In the beginning, I thought this would be over in less than two years. Going from a 45- to a 3-year-old in one year didn't leave much time for the disease to run its course. I could concentrate all my energy into what it would take to take care of her because she didn't have much time left. Whatever energy I had left would be put into taking care of the rest of my life. I shouldn't have to worry about running out of energy and willpower because her life would be over in a short time. It was like running a sprint, when the gun goes off, you run as hard and fast as you can; there's no need to hold back because the finish line would come before you exhaust yourself. As time went on, it seemed as if someone kept moving the finish line. I was running as hard and as fast as I could, but the finish line was not getting any closer. In fact, it seemed to be farther away than when we first started. Would my endurance last until I completed the race? What began as a dash was turning into a marathon.

I felt like I was dying with her. Some husbands have a psychosomatic pregnancy when their wives are expecting. I wondered if it could be the same when one's wife dies. I felt so empty and shallow. Death was taking its toll.

Lou-Ann didn't have a good weekend. We only walked around Starr Farm once because she was very shaky when walking. I had to hold her close so she wouldn't fall. She had started her period so that could have had something to do with it. She was given Anaprox in case she was having a severe case of cramps. If she could only tell us what the problem was. Guessing what it might be, with the possibility of being wrong and not helping her, made me uneasy.

I was gone for a day and a half to Portland, Maine, for a New England Math Conference and didn't return until Saturday afternoon. Maria picked Lou-Ann up from Starr Farm and it seemed that Lou-Ann knew who she was. Lou-Ann was sitting in the wheelchair when she saw Maria, and seemed to look at her with a special focus and intensity. She wheeled toward Maria and stuck her arm out to shake hands. She seemed more alert than usual because she got in and out of the car with less assistance than in the recent past.

When I took her back to the nursing home, she didn't want to get out of the car. I'd swing her leg out and she would pull it back in. She grabbed the seat belt when I tried to take it off from her. I had a real sense she had an understanding of what she was doing, that I was dropping her off and would leave. She finally got out when I explained that I would bring her home again the next day. As we walked down the hall, an aide took her hand and we walked to her room. Once she saw and entered her room, I was able to slip my hand from hers and leave. The next day she didn't seem to have that same level of understanding of what was happening around her. She reverted to what she had been before. At least we had one day where she seemed to have a little more understanding.

As I was visiting during the week, the daughter of a resident claimed Lou-Ann recognized her and said, "Hello, how are you Pauline?" She insisted that Lou-Ann said that even when I told her Lou-Ann didn't talk anymore and didn't even know who I was. I didn't even know Pauline's name, why should Lou-Ann know it? Things like this really irritated me. People wanted to insist that Lou-Ann still knew them. Why was it that everyone wanted to be recognized by her?

I asked her to write her name as I took her back. She wrote "Janet Williams" over and over again. I asked her to write my name after she wrote "Janet Williams" a few times but she continued to write that name. After I said her name a few times she wrote "Louise Ann" once then just scribbled.

November 22 — It was the day before Thanksgiving, exactly three years since Lou-Ann went to the doctors for the first time and was also the 22nd anniversary of my father's death. She had spent half of those three years in the nursing home. She was sitting in her wheelchair in the TV room and was found with vomit, full of cigarette butts, over her shirt and pants. Cigarette ashes were on her fingers and there were no butts left in the large floor ashtray. She had eaten all the butts and then vomited. What did this say about her ability to discriminate taste?

They had put her back in the geri-chair so she wouldn't get into the ashtrays again. I complained that she should not lose her freedom because others wanted to smoke. Since all residents needed to be supervised when they smoked, the ashtrays could be emptied when everyone was finished. She was put back into the wheelchair.

I purchased a birthday card for Keith and asked her to write "Mom" on it. She wrote "Lou-Ann" first then "Mom" when I asked her a second time.

I didn't know if it was because of the holidays but I had been thinking a lot about her death. It tore me apart to think that she wouldn't be here anymore. Even though she was so incapacitated, she still meant so much to me.

She wouldn't make any attempt to feed herself, so I had to feed her the entire meal. She kept bending her head to her chest and closing her eyes.

The dean asked me to be interim chair of our department for the next six months. This would be until the college could hold a search to permanently fill the position. A chance to try something like this didn't come along very often, so I decided to give it a try.

December, 1989

Lou-Ann continued to grab onto everything and wouldn't let go. When I took her belt restraint off to get her out of the wheelchair, she grabbed on and held tight. She then tried to wrap it around herself again to be tied in. When taking her shirt off, she tried to put it back on when I got it half off. She also grabbed at people who walked by.

Maria had a number of friends over for a Mary Kay party at our house. Lou-Ann was there and seemed to really love it. She sat still, for the most part, during the entire party. She was very cooperative and seemed to enjoy it when I put cream on her face.

Lou-Ann used to accompany a group called Musica Propria before she became ill. I decided to take her to the rehearsal for their annual Christmas concert so she could enjoy the music. Taking her to the concert would be too complicated. The nursing home didn't have her ready to go when I arrived so we got out late. It was around zero outside and I couldn't find a parking place near the church where the rehearsal was being held, so we had to walk a short distance. At her pace, it took awhile so she was somewhat chilly when we finally got inside. Tim and Maria met us there. We stayed for about an hour. During their break, three people came by to say hello. At times she would sit and watch the group intently, but at other times she would be distracted and lean over. Going to a concert together used to be a common occurrence.

A week later she came down with a cold. She was home and stuffed up so I got the aspirator we used with the kids when they were infants and tried to clear out her nose. She threw up her dinner so I put her to bed. She was warm and flushed. She slept for an hour and seemed to be better after that. The next day I came down with her cold.

Two days later at Starr Farm she had some more trouble. She couldn't breath through her nose and when she filled her mouth with food and didn't swallow, she couldn't breath. Her gag reflex caused her to throw up what she had eaten. It was not easy to get her mouth cleaned out since she couldn't rinse it out with water.

One of the concerns the doctors had mentioned was that she might aspirate something into her lungs, which could induce a case of pneumonia. Gagging with her mouth full was a possible situation that could cause her to aspirate some of her food. We were more than ever now living with the possibility that something could happen which would place her life in jeopardy. If she did come down with pneumonia, what then? I said I would withhold treatment with an antibiotic if she came down with pneumonia, but if it happened now, would I do it or not? I always pictured her being weak, thin, and sickly when that happened. Could I allow pneumonia to run its course when she seemed relatively healthy and fit?

Christmas Eve, 1989

I was going to take her to the candlelight service at church. I spoke to our minister because I didn't want to cause a spectacle and be a distraction to the service. It had been three years since she had been in church, and I wasn't with her that last time. I was conducting the service because we were between ministers so she was sitting by herself. She had gotten up in the middle of the service because she said she had "head twinges." I could still see her walking out of that service.

I bought her a special green dress and a colorful scarf for the Christmas Eve service. This would probably be the only time she would wear these clothes.

Peg was in the hospital for a hip replacement operation so both our families met there before the service. We brought some shrimp and cookies to have a little party. We were there for 45 minutes before leaving for church.

Lou-Ann was somewhat attentive during the music, especially the solos, but the speaking didn't hold her attention. She would lean over as she sat and move her hand in front of her. We didn't stand up for the hymns and stayed seated throughout the entire service. It was nice just having her there next to me. It was the completion of a little unfinished business of mine. I wanted to be in church with her one more time.

Some people made a point to say hello after the service, while a few ignored Lou-Ann. One person said hello to Tim, Maria, and myself but didn't say a word or even look at Lou-Ann. It was as if she didn't exist. A few others, though, made an effort to speak to her and shake her hand.

Peg's family joined us at our house for our annual Christmas Eve buffet. We were going to have it at Peg's, but she wasn't released from the hospital.

In order to hug Lou-Ann, I had to take her arms and put them over my shoulders. For awhile she had been backing away from me, but this time she stayed close for a few moments. As I hugged and patted her on the back, I felt her pat me also. It was the first time she gave me something in return in a long time. I felt like I did the time she put her head on my shoulder as we were lying in bed. There were times I knew she didn't have any idea of who I was, but at moments like this, I believed she had a sense she was with her husband.

That night when I first put her to bed, she wouldn't lay down. I told her it was okay, that she was spending the night with me and she should go to sleep. I had to physically lay her head on the pillow before she would relax. Once she did that she went right to sleep. She woke up twice during the night, tossed and turned before she went back to sleep. It was nice to wake up on Christmas morning and have her by my side.

We didn't eat breakfast until 9 a.m. and then opened our presents. She would just hold her presents on her lap. As I started to take the wrapping off she would help, but would often stop before her gift was fully unwrapped. We didn't finish with our gifts until noon.

New Year's Eve, 1989

The last day of the 80s, as I looked back they seemed to be a blur. The first half of the 80s was taken up by the middle teenage years of our kids, and the last half was filled with Lou-Ann's illness. No wonder I seemed to have a block about this decade.

I kept her home late. She wanted to sit and hold hands while we sat at the table after dinner. She wouldn't let go. I poured some eggnog and she seemed to really like it. I didn't think she had any real taste left (remembering the cigarettes,) so I wondered if texture was important to her? She drank the eggnog a lot better than she did her milk.

I was starting the job as interim chair and the amount of work frightened me. I no longer had my life with Lou-Ann to counter the pressures of the position. It was at times like this that I really missed her. I could always count on her to be there for me. She would listen and not only give me self-respect and confidence, but also give advice as to how to solve some of the things I faced at work. I missed her wisdom and insight, her love and support.

Chapter 9

The Fifth Year

January, 1990

I never expected Lou-Ann to still be with us at the beginning of this new decade when she became ill four years ago.

New Year's day — I was invited to the wedding of two of Tim and Maria's friends. Sitting through the wedding was difficult. Their marriage was just beginning, ours coming to an end. Pam was asked to sing, it was also hard for her since the plan had been for Scott to be an usher. She sang, but the void left by Scott's death was obvious.

Lou-Ann's grip was becoming more of a problem. She grabbed everything when being undressed or when taking off the restraint from her wheelchair. She wouldn't release what was in her grip, her hands had to be pried open.

For dinner I cooked steak for the two of us, cut hers in small pieces as one would do for a child. She held some of the pieces of meat in her hand while eating other food on her plate. She ate her peas by placing them on her fork with her hand. She tried to feed herself, but needed help to finish.

Keith was having some major problems with his roommate in Salt Lake City. In addition, his job situation hadn't work out, so he called and said he was returning home. He was going to contact the Culinary School to see about completing the second half of his program.

The wheelchair allowed Lou-Ann some mobility and gave her a certain degree of freedom. She would hold onto the armrests of the wheelchair as I helped her stand when we went for our daily walk. If I didn't pry her hands off the arm supports and get her to start walking right away, she would try to sit back down. In order to walk, she had to hold onto both my hands. She continued to step only on the shadows on the floor.

Eating was continuing to be problematic. When she was home for the weekend, she would hold solid food in her mouth and not chew. She would start to eat if I gave her a little milk. She also stuffed too much in her mouth making it impossible to chew. I had to remove some of the food, which wasn't easy because she wouldn't open her mouth.

She also started to exhibit some other new behaviors. She was found stretched out in her wheelchair, head rolled back and mouth open. She was difficult to arouse, but eventually sat up. This happened a second time after lunch. She was put to bed and immediately feel asleep. This behavior was to continue on and off for a long time. The doctors were never able to say exactly what was happening.

When getting into the car, she would let her right leg hang outside. She would grasp the armrest of the door and hold the door open. If I lifted her leg she would completely get in. While her leg was out, she would sit there looking somewhat bewildered.

February, 1990

Alone, depressed, nothing excited me, nothing to look forward to. My stomach had a constant knot in it. Life seemed desolate.

After walking, Lou-Ann seemed to become tired so I sat her back down in the wheelchair. She wanted to hold my hand so I thought we would sit together and watch some TV. After just a few minutes, she scooted off down the hall. She continued to reach out to anyone and hold onto them as she went. This caused problems with other residents who didn't like her grabbing onto them.

Keith started school and moved out of the house and into student housing. We had a decent time together while he was home, but it was nice to have the house to myself again.

Lou-Ann was having some trouble with constipation so the doctor gave orders for Milk of Magnesia. It worked, even better than some of the aides would have liked.

I received a letter notifying me that one of my students had charged me with sexual discrimination. It didn't have any merit, but who knew what could come of it. He failed my course because he only completed half of the requirements and received a low grade in a second course, all of which resulted in his dismissal from the fifth-year program. He claimed I gave special attention to the women in class, to his detriment. Another hassle I had to deal with. It would take time and effort on a number of people's parts to answer his charge.

I was also having a dispute with a faculty member regarding the teaching assignments for the next semester. Being interim department chair would end in June, and that day was looking better and better. I was sure it would have been different if Lou-Ann were well.

Lou-Ann had been having trouble trying to drink from a glass. She wouldn't tip it high enough for the milk to reach the edge and get to her lips. She couldn't figure out what to do to be able to drink.

Mark and Lori, Tim and Maria's friends, were over for a Saturday afternoon with Lou-Ann. We were downstairs watching TV when I had to leave for a while. When I returned she was holding Mark's hand. She seemed to want the assurance of touching someone.

I went to pick her up at Starr Farm after church and couldn't find her. She was roaming in her wheelchair and could not be found. I discovered her caught in the corner of a little corridor that led to an office. She seemed confused as to how to get out, and I imagine she would have been there for awhile if I hadn't come.

She would hardly do anything when we sat at the piano so I brought the Grieg sheet music home from Starr Farm. This marked the end of a major part of her life, playing the piano. Music didn't stimulate her like in the past. So much of her was now gone. I really missed her!

March, 1990

I received a call from the Chair of the Board of Deacons that the son of a couple from church had been killed in an accident. He was a member of the youth group when Lou-Ann and I were advisors. I had no reaction to this news. My heart really went out to his parents, but it was an intellectual reaction rather than an emotional one. I didn't seem to have any emotion left for other people's problems.

I dyed Lou-Ann's hair. As I dried her off after her shower, she took one of the towels and tried to put it on as if it were a diaper.

I received a call from Lou-Ann's brother that her father's condition had become much worse. He wasn't eating and had lost a lot of weight. They didn't think he would pull through.

Budget time at school. This meant establishing salaries for the faculty in the department, and this year, due to cutbacks, having to make a decision as to which one of two instructors would not be offered a contract. Personnel decisions are tough because one is dealing with other people's lives in extremely critical ways.

The counselor I was seeing every month thought I was going through another step in the separation process. I really missed coming home to a person who loved and accepted me for who I was. I had no one to share the pressures of the department chair position, no safe refuge where I could get away from the pressures of life and just be surrounded by the arms of one who totally loved me.

Lou-Ann's father died. Every member of the family was with him except Lou-Ann. It was a little more than a week since he started to fail. It saddened me that Lou-Ann couldn't even attend her own father's funeral.

I cried when I thought of how I would tell her. I wanted us to be alone so she wouldn't be distracted as I talked. The weather was nice so I took her out on the porch at Starr Farm. She gave no indication that she understood what I said. Not only would she not be able to go to his memorial service, but I wasn't sure that she even knew he was gone. A memorial service was held one week after his death. I met some of his relatives there whom I hadn't seen in 15 years. I took part in the service, in reality taking Lou-Ann's place since Janet and Lloyd also had a part in the eulogy. I was nervous, but it was a joy to be able to share some of my memories of him.

My 50th birthday — Both my grandfather and father died before they reached their 50th birthday. I used to tease Lou-Ann that we should not postpone things because I wouldn't live to be 50. "Don't talk like that," she would respond. How ironic that it was she who might not reach her 50th birthday.

Class lasted until 7 p.m., so I rushed to the nursing home to be with Lou-Ann. I had nothing special planned except to spend the evening with her. As I entered Starr Farm, one of the nurses said I should immediately go home. Something must have happened so I wanted to call to find out what it was. As I walked to the nurse's station to phone, I realized that Lou-Ann wasn't at Starr Farm at all, she was home. Tim and Maria had picked her up so we could have a little celebration together. Peg was there also.

After dinner I was handed a bowl that contained several folded slips of paper. Each had a birthday gift written on it. I was to choose my present by lottery. The one I picked said, "You get tomorrow off from work." All the slips were identical. Maria had called my secretary a month before so she could fill my day with fictitious appointments. It was a real nice surprise. I was able to spend much of the next day with Lou-Ann.

Lou-Ann was playing with a rattle when I arrived and wouldn't look at me. She was concentrating so intently on the rattle that, no matter what I did, she wouldn't look up. She finally looked at me when I took it from her. She readily gave it up.

A year before, Maria had wanted to begin to make plans for a celebration for my 50th birthday. I didn't want to celebrate unless I knew Lou-Ann could be with me. When it was obvious she could attend, Maria began planning with one restriction, no gifts. It would be a time for friends to get together, mark a milestone, and renew old relationships. This would be a time for Lou-Ann as well since most of the people invited had not seen her since she had gone into the nursing home, and some new friends had never met her.

Approximately 70 people came. There were people from church, school, past students, and family. I was the only person there who knew everyone. Lou-Ann wore her green Christmas dress with a colorful scarf around her neck secured with a brooch. She was all dressed up, complete with panty hose. She would wear this dress only one more time.

We arrived 15 minutes after everyone else so she wouldn't have to wait for everything to start. We slowly walked in hand in hand. At first she seemed confused, but settled down after a while. It was a great day, being surrounded by family and friends and having Lou-Ann with me in a social setting.

After Lou-Ann entered the nursing home, I had had a conversation with Maria regarding my future, which seemed to have been erased with the onset of Pick's disease. I needed to think of something I could look forward to after Lou-Ann's death, something to indicate there was a future. The first idea that entered my mind was flying. I was fascinated with flying as a child and built model airplanes. My father got his pilots' license before he was drafted into the Second World War and I had flown a lot with him, especially after he was discharged in 1946. We flew until I was around ten when he gave it up. Maria stored that piece of information for future consideration.

At the party, I was presented with a leather jacket and coupons for some lessons at a local flight school. She had written everyone on my Christmas card list, plus all my local friends, asking for contributions for this gift. The party provided a chance for people to show their support for the family. It turned out to be one of those events I would never forget. Becoming 50 was a joyous occasion.

April, 1990

At Deacon's meeting, a member asked for prayer for a family whose 29-year-old son had committed suicide. Our minister said, "There can't be anything that would hurt more." His statement hit me hard. Severe hurt and pain could be prioritized? Losing a child by suicide hurts more than losing a child by other causes, hurts more than losing a spouse, hurts more than . . . Losing a leg hurts more than losing an arm, hurts more than losing a foot hurts more than . . . What makes a person make such a statement, especially in the presence of people who are going through severe loss? The kind of relationship between the individuals involved didn't seem to matter. It wasn't the fact that they try to express some compassion for the loss, but that there was a judgment regarding how much the loss hurt, when in fact they had no basis to make such a conclusion. More appropriate comments would be, "I can't comprehend how one deals with such a loss," "This must be one of life's most difficult things to go through," "I can't imagine many things that would hurt more than this."

Lou-Ann picked all the buds off our Christmas cactus two years earlier and it hadn't bloomed since. It was now blooming, just in time for her birthday.

Lou-Ann's mother and sister came for the weekend to celebrate both Lou-Ann's and Maria's birthdays. It was nice to have them spend a little time with her. I also got to eat a good meal or two. I brought Lou-Ann home on her birthday but we didn't do anything special.

Lou-Ann was having problems choking again. This time she started while eating soup and didn't stop until she threw up what she had eaten. She continued to hoard food in her mouth.

In casual conversation with a couple of the nurses, they commented that they had seen her decline in the last month. One of them only worked on the weekends so she didn't see her on an everyday basis.

Lou-Ann was becoming difficult to get up, but once up, she moved around at a slow pace. She bit her fingernails, which she had never done before, and continued to reach out to anyone within arm's length. If I stopped when walking with her, she would stand in the same spot and not move. She propelled herself in the wheelchair with her feet. Often when she got to the end of the hall, she would get stuck in a corner and couldn't get out.

She seemed more reserved when I dyed her hair and gave her a shower. She didn't grab the shower nozzle as much as in the past and tended to just stand there. When I dressed her, I put on one sock. As I picked up the other sock, she put out her foot to help me, the only trouble was that it was the foot with the sock. It took some talking to get her to lift her bare foot.

I found Keith at home when I returned from Starr Farm. He was having problems at school, keeping focused on what he was supposed to be doing. He didn't go back for two days. While he was home we had a talk about how things were going and his plans for the future. When he returned they told him to take the rest of the week off to get himself back on course. He sapped the energy from me, but I didn't really have much left for him. How was one supposed to be there for their children and at the same time take care of their sick spouse?

It was six months since Lou-Ann's last visit with Dr. Gomez. He changed her to a soft diet. He said her reaching out was natural for where she was in this disease. Physical changes seemed more evident. She had slowed up so much. The end to this disease could potentially come at any time. The next big physical decline could lead to a direct cause of her death.

The void in my life just seemed to get bigger and bigger and bigger.

I brought Lou-Ann to Tim and Maria's for a small party. She didn't seem comfortable all evening. Sitting on the sofa seemed hard for her because she wasn't able to sit upright, she was always leaning to one side or the other. She lay down on the sofa but didn't relax until I lay next to her with her head on my shoulder. We put her to bed for an hour but she wasn't able to relax so we got her up. She sensed she was out of her element, strange noises, strange sights.

Riding in the car had become harder and harder for her. She didn't seem to be comfortable. Since she couldn't get into the car by herself, she couldn't adjust herself to a comfortable position. Her posture was where she ended up after I swung her legs in. I straightened her up, but she couldn't always hold herself erect and ended up slumping to one side or the other.

May, 1990

Lou-Ann lay down and fell asleep when I had her home on a Saturday. I couldn't wake her for dinner. I shook her, patted her hand, but nothing worked. I sat her up and she just collapsed. I lifted her to her feet and her knees buckled four or five times before she finally woke up. After dinner we got ready to go back to Starr Farm. Upon reaching the edge of the breezeway, she stopped and would not take the one step down to the driveway. I had to pick her up and lift her down.

Every day seems to be a "what could go wrong today?" sort of day. When I got home from a meeting, I found a note from Keith saying that he wanted to quit school. This wasn't a total surprise after the talk we had had last month.

The next day I was called into the Dean's office and encouraged to make an appointment with the Employee Assistance Office. Someone, they wouldn't say who, felt I was under great pressure and needed help. They refused to tell me what led to this meeting. I left the room angry because I felt I was being accused of doing something that was being attributed to the fact that I was under stress because of Lou-Ann, and no one would tell me what I supposedly had done.

I changed our walking schedule at the nursing home. Twice around the facility, watch some TV, a couple of more times around and more TV.

She stopped a lot as she walked. We were together for almost two hours and I didn't hear one sound from her.

A nurse saw her stand by herself. She hadn't done that in months. She came up behind another person who was in a wheelchair, grasped the handles at the back of the chair, pulled herself up and pushed it for a short distance.

Keith moved home from school. He took a leave of absence even though he didn't think he would be returning. He lived home for two weeks until his summer job began at Basin Harbor.

Mother's Day — The kids bought Lou-Ann a mylar balloon. At first she ignored it. As we were lying down watching TV, I pulled it down so she could see it. She took the ribbon, pulled the balloon down and held it tight. She didn't let go of it the rest of the day. She even ate one-handed. I pulled it out of her hand when I changed her, but other than that she never let it go. As we put her arms in her coat, she transferred the balloon from hand to hand and repeated it when we took her coat off at Starr Farm. We walked around the nursing home twice before she sat in her wheelchair. She still had the balloon in her hand when I left.

She went back to staying in step with me as we walked. She did this for two days. I skipped to put us out of step and she would change her gait to get back together. She still walked on the shadows and stopped more and more as we went around the nursing home. Once she stopped, it was hard to get her moving again.

As she sat in the wheelchair, she would cross her ankles then immediately uncross them, move the chair ahead one step, cross her ankles, uncross them and continue this pattern for quite some time.

Memorial Day — Two years since Lou-Ann entered Starr Farm. I never expected her to be there one year, let alone two.

Walking outside was becoming more of a challenge. The shadows from the trees made an interesting pattern on the sidewalk. She tried to walk only on the shadows but that became a problem when there was a larger patch of sunlight. Walking was stop and go.

Our walks were one of the few "normal" things we could still do. Strolling hand in hand, whether talking or not, was something we used to do. Now that has been taken away. Everything was starting to take so much effort.

Keith started work at Basin Harbor. It was good to get my house back.

I started my flying lessons. It was not the thrill that I expected it to be. Flying was more involved now than when I flew with my father some 40 years earlier. There was a big difference when one had to concentrate on what was happening rather than looking out and enjoying the view.

June, 1990

Lou-Ann reached the point where she couldn't feed herself anymore. She was changed to a mechanical soft diet. Her food was chopped to a fine consistency, but not to a pureed state.

I bought two pairs of jeans of the same size I had previously purchased. They were very loose when I tried them on her. I checked her weight in her chart and she had lost five pounds, down to 165. It was her first weight change in more than a year.

She was having trouble going down the steps to the basement. Tim and Maria rented a couple of movies so we all went downstairs to see them. We could only get her to take one step at a time. When taking her back to Starr Farm, I couldn't get her to step off the breezeway so I had to lift her down to the driveway again.

As I was talking with Maria, she mentioned she hoped her mother would continue to decline and not level off. It took me back when she said that, even though I had the same desire. Part of me wanted that to occur but part didn't. I was being pulled in two opposite directions again. I could still hold her, touch her, sing to her, kiss her, caress her, and take care of her. When she was gone, it would be all gone.

The end of June, the term of being Interim Chair came to an end. I learned two things from the experience: first, I could do the job and second, I didn't have the desire to do it.

After three months, Lou-Ann had her period. She was not as regular as she had been. I had to ask that she be given Anaprox so she would be more comfortable.

When she lay down, she held her head off the pillow. She would eventually lay it down, but not right away. She also leaned way over at the waist while sitting in her wheelchair. At times she fell asleep in that position.

July, 1990

July 7, our 28th wedding anniversary. I had my first solo flight in the morning. In the afternoon, Tim and Maria came over and we had a little celebration to mark the day. Lou-Ann had to go down the stairs again since we had the party in the basement. In the past, once we got her started down the stairs she would continue, but this time I had to move her leg down each step. Going up the stairs did not present the same difficulty. She walked up by herself, but stopped with three steps remaining. We moved her foot to the next step which got her going again, and she took the final steps without assistance.

After her period she seemed to be doing well. Then all of a sudden she had trouble walking. She was unsteady when she first stood. The only way I could get her to walk was to stand directly in front of her, take both her hands and walk backward. It seemed as if I was almost pulling her around as we walked. She didn't stand erect, but stooped over as she stood.

I received a call from the nursing home saying they wanted to put her back into a geri-chair. She had been leaning way over in the wheelchair with her head below her knees. She also had slid out of the chair onto her knees a few times. It took three people to get her back in because she provided no assistance when they tried to lift her. She also hadn't been moving around much in the wheelchair. It ended up that she started spending more time in the geri-chair but still spent some time in her wheelchair. All these changes had taken place over the course of just a few days. She had also started to drool a lot more.

When she lay down now she repeatedly raised her head off the pillow, held it there for a second or two, then rested it back down. Two seconds later, she repeated the entire process. This would go on for a while when she first lay down.

Choking while eating was still a problem. The mechanical soft diet did not seem to help with this, so she was changed to a pureed diet. This wasn't the most appetizing way to present a meal.

We went to the Neurology Clinic for her regular doctor's appointment. The nursing home staff weighed her before we left and she was down to 159 pounds. She had now lost 10 pounds in the last three months. I had made a list for Dr. Gomez of the major changes since her last visit three months ago.

  weight loss (10 pounds)
  drooling
  leaning over a lot
  harder walking (getting started and keeping going, she doesn't seem to
  know what to do with her feet)
  stairs (have to place her feet when going down)
  lifting her head when she lies down
  just put on pureed food
  pained expression much of the time
  on daily Tylenol (every 4 hours)
  far away look
  hardly opens mouth when eating
  takes time to gain balance when she first stands up
  leans to side when walking

Her drooling indicated that she was not swallowing. This was of some concern because she might aspirate what was in her mouth, which could lead to a respiratory problem.

We discovered she had a urinary infection a few days after her doctor's appointment. Who knew how much this had affected the way she behaved? She started doing a little better once they put her on antibiotics. She moaned every time she urinated so it must have been very uncomfortable for her.

August, 1990

When I first arrived at the nursing home she didn't look at me. She seemed to be staring out into space. I could put my face in front of hers and even then she usually wouldn't focus on me. I took her glasses off to clean them and handed them to her to put back on. She tried to put them on my face even though I was already wearing glasses.

She still ate 75% to 100% of her food, but it took a long time. I tried to be sure to be there by dinnertime so I could feed her. I had the time to take with her to see that she ate as much as she could.

I brought her home for the first time in a couple of weeks. She seemed upset when she got in the car. She wouldn't let go of my hands so I could go around the car and get into the driver's seat. I had to talk to her for a while before I could pull away. Once she got home, she seemed more relaxed. I swung her legs out and she stood up as I took both hands and gave a slight pull. She hadn't gotten up that easily in a long time. I usually had to lift her to her feet by lifting under her arms before she would support her weight.

While we were laying down together, I had to get up to help Maria at the computer. Lou-Ann became upset and made noise until I returned. She had stopped talking completely and the only sound she usually made now was a whining noise.

Since she had trouble swallowing, she had problems when laying down. She choked on the saliva that built up in the back of her throat. She constantly drooled when she was up.

I met with Dr. Martenis to talk about the future decisions we might have to make as her condition degenerated. What actions should be taken and when should treatment for a condition be withheld? Fortunately we were thinking along similar lines. In general, we decided that if something happened that was life-threatening, such as a massive infection or pneumonia, we would not treat and let it run its course. Our concern would be for her comfort, but not with the intention of stopping the pneumonia or the infection. Everything else would be treated in a normal manner. She had been put in a no-code classification, meaning the nurses would not attempt to resuscitate her if for any reason her heart should stop. These decisions were not too hard to think through and make when the emergency wasn't present, but I wondered how hard they would be to carry out when the situation arose.

She continued to slide out of her wheelchair. The last time she had her ankles crossed so when she went to her knees they had a hard time getting her up.

September, 1990

She seemed to have been uncomfortable for a while so they tested her for a urinary infection again. It came back negative. She seemed to be going through menopause because her period had become so irregular. How much of her recent discomfort was due to this or to Pick's.

The church, the one place I had thought I would be able to look to for support and comfort, had been totally eliminated. This month's Deacon's meeting turned confrontational. When the dust cleared, four of the six board members resigned. There was no way I could continue attending that church. It really hurt because Lou-Ann and I had done so many things there, in addition to the fact that Tim and Maria were married in that building.

There were some good people in that church; I would miss them.

I flew the final long cross-country flight of my training on Labor Day. A few more hours of flight time, and I would be ready for my flight test. I had passed the FAA private pilot written exam earlier.

I was supervising a student teacher at the school where Pam, Maria's friend who was widowed a year ago, was teaching. Pam invited me for dinner after I had visited my student teacher. While we were eating, Joshua, her 15-month-old son, was trying to feed himself with a spoon. As I watched him it struck me that when it came to feeding, he was more advanced than Lou-Ann.

Lou-Ann was having trouble standing. Recently while I was changing her at home, she had lost her balance three times. I had to sit her on the toilet so I could dress her without fear of her falling.

A resident at Starr Farm picked up my spirits. One woman and I always exchanged greetings as we passed. As I was walking Lou-Ann, she came up behind us, pushed in her wheelchair by a relative. I heard her say, "There's a man who loves his wife." It was things like this that kept me going.

Lou-Ann couldn't be left standing by herself anymore. While changing her, I sat her on the toilet to take her pants off. I changed them and stood her up so I could pull them up. I decided to get her a new shirt so I left her standing for a moment while I went to the closet a few feet away. I had only gotten three steps from her when she stumbled backward and fell to a seated position on the toilet. She was able to catch herself a little on the grab bars, but her face showed that she had scared herself. To see an energetic and physically fit person decline to the point of not being able to stand alone was hard.

October, 1990

Lou-Ann's mother and sister visited Lou-Ann for the first time since her birthday in April. She had changed a lot since then.

Since she was now on a pureed diet, I had to change what I fed her when she was home. I tried baby food and that worked out well. This made it easier to have her home. It had been a long time since I had to make choices regarding baby foods. I would stand in the baby section of the grocery store with all the young parents picking out the things I thought Lou-Ann would enjoy. The contrast of life beginning and life ending was very vivid as I stood with mothers who had their infants along with them.

She seemed to be shuffling her left foot as she walked. She wouldn't step off the breezeway at all anymore. I had to give her a big hug and lift her down every time now.

She had begun to give specific indication of pain. One nurse found her moaning and cupping her hands over her ears. There were tears running down her cheeks. I hadn't seen her cry in a long, long time. She was given Tylenol. It was hard to know what she was feeling since she could no longer communicate, either verbally or nonverbally.

A week later, I put her back into the wheelchair and put on the restraint so she wouldn't fall out. She seemed fine and was helping me when suddenly she let out a short cry, grabbed her forehead, and leaned over. She had been holding her head a lot lately, but nothing as dramatic as this had happened.

She seemed to have a few good days and then became restless and had pain. She was put to bed after lunch when she moaned a few times and grasped her head. She was medicated but did not go to sleep. When checked, she was found awake with her head raised off the pillow, moaning and grasping her head. The head of the bed was elevated to 30° in an attempt to make her more comfortable. When the aide checked her a half hour later, she was asleep.

The staff sometimes had trouble medicating her because she wouldn't open her mouth, and this caused trouble at meals also. She seemed to be more tired lately, so every afternoon she was put to bed for a nap.

On Sunday I fed her lunch and we watched some football on TV. I had to leave at 2:30 for a 3:00 flying lesson. When I got home at 5:30, there was a message on my answering machine to call Starr Farm. They couldn't wake her from her nap. I went back to stay with her. She seemed to be waking a few times as she moved and reached up to scratch her nose, but would drop off again. She didn't come around until 9:15 p.m. She had been in that state for more than seven hours. When she awoke, she moaned and held her head. Her vital signs were steady throughout this whole affair. No one had any idea what caused her to do this. A similar situation had happened a week before when they couldn't get her to wake up for breakfast. She woke at 9:30 in the morning and had a fine day after that.

While this was happening, the daughter of Lou-Ann's roommate was visiting her mother. I had had the daughter in class a few years previously and she now worked at the university library. She looked tired, but since Lou-Ann was having trouble, I didn't want to engage in much conversation so I said little to her. She left around 7 o'clock in the evening. She didn't show up at work the next day and didn't call in sick. She lived by herself so someone went to her house to check on her and found her dead on the sofa. She must have lain down soon after arriving home and died before she could get up and go to bed. She was in her late forties. I was probably one of the last individuals to see her alive. It seemed as if death had been in Lou-Ann's room that night but was not there to call Lou-Ann.

The next day Lou-Ann had an appointment with Dr. Gomez. I took her in a wheelchair because walking had become such a problem. He didn't have any idea what would be causing the deep sleep or the headaches. He changed her medication to Tylenol #3 which contained codeine to try to make her more comfortable.

While being fed breakfast, she began choking on her cereal. She couldn't clear her throat and couldn't catch her breath because her nose was stuffed. She started to turn blue until she finally was able to breath through her mouth.

November, 1990

I had to be in Rhode Island for a three-day math conference. I really missed her while I was away. It was always hard when I first saw her after being gone. I so wanted to tell her about my trip, so wanted to hold her and be close, but when I saw her, there was so little reaction or interaction.

Where were God's people when I needed them? What I needed and missed were: comfort, someone to share my struggles with, a Christian perspective (not judgmental or having the "right" answer), a sounding board, a friendly ear, a haven, a support for my Christian faith when I couldn't supply the support and strength myself. This disease made me feel so isolated and alone.

The 17-year-old daughter of a member of our summer baseball team was killed in an automobile accident. She was very popular and the school auditorium was filled to overflowing for the memorial service. Before Lou-Ann's illness, I was so insensitive to people's losses and grief. It seemed as if so many people I now knew were facing some tragedy in their lives.

I weighed Lou-Ann after I dyed her hair. She was down to 150 pounds. She had lost about 20 pounds over the last seven months, three pounds per month.

Eating was becoming a constant problem now. She seemed to choke at every meal and was still seemingly having problems with headaches.

My flight test had to be rescheduled four times because the weather had been so poor. It was finally scheduled for 1 p.m., and by 11 a.m., I was a nervous wreck. I spent the morning reviewing basic information for the oral part of the exam and couldn't relax so I went to visit Lou-Ann. She was the one person I felt I could turn to in order to relax. I felt better after spending some time with her. That afternoon, I passed my flight test and received my private pilot's license.

Marguerite, one of my favorite residents, died a couple of days before Thanksgiving. I would miss her and her family. We had seen each other every day at dinnertime. It had always been nice to talk to her family. Her husband was 90 but moved around like he was 75. I'll never forget the day when her son, Father Jay, had taken her for a little walk and as they rounded the corner of the TV room, she spied her husband and said, "There's my man!" This was one resident's funeral I wanted to attend, but I couldn't because my aunt and uncle were celebrating their 50th wedding anniversary back in Buffalo, and I had said I would be there.

November 22, Thanksgiving — Twenty-three years ago my father died. Four years ago Lou-Ann had her first doctor's appointment. Four years isn't a long time, but these four years seemed like an eternity.

The nursing staff suggested Lou-Ann's wheelchair be equipped with a roll bar restraint. This was a padded bar that fit across her waist and acted like a seat belt. She could bend at the waist but couldn't fall forward and out of the chair. I preferred this to the geri-chair because she could still move around the facilities, propelled by her feet.

December, 1990

When I came to visit, she was leaning over to one side of her wheelchair, starring into space, drooling. She looked like a person who was overmedicated, when in fact she wasn't on any medication. She now tended to lean as she sat in the wheelchair.

Dyeing her hair was becoming more difficult. As I put the dye on, she wanted to run her hands through her hair. I solved that by putting rubber gloves on her to keep from getting dye all over her hands. She then tried to hold my hand as I applied the dye. I gave her a towel to hold and that seemed to keep her hands occupied.

On the evening of our support group, I would come in early to visit so I could spend our usual amount of time together before I had to leave. She was in obvious discomfort so was given Tylenol #3 which helped. While I was kneeling in front of her wheelchair with my hands on the arm rests, I rested my head on one of my arms. She leaned over, softly placed her head on mine, tenderly touched the side of my face with her hand, and gently started to pull my head around so I could kiss her. Such a tender moment when I least expected it. It was as if she was telling me she loved me. She had such a difficult couple of months and then did something like this. How much did she really understand?

Lou-Ann lost the use of her right wrist. She could use her fingers but couldn't raise her hand from a limp position. She saw the physical therapist and had to wear a splint. They added a padded lap tray across the arm supports of her wheelchair to keep her arm from getting caught by her side. The doctor thought her limp wrist was caused by a pinched nerve. He expected it to clear up over time.

I brought Lou-Ann home on Christmas Eve and kept her overnight. This was the third year we've been able to do that. She didn't get to bed until late and fell right asleep. She woke at 2:30 a.m. and slept very little the rest of the night. She was having a difficult time breathing because of the phlegm in the back of her throat. She kept picking her head up and laying it back down, which made it hard for me to rest. She finally lay still and stared at the digital numbers on our clock radio. Neither of us got much sleep the rest of the night.

Maria was sick during the night, so Christmas was a slow, low key day. Keith was working at the Trapp Family Lodge over the winter so everyone was home for this Christmas. He was planning on working in Florida during the winter next year, so this would probably be the last Christmas we would all be together as a family. The way Lou-Ann was going, it was questionable if she would still be alive then.

The last day of the year and we ended it with a bang. I took her for a walk after lunch, and when I sat her back down in the wheelchair I noticed the pad on the lap tray was coming off. I decided to retape the pad before I reattached the tray to the chair. This tray also acted as a restraint and took the place of the roll bar. I didn't think a couple of minutes with it off would be a problem. As I was taping the pad at the nurse's station, one of the aides called for help to get Lou-Ann up. She had leaned forward and fallen out of the chair, flat on her face. Her nose and lips were rug-burned and her glasses were pushed into her face, causing bruises above and below her eye. She had declined so far that she even lacked the ability to put her arms out to break the fall. She didn't exhibit any discomfort and didn't cry out, but there was no way that this could have happened without pain. I felt bad because it was all my fault.

The winter season could be hard in a nursing home. Four people died the last week of the year. Three had been there as long as Lou-Ann.

Chapter 10

The Sixth Year

January, 1991

It was so cold out New Year's Day that I decided not to bring Lou-Ann home. We spent the day together at Starr Farm. At 2:30 she took a nap and went into one of her deep sleeps. She couldn't be aroused until 7 p.m.

Lou-Ann's cheek as well as her eye turned black and blue from her fall. It looked as if she had been mugged. Her bad days seemed to be more frequent. She was very unstable either walking or standing, and choked on much of her meal, especially liquids. The nurses noticed her crying more than before.

The son of a friend, who had graduated from high school with Keith, was diagnosed with leukemia. I visited him and his mother in the hospital. He had one course of chemotherapy and came down with a severe infection. He was a very sick person. His mother, who is a teacher, took a leave of absence from school so she could spend all her time with him.

The last few months had been very trying — a number of friends at Starr Farm died, the son of a friend was critically ill, and Lou-Ann was having more and more trouble doing the basic things of life, like eating and breathing.

February, 1991

I had to stay away from the nursing home for five days because I came down with a cold and a sore throat. I realized that we would never know if Lou-Ann ever came down with this type of sickness because there was no way for her to let us know. How often did she have similar problems like a sore throat and we never realized it?

I think Lou-Ann realized I had not been with her because she held on to me while we were together. She held both my hands, very tight, even when I tried to feed her. I took the splint off her right arm while she was eating, she picked up her spoon and tried to feed herself. She used her left hand, even though she was right-handed, but she couldn't hold the spoon level without my help.

I invited a couple from our old church to our house for dinner. Lou-Ann as well as Tim and Maria were there. Maria helped with the preparation of the meal. It was nice to have an evening with other people. It was as close to "normal" as our life could become.

It had been almost six months since I last attended church. With Lou-Ann declining so precipitously, it became a pressing concern to find a church from which to bury her. I heard a number of good things about the new minister of a church we had attended 15 years before when we first moved to Burlington. I decided to try that church, but as I was getting ready to go for the first time, all the negative thoughts about our past church situations came rushing back. I had to put all that behind me and move on with this part of my life, but that was easier said than done.

After the service, a number of people I knew but hadn't seen in years came up to say hello. Many of them knew of Lou-Ann's condition. I didn't remember who everyone was. On the way out, a friend introduced me to the minister, Roland Coffey.

The head nurse claimed that Lou-Ann said, "Nurse, nurse, nurse," in a clear voice while she was having a difficult time eating. I had a hard time believing she really said something, but they insisted. I wished I had been there to hear it.

It was time to dye her hair. I weighed her after her shower and she was down to 142 pounds.

Our walks around the nursing home were taking longer and longer. It took over more than 12 minutes; at the beginning we could make a trip in three minutes. She also began to walk on her toes or the balls of her feet, instead of her full foot.

I went to church again and felt so alone sitting by myself. Thoughts of Lou-Ann's funeral kept going through my mind. Peg's daughter sat with me after she sang with the choir. It was comforting just having someone to sit with.

I didn't see Lou-Ann on Saturday. She had a couple of poor days in a row and the day before, I was near tears all the time I was with her. While eating, she started to stick her left hand into her mashed potatoes. I seemed to be jumping on every little thing she did. I also questioned the nurses about things I hadn't questioned before. One of the nurses said I seemed more depressed. I needed a day for myself so I went to a UVM basketball game and then to a movie.

March, 1991

Winter was dragging on, which was having its effect on my emotions. I couldn't wait until spring recess came. I saw the movie with *Sleeping the Enemy* and had a hard time watching the suspense scenes. Every love or tender scene seemed to accentuate my loss.

Lou-Ann's weight loss was becoming more and more evident. Her shoulders seemed so shallow and one could even see the thinness of her legs through her sweat pants. Major physical movements like walking took so much effort for her. Since she was having a hard time sitting upright, we had to stuff a blanket or pillow on the left side of the wheelchair to give her support.

Flo, a resident who always looked out for Lou-Ann, died. Everyday she would tell me how Lou-Ann's day went. She always made sure no one took Lou-Ann's wheelchair while we were walking. Flo and Doris, another resident, used to spend their entire day together. Doris was really going to miss her. They both smoked and sometimes I stayed with them in the TV room so they could have a cigarette. A resident couldn't smoke unless there was someone other than another resident present. I would give them a hard time about smoking, and they would always kid back. We enjoyed our times together.

After attending church for a month, I decided to meet with Roland Coffey, the minister. On the way out after the service, I asked, "Could we get together sometime so you could get to know me and I, you?" "Give me a call tomorrow, and we can set up a time to meet," he replied.

I called and we made plans to meet the next day for lunch. "I would like you to meet me at the Starr Farm Nursing Center so you can meet Lou-Ann, my wife."

I didn't know if he knew of our situation. I had Lou-Ann in her wheelchair in the front reception room when he arrived just before noon. "Reverend Coffey, I'd like you to meet my wife, Lou-Ann." He looked directly at her, reached out, took her hand, and said, "Lou-Ann, I'm very glad to meet you." She looked right at him as he talked to her. We remained at Starr Farm for about five minutes before we left for McDonalds.

The next hour and a half was the best time I had spent in a while. I learned more about him and his family in that brief period than I ever knew about my last minister. His youngest son had been killed in a traffic accident eight months before he and his wife moved to Vermont, a little more than two years before. He was able to relate to my situation in a more understanding way than many others. One of the things I liked about our visit was that he didn't give any pat clichés and was able to see things in terms other than black and white. Some ministers I've had dealings with always felt they had the definitive answer to everything and would not hesitate to tell me.

At the end of the month, we went for Lou-Ann's usual three-month doctor's visit. Dr. Gomez said she was showing some Parkinson's symptoms like walking on her toes or the balls of her feet. Her wrist movement had returned so the splint was removed. She was having more trouble initiating any activity. She balked at taking the one step up to the breezeway, so I now had to lift her up as well as down.

April, 1991

With classes on Tuesday, Wednesday, and Thursday evening, the spring semester had been very time-consuming. I didn't have much free time since the weekends were taken up with Lou-Ann, so I asked Maria if she could visit her mother on Mondays to give me some time for myself. Tim and Maria walked her and said she seemed tired after only once around the halls. It took about 15 minutes to make one trip around when I walked her, they did it in 5 minutes. No wonder she was pooped after their walk.

One night Denise, Maria's best friend from high school, was eating at a restaurant in downtown Burlington that featured live entertainment. Kathleen, the daughter of a neighbor four houses down from us was beginning a career in singing and song writing. She wrote a song inspired by Lou-Ann's condition and sang it at the restaurant, including a little explanation about its origin. I was not aware of this song until Denise told me about it. A year earlier, Lou-Ann and I had been walking on the bike path behind our house when we came upon Kathleen's family. We only spent five minutes talking together. Lou-Ann didn't recognize any of them and kept wandering away. I had to continually get her and bring her back. The song was about the loss of memory.

I now saw more variation in her from day to day. There were some definite bad days where she couldn't walk well, couldn't stand or sit straight up, and had extreme difficulty eating. She started to grind her teeth and bite down on the spoon when someone tried to feed her. When she clamped down on something in her mouth she wouldn't let it go. She had a difficult time being able to relax her bite and release what she had in her mouth.

The nursing home had placed her in a high-back wheelchair so she would have more support since she was having such a hard time sitting without leaning to one side. The back could also be adjusted so she could lean back more to make her more comfortable.

She went into that unresponsive state again as she sat in a geri-chair before lunch. She didn't come out of it until I arrived at 4:30 p.m. I got her up and she was very unsteady. As I stood her up and let go of one hand to reach for some clothes, she started to spin backward.

She ate her dinner well, especially the ice cream, and we were able to go for a walk, although she was leaning to the left all the way around. After, we sat in the TV room and she took both my hands and kept moving them up and down a few inches.

Lou-Ann turned 50 on the 19th. It was an exciting day because it was also Carolyn's wedding day. It was a monumental day for me, seeing Lou-Ann reach that milestone, and also seeing a close friend begin a whole new chapter in her life. About a year before, Carolyn had started to go with this fellow whom she met on a blind date.

We celebrated Lou-Ann's birthday on Sunday by having the family, as well as Tim and Maria's close friends, Mark, Lori, and little one-year-old Ben, over to the house. Lou-Ann seemed to enjoy the time and watched Ben very intently. She ate all her Ben and Jerry's ice cream.

Hair dyeing and weighing time. She had continued to lose weight and was down to 131 pounds. Still three pounds a month since her weight loss started. At this rate, she would be under 100 pounds in less than a year. How long could she continue to lose weight before it affected her health? She looked so thin laying on the bed when I dressed her after her nap. She hadn't been this light since junior high school.

They added a fortified pudding to her diet, which increased her caloric intake for each meal by 300 to 400 calories. Liquids were becoming especially hard for her to take. She didn't begin to swallow when a cup was placed to her lips but once she began she continued. It became tricky to know how long to keep her swallowing so she would get the maximum amount down, but at the same time wouldn't cut off her breath to the extent that she would begin to choke.

Lou-Ann was no longer able to sit without leaning and couldn't hold her head up. I had to reach around the back of her shoulders with my arm to lift her head to an upright position to feed her. Without doing that, the spoon couldn't be held level enough to keep food on it.

May, 1991

She started the month with a turn for the better. She was standing much straighter, although she wasn't as erect as she was the beginning of last month. Since she bit down hard on anything that was put in her mouth, she was now being fed with a rubber covered spoon. This was to protect her teeth from chipping on the hard surface.

She continued to fall into those deep sleep episodes. During the last one, she opened her eyes for a few seconds, gave a big sigh, then put her head back down and dropped back into the unresponsive state.

I received a call that she had fallen from her wheelchair as they gave her a shower because she had to be cleaned up after a bowel movement. She had been having difficulty defecating even though she got Milk of Magnesia every other day. I came in after they called and found her in the wheelchair, backed into a corner by the nurse's station. I got her up for a walk and she started within a few steps. She walked so well that we went around the corridors twice.

She ate everything for lunch, but it took an hour to feed her. After eating, she was falling asleep in her wheelchair so I put her to bed. Once in bed, she would not rest so I got her up and then realized that she had to be changed again. She was as alert as I had seen her in quite awhile.

The nurses recommended, and her general physician, Dr. Martenis, concurred, that her swallowing be evaluated by a specialized speech pathologist. The specialist observed her eating twice, at an evening meal and the following day for breakfast.

The first time she was observed she was asleep when her tray for dinner arrived. She seemed lethargic throughout the meal and frequently yawned. She repeatedly bit down on the spoon when fed warm pureed food. There was a significant delay in the onset of swallowing after the food was in her mouth and this was followed by her pumping her tongue up and down. She did a little better with cooler food, such as pudding. Her response to solids was better when they were preceded by a small amount of ice cream. She had only consumed about 25% of her meal after an hour.

The next morning, she was more alert for breakfast and often grasped the aide's hands. She ate her oatmeal well but choked severely when fed scrambled eggs. She again had long delays, even over a minute, between the time when food was placed in her mouth and when swallowing was finally accomplished. Swallowing was sometimes stimulated when an empty spoon was placed in her mouth. She ate 75% of her meal after one hour.

The speech pathologist had a number of recommendations after her observations such as: no eggs; thickened liquids only — from a spoon; bite-size servings, 1/3 to 1/2 teaspoon amounts maximum; do not rush; minimize external distractions while feeding; clean mouth of food after feeding and do not allow her to lie flat for 30 minutes. The last recommendation was because Lou-Ann was at great risk of inhaling food into her lungs and choking due to the delay in swallowing.

Her weight was still at 131 pounds when I dyed her hair at the end of the month. This was the first time her weight had not dropped since she started this decline. I didn't know how to react to this. These things always left me with mixed emotions. On one hand, I didn't want her to remain in such a diminished state for a long time, but on the other hand, I wanted her to be with me as long as possible. She seemed to react less and less to my presence.

June, 1991

Eating had become so difficult that some of the aides didn't want the responsibility of feeding her. She needed patience and time to eat, and anyone who didn't want to feed her would be short on those attributes. She wouldn't open her mouth, or if she did, she would only separate her teeth far enough to let the spoon in. Everything on it was then pushed off as it was slipped into her mouth. An alternate way to feed her that sometimes worked was to put the food inside her cheek, and she would then suck the food into her mouth through her teeth. I tried to make sure I was there at dinnertime to feed her. That way, I knew she would be given the time she needed to eat.

On Sunday, after my baseball game, I took Lou-Ann out for a ride. It was the weekend for the hot air balloon festival, so we rode over to where we could see the balloons flying. They didn't seem to catch her eye, and after an hour in the car, she seemed to become uncomfortable. We were out for an hour and a half. She didn't have an easy time walking to and from the car. When she walked she was breathing through her nose, which was stuffy. She wouldn't breath through her mouth.

Lou-Ann came down with a low-grade fever. The Tylenol seemed to break it. I couldn't get her to eat anything for dinner that night. She wouldn't open her mouth for me.

At her doctor's appointment, Dr. Gomez said he spoke to some colleagues at a medical meeting and they felt people with Pick's were living longer today because of the improved care they were receiving. He asked if she was having any difficulty breathing because that could become impaired. It was possible she could reach a point that she could forget to breath. Breathing is not the same as the involuntary reflex of a heart beating since a person can consciously stop breathing, i.e., hold their breath, whereas someone cannot stop their heart from beating.

July, 1991

Lou-Ann started the month with the flu. During her nap she vomited and had diarrhea. Her temperature was up to 102.9°. She was cleaned, given some Tylenol, and put back to bed. I arrived just as the staff had finished so I lay with her until 6:30 p.m. when I had to leave for an evening meeting. She had rested pretty well, but held on to me when I tried to go. I called the nursing home at 11:30 that night when I got back home and her fever was coming down. She took some liquids but wouldn't eat anything.

The next morning, the 4th, she was in a deep sleep and they couldn't wake her for breakfast. She woke just as I was arriving at 10 a.m. She was alert and took liquids for lunch. She was back on her pureed diet for dinner. Her temperature remained elevated for the next few days but she stopped vomiting.

July 7th — we celebrated our 29th wedding anniversary. It fell on Sunday, so I brought her home right after lunch and we spent the rest of the day together. Peg brought over a yogurt pie for a little celebration.

The following week, I went to my 30th college reunion at Clarkson University. Five years before, Lou-Ann and I attended my 25th reunion. She was just coming down with Pick's then, but we were not aware of what was happening. I spent a lot of this reunion going to many of the places that were important to the two of us, the place where I proposed to her, the walk we always took from where we lived to our church. This was where we met, where we courted, where we became engaged. I wished we could have shared it again. The place was not the same without her.

She weighed 124 pounds after her shower. I was surprised her weight wasn't lower since she hadn't eaten well when she had the flu.

One day it took the aides an hour and a half to feed her lunch. That night it was so nice out I took her into the courtyard for dinner. It took her two hours to eat 80% of her meal. She refused to open her mouth. It sure took a lot of patience to get any food in her.

I took her for a walk after dinner, but she couldn't straighten up and walked hunched over. I put her in the wheelchair and pushed her around the corridor. If she didn't walk with her feet as I pushed her chair, they would get caught under the seat. We would go a couple of steps then she would stop walking. I'd have to back up once her feet got caught under the chair, in order to get them out in front of her again. Then we could go forward until they got caught again.

After the walk, she held my left hand tightly with both hands. As I sat to her right, I put my left arm around her and she still wouldn't let go. As we were sitting there, I told her I had to go to the bathroom and that I'd be right back. She let go of my hand as I slid it out to get up. I felt she truly understood what I said. There were times in the past when under similar circumstances she didn't let go. Later, she didn't willingly let go when I was ready to leave.

Roland Coffey stopped by the house. We had gotten together a few times since that first lunch at McDonalds. This time we talked about Lou-Ann's funeral and some of the ideas I had about what I wanted in her service. Instead of organ music at the beginning, I wanted to have some songs by Amy Grant and a new singing group, Take 6. I played them to get his reactions. I could tell the songs had an effect on him. I didn't know it at the time, but that day was the third anniversary of his son's death.

While we talked, he shared his first impression of us when we met at Starr Farm. No one had told him of Lou-Ann's condition so he didn't know why Lou-Ann was in the nursing home. He said he thought she must have had some kind of terminal or debilitating illness and suspected that I was going to ask him if it would be okay for me to divorce her or start a new life without her. He was going to have to say that as a Christian it wasn't right to do any of those things. But he said, "As soon as I saw the two of you together, I knew I had jumped to the wrong conclusion. Here was a couple who loved each other and she was not about to be abandoned in the nursing home." The fact that the strength of our relationship showed was encouraging.

In our conversation, I mentioned that she sometimes seemed to understand what I was saying, like when she let go of my hand after I told her I had to go to the bathroom.

He immediately asked, "Do you think she would understand communion?" I had never thought of that and responded, "Only God knows if she would understand, but that is no reason not to serve it to her."

A few days later, at 10:30 in the morning, the three of us had communion together in the coordinator's office. Roland read some scripture and said a few things directly to Lou-Ann before he served communion. He handed me the wafer to feed her and suggested I first dip it in the juice. She opened her mouth and immediately tried to eat it. She had a little trouble, but I gave her the cup right after and she drank a little, which helped. After, the three of us held hands as he prayed. It was a very meaningful time for me. I don't know whether she knew what it was all about, but I know the Lord honored what we did. I was also a little bitter that no other minister had thought of doing this before, when there was more of a chance she could understand. This was something a minister should be sensitive to and could do for many people in similar circumstances.

Roland also shared with me that he used us as an example in his premarital counseling as to what it means when couples say their marriage vows. It was encouraging to know that some good was coming from what we were going through.

Penny, one of the aides who had taken a special interest in Lou-Ann, approached me and said I didn't have to come in every night to feed her. They would make sure she ate and I could come in around 6 p.m. to finish her up. They had the staff to do it, so it wasn't as critical for me to be there for every dinner. It was a help to have her say that to me. Feeding her was getting me down because I had to rush to be there by feeding time, and it was a heavy emotional weight to carry because she had so much trouble eating. One of the pleasures of life had turned into one of the most dire experiences of her day. This also allowed time for me to eat before I came to see her instead of having to wait until 9 or 10 p.m. to have dinner. More important, it was as if Penny had said, "I know what you want for Lou-Ann. I promise that her care will not be less when we feed her than when you do." There were some aides who I knew had a special relationship with Lou-Ann, and I could rest easy when they were assigned to her. They would treat her with as much love, respect, dignity, and kindness as I could. Their work in the nursing home was more than just a job to them.

During rounds she was found, call bell cord in hand, pressing the wooden ball at the end into her left eye. She had pressed so hard that her eye became swollen and reddened. No other damage resulted from this, but we never could figure out why she did that. It was difficult to determine reasons for many of her actions.

Keith stopped by to introduce us to a friend who worked with him at Basin Harbor. Her name was Maria. This was a very unusual event. This was the first time he had ever brought someone home to meet the family. Keith had dated before, but his relationships had never lasted very long. He used to say, "If I go with a girl for three weeks, it's a long-term commitment." He wouldn't bring a girl around unless there were something special to this relationship. "I'm never getting married," might be a statement he was going to have to swallow. They had some things in common. Like Keith, she was a minority, Korean, adopted into a Caucasian Vermont family as an infant, and grew up 20 miles south of Burlington. Tim and our daughter Maria were also at the house along with Lou-Ann so Maria, Keith's girlfriend, had a chance to meet everyone. She was relaxed and natural around Lou-Ann as well as the rest of us. Keith had brought home someone who everyone liked instantly.

August, 1991

This disease kept yanking me up and down. I was up when Lou-Ann had a good day and down when she was not so good. Last month I wasn't sure whether she would make it to Christmas, then this month started with her having some good days. She was more responsive and alert and was walking in a more upright position.

After a couple of weeks of good times she went back to vacillating between good and not so good days. She had some more time of being unresponsive and she began to have a low-grade fever along with a little vomiting and diarrhea.

Her weight had decreased to 120.5 pounds. At this rate, she would be under 100 pounds by February or March.

I talked to Don Goff, her boss when she worked for the Champlain Valley Office of Economic Opportunity to see if he would agree to deliver part of Lou-Ann's eulogy. I wanted him to speak about her as she was in the workplace. I had asked Peg to also be a part of the service and talk about her as a friend. I planned on finishing the picture by talking about her as a wife and mother. I wanted to plan as much of the funeral as possible so it wouldn't be thrown together at the last minute. I wanted the funeral to be a pleasant time, remembering her as she was before Pick's. I didn't want to dwell on the fact that we lost her, but take pleasure in the fact we had known her.

A friend from our past church who left the Board of Deacons at the same time I did would come to see Lou-Ann every week. She came with her young daughter while her older daughter was at dance class. They would push Lou-Ann in her wheelchair around Starr Farm and visit with other residents. The residents looked forward to their weekly visit, especially the opportunity to spend time with her daughter. It was a special time when children visited the nursing home. For me, knowing someone else was spending time with Lou-Ann meant that another person was helping to carry the weight of this disease. These acts of support and kindness helped me get through each day.

September, 1991

Lou-Ann came down with a cold. She had all the symptoms, a red, runny nose and a slight fever. Since she could not blow her nose, we tried to clear it with a syringe. A stuffy nose was very uncomfortable for her.

Another visit with Dr. Gomez. There was nothing new except her weight loss. She was healthy and not close to being malnourished. It appeared that we still had a way to go before this was all over. I didn't know how to react to that. It hurt seeing her struggle to make it through each day. Dr. Gomez didn't think she understood words anymore, but I was not sure what lead him to that conclusion. Since the only change from her last visit was the weight loss, he decided to wait until January to see her again. This was a change in our schedule from the three-month span between visits.

Friends from western New York visited along with their daughter. They hadn't seen Lou-Ann in four years. Lou-Ann made tuna casserole when they were last in Burlington. They were surprised at how good she looked. They expected her to look worse than she did. Except for her thinness, she still appeared relatively healthy. Their daughter reacted very protectively toward Lou-Ann. Their daughter had some serious physical problems when she was young, which left her with some learning difficulties. She wanted to sit next to Lou-Ann and hold her hand. She came with me when I took Lou-Ann back to Starr Farm. We talked about being physically close to Lou-Ann, which would make her feel more comfortable. She said, "I was patting Lou-Ann on the back because that way she would know we love her." Many adults didn't have that degree of sensitivity.

A long day. I had an early flying lesson and my flight instructor didn't show up. He had forgotten we were scheduled. He arrived and when we got to the plane an instrument, the turn coordinator, wasn't working so we couldn't fly. I went to my office and was working at my desk when I realized it was one o'clock so I rushed down to my class. No one showed. I couldn't figure out what was wrong. It finally dawned on me that my class wasn't until two.

That evening, I arrived at Starr Farm just as they were finishing feeding Lou-Ann. As I wheeled her down the hall she vomited. She had come down with the 24-hour bug. Starr Farm was short on help because many of the staff were out sick for the day, so I helped clean her up. It was the perfect way to end this day.

A new person came to the support group this month. She was a disruption from the beginning. Within five minutes, she started to make suggestions to people who were sharing how things had gone for them the past month. We went around the room and each person gave a brief update on what was happening to them. She started to tell me what I could do for Lou-Ann and I got very angry. "You don't understand my situation!" I told her. After the meeting she came over to talk and during the conversation she said, "I know how you must feel." I left that meeting in a worse mental state than when I arrived. She was a caregiver who worked for others and didn't have any family members who had Alzheimer's. She had tried too hard to be a part of the group. Later, she became a valued addition when she didn't try to prove herself and had developed more of an understanding of where each of us was coming from.

October, 1991

Lou-Ann continued to lose weight at a rate of about three pounds per month. She was now down to 115 pounds. She was also losing what balance she still had. In the past, her balance from front to back was a problem because she had to lean forward to move, but now she tended to fall sideways. Walking consisted of having to hold her upright as we moved. We were only able to walk from her room, around the nurse's station, and back — a total of about 50 feet. She was so thin she didn't have much muscle mass left and who knew how this disease had affected the part of the brain that controlled balance? She was sitting hunched over in her wheelchair, which made breathing difficult. She was given Tylenol, put to bed, and her breathing returned to normal.

She also began to clench her teeth more. The problem of getting food into her mouth was becoming extremely difficult. Things that stimulated her swallowing, like stroking her throat or cheek, or tilting her head back slightly, were not working as well as they had before.

On a Saturday afternoon, I found Lou-Ann in the activity room playing a game with other residents. The activity director had put three tables together to form a 10-foot by 10-foot square. Residents were sitting around the tables, hitting a large beach ball back and forth. Lou-Ann was sitting with the group in her wheelchair. When the ball came toward her she would reach for it. She didn't have the coordination to catch it, but at times she would hit the ball as she reached for it. When the ball fell to the floor I put it in front of her. All she could do was hold it with both hands but nothing else. I had to tap it out of her hands or else she would have just sat there holding onto it. It was exciting to see her react to a stimulus. It was amazing that something as simple as reaching for a ball, an action that an infant does, was now something I found exciting to watch.

November, 1991

Because she has been having trouble with the pureed food, they put her on a blended diet. All her warm food was put into a blender and mixed with milk. She took her juice and the cold dessert but wouldn't drink the warm food.

Since she was having trouble sitting up in Starr Farm's wheelchair, the director of the nursing home suggested we get one that was fitted to Lou-Ann and her needs. I met with the physical therapist and a representative from a medical supply store to determine what would be best for her. A narrow, high-back chair with side supports and a lap tray would meet her needs.

Once it came, we had to try various configurations to see what would give the most support without limiting her movement. Feet supports were used to keep her legs from getting caught under the chair when she was pushed forward, and this also seemed to help her sit back in the chair. They also installed supports for her sides, which helped to keep her from leaning over the edge of the chair.

She didn't seem to move her feet quite as much as in the past, although the crossing and uncrossing of her feet kept her joints moving so she wouldn't get so stiff. One reason I still tried to walk her, even if it was for only a short distance, was to have her skeleton support her weight and give her joints a workout.

The cost of the wheelchair was shocking. That wheelchair cost more, over $1600, than the new car we purchased in 1969. I also wanted a lap tray that would fit over the arm rests. We had kept one on her chair since she had the dropped wrist problem. It worked at keeping her arms from getting caught by her side and also acted as a restraint in keeping her from bending way over. The medical store brought a Plexiglas tray that cost $165, but I didn't like it. It was too expensive and took too long to remove. I wanted something that could be taken off in a few seconds in case she choked and it had to be removed quickly to get her out of the chair. I designed and built a wooden lap tray for under $10 that could be removed in two or three seconds.

Lou-Ann's mother and sister visited so I brought her home before they arrived. As she came to the breezeway she stepped up without my help, but couldn't lift herself completely with her forward leg. As a result, both knees were bent when she stepped up with the trailing leg. I was in front of her holding on to both her hands for balance when she slowly sank to her knees. I know she was trying to hold herself up because she didn't suddenly just drop down to the breezeway. She lacked the strength to straighten up when her legs were slightly bent.

The Commission on Vermont's Elderly asked if I would be willing to be interviewed by the *Burlington Free Press* for an article regarding the financial concerns associated with long-term care. The state legislature was debating a bill on long term care and the paper wanted to have some personal experiences in the article. A reporter called while I was at school and we talked for about 20 minutes. We talked more about Lou-Ann and Pick's disease than we did about the financial concerns. At the end, she asked if they could sent a photographer to the nursing home to get some pictures of Lou-Ann and myself. I was leaving the next day for a four-day math conference, so we had to do it that night.

I had Lou-Ann in the front reception room when the photographer arrived, but she wanted to take the pictures in Lou-Ann's room. The photographer had a couple of cameras over one shoulder and carried a tripod in the other, which was next to Lou-Ann as we walked down the hall. As I wheeled Lou-Ann back to her room, she reached out and placed her hand on the tripod. She left it there until we entered her room. The photographer and I talked as she set up the room for the pictures. I mentioned that I was going to dye her hair the next morning. Both the photographer and the journalist asked why I dyed her hair. I was surprised by their question. No one had ever questioned that before. I guess it didn't make sense to them to dye the hair of someone living in a nursing home.

I kneeled in front of Lou-Ann, who was sitting in her wheelchair. The photographer took our picture as we talked. She asked questions about Lou-Ann, the disease, and what she had done before the illness. After taking a number of pictures, I realized she had stopped. I looked up and tears were in her eyes. Our situation had touched her. She apologized and began to take more pictures. She exposed two rolls of film.

As she was putting her equipment away, she asked for some general information.

"How old is Lou-Ann?" "She turned 50 last April," I responded. "Last July we celebrated our 29th wedding anniversary and I pray she lives long enough so we can celebrate our 30th."

I surprised myself when I said that. Previously I had never expressed a desire that she would live to see a given event or date. I had always wanted us to live long enough to celebrate our 50th anniversary but now that was impossible. While making that statement to the photographer, it hit me that we would never make 50, but 30 was not out of the question and 30 sounded better than 29. Living to see our 50th was something I had never shared with Lou-Ann. As the photographer left she remarked, "You certainly are a man who loves his wife." That meant a lot to me.

I was out of town at the conference when the article was published. It was on the front page and our picture was three columns wide.

I was excited about having the picture in the paper. For people who knew us, it was a way for them to get to see her again because only a couple of friends still stopped by to see her. It also gave confirmation of her existence. It brought her back to people who wanted to put her out of their lives. She shouldn't, and couldn't, be that readily dismissed. That was the sad thing about many of the people in the nursing home. People had put them there and it became convenient to just forget them, put them out of their lives as much as they could. I imagine the movements surrounding MIAs and hostages stem from the same concern. Don't forget them, or her. In many ways their existence depended on us not forgetting about them.

The wife of a fellow choir member had been ill for a long time and had to be placed in the hospital because her condition had become critical. The choir director had prayed for her and her family at practice and also Sunday before we warmed up before the service. As we were walking into the sanctuary, she came to me and said, "Our prayers for Chuck's wife must be hard for you since we have never prayed for Lou-Ann, and she has been sick for such a long time." I appreciated her sensitivity, but it would have also been nice if they had prayed for her once in awhile.

December, 1991

Lou-Ann came down with another cold. She was flushed and had a temperature and a stuffy nose. She had trouble breathing because she continued to try to breath through her nose.

Maria and I went Christmas shopping for Lou-Ann. We bought some shirts, jeans, sweatpants, and socks.

Lou-Ann now stayed in her wheelchair for her haircut. I also had to hold her head steady much of the time as Hope cut her hair. Hope styled her hair in a shag so she wouldn't have to shave the back of Lou-Ann's neck.

Later I dyed her hair so she would look nice for Christmas. She didn't have to wear rubber gloves because she no longer tried to run her hands through her hair after the dye was put on. It was becoming increasingly harder to dye her hair because she couldn't, or wouldn't, keep her head up or hold it still. After her shower she weighed 112 pounds, the same as last time. This was only the second time in 20 months that her weight hadn't dropped.

On Christmas Eve the kids went to church and I stayed with Lou-Ann at Starr Farm. She leaned over a lot and ground her teeth. I wish I knew if that indicated pain. I hated to think she might be uncomfortable and we weren't doing anything about it. I decided that Lou-Ann should stay at Starr Farm until Christmas Day. Christmas Eve had been the only night she slept in her own bed at home since she entered the nursing home, but given the state of her condition it would have been too much to have her overnight.

I really missed not having Lou-Ann with me when I went to bed. It was the first Christmas Eve we had spent apart since we were married.

On Christmas Day I went to get Lou-Ann a little after 9 o'clock in the morning. No one was hungry for breakfast when we got home, so I got Lou-Ann settled on the sofa. After changing her once, we opened our gifts. Lou-Ann couldn't do anything including sitting up. She lay back down on the sofa and it didn't take long before she fell asleep. She went into one of her deep sleeps and didn't wake until 2:30 in the afternoon. She looked so relaxed while she slept. It was good to see her comfortable. When she was awake, she seemed to have to struggle and fight so much.

Keith wasn't home since he was working in Florida for the winter. Maria, Keith's girlfriend, came to visit for a few hours in the early afternoon. She was a great person and I knew Lou-Ann would have been very fond of her. Everyone was so relaxed when we were together. It seemed as if she had been with the family for quite a while even though she had only visited a few times. She was a senior at the University of New Hampshire, so she was only around during school vacations.

For Christmas dinner Tim, Maria, and I were invited to the home of a person who worked with Maria, so we dropped Lou-Ann off at Starr Farm on the way to their house. It was nice not to have to worry about fixing a big meal, and all the hassles that went with that.

Lou-Ann seemed to constantly hold onto me while I was with her, especially if I tried to get up, even if it was to walk her or push her wheelchair. It was difficult to leave her since she would reach out to me and watch me walk away down the hall.

She was such a shell of herself. Oh, how I wished I could talk with her, hear har voice and laugh, and see her face shine. As she died, a lot of me died with her. "And the two shall become one . . ." It seemed as if we continued to be "one" even in death.

Chapter 11

The Seventh Year

January, 1992

New Year's Day used to be a secular holiday in our house, something we called "pig-out day." A day of parades and college football bowl games, potato chips, pretzels, cheese curls, Pepsi, and roast beef sandwiches. Lou-Ann would watch some of·the parades then spend the rest of the day upstairs reading and knitting while the kids and I would camp downstairs. She'd come down every once in awhile to check on us, to make sure we were still alive, but for the most part she'd let us break all the house rules on healthy eating. Keith would stay until he had met his limit on food, Maria would stay a little longer into the second game, and I would end the day watching the Orange Bowl by myself.

I brought Lou-Ann home for New Year's Day. Tim, Maria, Mark, and Lori stayed overnight. Not only do my kids come back to stay, they bring their friends along. Instead of trying the impossible of walking Lou-Ann downstairs, we took her down in her wheelchair. It took two people to negotiate the stairs with her in the chair. During, the afternoon she seemed to watch everyone and was particularly fascinated with Mark and Lori's little boy, Ben. This would be the day Ben would take his first steps. The wheelchair gave Lou-Ann more flexibility around the house. Before it took so much effort to just get her from one room to another.

The next day she had her regular appointment with Dr. Gomez. Kathy Slinker, our friend and social worker, asked if she could come along for this visit. This day her presence was particularly helpful. I always packed a bag of necessities for Lou-Ann everytime we went to Dr. Gomez's office, extra diapers, pants, socks, baby powder, etc. I'd pack it, bring it, and take it back. The aides were just finishing getting Lou-Ann changed and dressed in clean clothes when I arrived at Starr Farm. Since she had just had a bowel movement, I decided to take the risk to forego the traveling bag.

As I got her out of the car at the hospital where Dr. Gomez's office was located, I smelled a familiar odor. The one time I left her changing things, I needed them. Kathy met us at the door and I told her our predicament. Fortunately, as a geriatric social worker, Kathy had some adult diapers in her car. We took her upstairs and Kathy helped change her. Saved by a friend.

Dr. Gomez didn't expect Lou-Ann to look as good as she did. He wasn't sure she sensed pain in the same way as a healthy person. He divided pain into three parts: perception, recognition, and reaction. He wasn't sure if she could recognize what she felt. Her reaction, or lack of it, certainly wasn't the same as a healthy person. He wanted to see her again in three months.

He mentioned he saw the newspaper article and felt we would be celebrating our 30th wedding anniversary in July. How long would this go on?

Lou-Ann wasn't reaching out as much as before. She now sat much of the time holding one hand in the other.

A family in a neighboring town saw the newspaper article and sent a letter of encouragement. Their daughter had died from Pick's. Lou-Ann was the only other person they had heard of who had the disease. She included their telephone number so I called them. We talked for a long time.

In a Christmas letter, a friend included a booklet written by a man whose wife had Alzheimer's. This man resigned from his position as a college president to take care of her. In his booklet he told of his wife walking, about a mile, many times a day to his school to see him. Their family doctor had a theory that it was strong personality characteristics developed across the years that came out at times like these. I hated it when people made such grandiose statements. Not wanting to be away from the one they knew the best was not unusual. A friend's wife followed him around the house all the time, even getting up from a meal if he got up. What about the minister I heard of who swore all the time after he came down with Alzheimer's? Was this a characteristic that developed across the years? People try to make so much more out of a situation than they have the right to. Who knows why people do what they do when they have Alzheimer's? Are they willing to attribute all their actions to past life? I doubt it. How can they choose what to ascribe to past experiences and what they want to ignore? Such a comment, coming from a doctor, showed there were physicians who were not familiar with dementia and could give questionable information about the disease.

Friends who were missionaries in New Guinea and home on furlough, stopped by with their son to see Lou-Ann. It was nice that they had a chance to see her again. She seemed more alert and watched what was going on around her. She was home for over six hours. Having our friends around the house seemed like old times again.

Lou-Ann's weight seemed to be holding, but she was having trouble standing and walking. She had fallen twice in a few days. The first was when I had just finished changing her. As I closed the door to her bathroom, my attention left her for just a moment, she slowly spun in place and settled on her bottom on the floor. I couldn't catch her as she went down. It was similar to toddlers who were just getting their legs under them, their feet get twisted and they spin down like a top. The other time she was sitting in the bathroom after I had changed her diaper and sweat pants. I reached under her arms to lift her since she couldn't stand up by herself anymore. As I released my support from under one arm to reach for her hand, she started to spin down. By the time I grasped her hand, she had gone too far to keep her upright so I just guided her down to a soft landing.

She had trouble getting her feet to move when she tried to walk. Once she eventually got moving, she would wobble because she was so unstable.

Tim and Maria wanted to talk to me about their plans for the future. They want to build a house, have a family, and take a six-month trip around the world. They had been trying to decide in what order to do them. The trip was to center around trekking, visiting places like Egypt, India, Nepal, and China. The big issue about being gone for that length of time was the condition of Lou-Ann, and the possibility she could die while they were gone. If they didn't take the trip at this time, and instead started their family, it would be at least 25 to 30 years until they would be able to go. They had no guarantee they could do it 30 years in the future. Lou-Ann's condition drove that home. They decided to make the trip and leave at the end of August.

February, 1992

Lou-Ann came down with a gastrointestinal virus. She had a fever and diarrhea. Every time she got sick with something like this I became concerned about further complications.

She had gained three pounds since I last weighed her. She was up to 115 pounds. If she had continued on the decline she had had over the past two years, she would have been down to 103 pounds. Under those conditions, her weight would have become critical sometime during the summer. Her weight loss had provided a timetable regarding her possible death, but now I had no idea of how long she was going to continue in this state.

Some of the other residents at Starr Farm seemed to be becoming more demanding. One woman in her early 90s occasionally thought I was her husband. He had been dead for a number of years. She sometimes became upset when she saw Lou-Ann and I walking and said all sorts of nasty things to us because she thought she was being two-timed. On one occasion she began to hit me on my back. Another woman, who was a school teacher, was concerned about having someone with her class and she kept asking everyone to cover for her. It was hard enough trying to keep Lou-Ann upright and moving when walking without these interruptions from other residents. Other residents wanted me to immediately push them to their room if I was nearby and would get mad if I said no or ignored them. Starr Farm didn't seem to be as relaxing a place as it used to be.

It was hard to keep up with Lou-Ann's mouth hygiene because she wouldn't open her mouth and let others brush her teeth. Her bite was so hard that she once bit her toothbrush in half when the staff was trying to clean her teeth. They had quite a time removing the half that was in her mouth. I tried to clean her mouth and teeth by wiping them with a towel when she yawned. On one occasion I wasn't fast enough and she closed on my finger. She bit down hard and wouldn't let go. For a moment I didn't know if she would break my finger. I told her to open up in a loud and frightened voice and had to force her mouth open with my other hand. She released my finger only after a second or two, but she left her mark. It was just a reflex she could no longer control. When I looked at her it was obvious that she didn't have a clue about what had happened.

Big news in our house, Keith gave Maria an engagement ring — this from a guy who always said he was never going to become married. Everyone was excited! Lou-Ann would have been so happy.

Lou-Ann missed another big event this month. Denise, Maria's best friend who spent a lot of time in our house over the years and became a surrogate niece to us, was married. Maria was the Matron of Honor. Lou-Ann would have wanted to be a part of the celebration.

Days were becoming longer and longer for me. I didn't seem to get anything accomplished. When I was home on the weekends, I found myself sitting in front of the TV watching things I really didn't care about instead of becoming involved with something constructive. I decided not to see her one day because I didn't have the energy, but I felt so torn about staying home. The times that seemed the nicest now were when she was lying down and I could lie next to her. It was so good to see her relaxed and it was also nice to feel her next to me. It had been so long since I had any meaningful physical contact with her. She had to struggle so much to accomplish life's basic needs, like eating, that the peace she had when sleeping was comforting to me. She often looked at me when she was lying down awake. When she was up she didn't tend to that.

Walking was definitely coming to an end. I was able to get her standing, but when we started to walk she would only take two steps and stop. It was as if her feet had become attached to the floor, they would not move. I tried pulling her forward until she was almost falling over, but she still wouldn't step out.

March, 1992

She was able to take a few steps in the beginning of the month. We went from her room to the nurse's station, 20 feet, but there were too many people standing there for us to go around, and I didn't think she could go that far. She couldn't figure out how to turn around to head back so I picked her up, turned her, and we started back to her room.

Another fever of 101°, so early to bed with Tylenol and codeine. I felt so helpless as I lay next to her. It took me back years to when our children were infants and sick. They couldn't tell us what was wrong, but could only look up at us. As I cradled Lou-Ann's head in my arms she just kept looking up at me. I wish I knew what was going on in her mind.

Keith and Maria set their wedding date for June 27. Keith's work schedule dictated that date and hence they didn't have much time to put it all together. It was going to be different going through this as the father of the groom rather than father of the bride.

At home, Lou-Ann was now either in her wheelchair or in bed. Moving her from her chair to the car, and vice versa, was quite a feat since she could no longer give any assistance. She was dead weight.

April, 1992

Congested, feverish, needing to be suctioned in order to have a clear throat, this was how the month began for Lou-Ann. I stayed with her until she dropped off to sleep. She couldn't cough until whatever was in her throat began to inhibit her breathing. The next day as she coughed, I was able to get some of the phlegm with a towel.

I was asked to speak about dementia to two psychology classes at St. Michael's College, a local Catholic college. One of the aides at Starr Farm was in the class and had given my name to the professor. I was always happy to share what was happening to us because so many people didn't have any idea of what Alzheimer's or Pick's. There were students in the class whose families were dealing with a parent or grandparent who had dementia, those students asked the best questions and often gained the most, especially about resources for support.

I was spending a Monday at Burlington High School visiting student teachers. At noon I had to go back to the office because I forgot some papers I needed. There was a message on my door to call Dr. Martenis. He was at lunch and wouldn't be returning for half an hour. I called Starr Farm to see what was happening. They thought Lou-Ann was coming down with pneumonia. Treat or not treat? This was the first time I had to make this decision. There was no one to talk to at that time, I was left to myself. I was numb. People were all around me as they went about their business, but I felt in a world of my own. I knew what was right, but saying it when it counted was not easy. I called Maria.

"Maria, they think your mother is going into pneumonia."

"How serious is it?"

"I don't know. Dr. Martenis is at lunch and I can't talk to him until 12:30. I may have to make a decision as to whether to use antibiotics. If I have to I am going to say no."

"It's okay, Dad."

Those few words were a big comfort to me. I was making the decision, but she was standing behind me in it.

The decision was to do nothing until Dr. Martenis could see her that night. She was alert and completely clear when he saw her. When she laid down after he left, one could hear the rattles in her chest again and she seemed uncomfortable. The next afternoon she went into another episode of deep sleep. She drank a little milkshake for dinner, was bathed, and was returned to bed. She had a hard time breathing without moaning. They propped her on her side so any drainage would not settle in the back of her throat.

She had an appointment with Dr. Gomez two days later and by then was not having any problems breathing. He didn't see much change in her since our last visit three months ago.

The following Monday morning, at 1:30 a.m., I received a call from Starr Farm saying they had suctioned a lot of mucus from Lou-Ann's lungs and it sounded as if her right lung was filling up. They wanted to call the doctor for some morphine to settle her down. Morphine, how serious was this? I related the use of morphine with an extremely critical situation. Being woken up at that time of the night didn't help me think with a clear mind. Was this going to be it? At 2:15 they called again to say she was on oxygen and settling down.

How did one go back to sleep at such a time? My mind wandered through all kinds of scenarios as I lay there wondering how she was. Her birthday was next Sunday, Keith would be coming home from Florida in two weeks, Keith and Maria were getting married in 2½ months. She just couldn't die at this time, there were too many things coming up in our lives. But there would always be something coming up. Was there an appropriate time to die? Thankfully this was in God's hands, and I had to leave it there.

I went in at 7:30 the next morning. She was awake in bed. She was still on oxygen but breathing easily and very relaxed. She looked at me as I approached, not just looking in my general direction as she often did, but really focused on me. I gave her a little hug, kissed her forehead, and stroked her cheek. "Hi honey, I'm here now. How are you doing?" She slowly rolled her head to the side and closed her eyes. It was as if she really knew who I was and felt secure, safe, and could rest. After I left, the staff found her lying in bed, doubled over at the waist with her chest by her knees. She remained in that position until physically pushed, with resistance, to a supine position. Later they got her up and gave her a bath. She was feeling better when I called from school at noon.

When I arrived at 6 that night, things had turned around again. Her temperature was up to 103° and she was very congested. She was sitting up. I worried about what would happen when she was laid down to sleep. She seemed to be in more discomfort than the night before. I knew they wouldn't call during the night since they had a standing order for morphine. Another sleepless night.

I arrived early the next morning and again her condition had changed. They only gave her Tylenol with codeine during the night. It took three more days to throw off what was giving her these problems and get back to what was normal for her. I felt like I was being dribbled like a basketball, slammed down, bounced up, only to be slammed down again.

Her biting caused problems again, but this time it was to herself. While eating, her lower lip got caught between her teeth. As she closed her mouth she didn't stop until her two front teeth cut into her lip. Did she not feel pain, and hence had no reason to stop, or did she feel pain, but didn't have enough control to stop biting down?

By the end of the month she seemed so tired. She could not hold her head up. I tried to stand her up but she was like a rag doll. In the past, she would help lift herself with her legs as I pulled her to an upright position from her wheelchair, but now she gave no assistance. She had to be lifted under her arms to get her up.

May, 1992

Keith returned from Florida. Tim, Maria, Keith, Maria, and I went out to eat to celebrate Keith's return. It was a fun and relaxing evening. He seemed to be happy to be back home, but that was probably due more to his being closer to his fiancée, Maria. At dinner he bestowed on me one of the biggest honors a son could give his father; he wanted me to be his best man. Tim was asked to be an usher.

We stopped at Starr Farm on the way to the restaurant since Keith hadn't seen his mother in six months. She was alert but couldn't focus on anything.

Her diet was changed again, and this resulted in her eating better. The warm part of the meal was dropped and cottage cheese, for protein, was added to the cold portion of her meal.

The weather was so nice on a Saturday that I decided to take her for a ride. She was able to sit up reasonably well and looked around as we drove. We ended up in Richmond, a neighboring town, so we went to a friend's home in the area who we hadn't seen for a few years. We stayed in the car, and after 20 minutes Lou-Ann became restless. She quieted down within a mile or two after we left. She was tired when we returned to Starr Farm.

The next Saturday we took another ride to visit other friends who had not seen her since we had had them over for dinner a few years ago. I took her out of the car and wheeled her onto their deck where they were cooking dinner. Even though I hadn't planned it, this was a chance for them to see Lou-Ann while she was still alive, since except for a couple of friends, only the family came to see her in the nursing home. It was important for me that she still have the opportunity to be about in the community and not be shut up at Starr Farm. It seemed like this preserved some of her personhood. We were still a couple and it was nice to be seen that way.

Five days later, at 7:15 in the morning, an aide went to get Lou-Ann and found her lying in bed, eyes rolled back, lips and fingertips blue, and not breathing. The aide pushed down on the mattress to stir her. That movement was sufficient to rouse her, and she took a breath. Dr. Gomez had said she might get to the place where she would forget to breathe. Another thing to add to the list of possible daily occurrences. How many more things would she have to deal with? Would she have started to breathe on her own if the aide hadn't entered when she did?

June, 1992

Lou-Ann's recent problems had affected me more than I realized. On Monday I stayed with her until 6:30 because I had a softball game that night. The phone rang just as I got in the house. It was Keith, "Hi, Dad." Nothing hit me until he continued, "Did you forget something?" That was the night we were to get measured for our tuxes. This was an event I had really looked forward to, but since I hadn't written it on the calendar, I completely forgot about it. It was a rite of passage and I had missed it. A few days later I went to the store by myself and got measured.

Six days after that first episode of not breathing, it happened again. After lunch an aide went to put her to bed for a nap and found her in the same condition, lips and fingertips blue and not breathing. As the aide picked her up to get her out of the wheelchair, she began to breathe. This had happened twice in less than one week. Was this to be a regular occurrence?

June 27 — a beautiful day for an outdoor wedding. Keith and Maria were married on the front lawn of her parent's farm. It was an exciting time for all. Richard Esty, the minister we had worked with for a long time in the church we attended before Lou-Ann became ill, officiated. The weather was perfect and much of our extended family was there.

We had arranged a little reception at the nursing home as we had done at Tim and Maria's wedding. It was a good opportunity for everyone to see Lou-Ann back at Starr Farm. At the reception four years ago, Lou-Ann was up, moving around by herself and singing, but now she was in a geri-chair, having a hard time just holding her head up, but she was there for both her children's weddings. She at least had been present for the climax of all the work, prayers, and tears she put into the raising of our children. She didn't get to bed until 11:30 that night. She was tired for the next three days.

July, 1992

To celebrate our 30th anniversary, I had planned a family picnic on Sunday at the downtown waterfront. Instead, the family across the street organized a surprise neighborhood party. I had an idea something was up, but I didn't anticipate anything of this magnitude. It was very touching. In the 22 years we had lived at our present address, the neighborhood had never gathered together. Many had not seen Lou-Ann since the open house for our 25th anniversary. Lou-Ann handled the excitement well. I supported her sides with rolled blankets so it would be easier for her to sit up in the wheelchair without leaning. I was thrilled to see a number of neighbors shake her hand and talk to her. One could tell they felt a little awkward, but they did it. It was always exciting when she was among a group of people. Again, this would be the last time most of them would see her while she was still alive. They tried to make it special, and it was.

She wasn't feeling well on our actual anniversary and slept much of the evening. She had a fever again. But we had made it to another milestone.

Her appointment with Dr. Gomez came again. When we first entered he thought she had aged quite a bit, but Lou-Ann 's head was forward on her chest so when I straightened her up, some of the wrinkles smoothed out and she looked more like her old self. He said he was always surprised by how well she was doing. She moved her limbs very little at this point, so he was concerned about her joints becoming stiff. He wanted her evaluated by the physical therapist to determine what exercises would be best "to keep her out of the fetal position as long as we can." This was important because some people with dementia revert to the fetal position before they die. If she assumed this position, it would both reduce her comfort level and make it more difficult to care for her. He felt she had the potential to go on for quite a while. She was going to take this disease as far as she could. She never was one to give up on anything.

All month she had had a low-grade fever, hovering around 100° and Tylenol didn't seem to bring it down, but we knew that the Tylenol kept her more comfortable since her moaning would diminish after taking it.

August, 1992

I exercised Lou-Ann's arms and legs every day. This would help her keep her flexibility, and I hoped it also felt good. When my father lost the ability to move his legs due to his cancer, he said it felt wonderful when his legs were exercised. It was frustrating not knowing whether she could experience pain or pleasure.

She began to bite her lip and took a dime-sized portion of skin off the inside of her lower lip. It swelled to twice normal size. I put ice in a rubber glove to put on her lip, but the rubber proved to be too insulating so I put the ice directly on the lip, making sure I didn't hold it in one spot. The swelling diminished within a couple of days. I also used Vaseline lip balm to keep her lips from drying out. She used to put that on all the time when this disease began. She seemed to enjoy the lip balm.

For a week she was more relaxed and alert. It was comforting to see her this way after all the problems she had been having. Another one of those delightful moments happened during that time. I was cradling her head in my arms when she fell asleep. It reminded me of the times, before she was ill, when we would be watching TV or listening to music and she would cuddle up in my arms and fall asleep. I treasured these last few times we had together like this.

Her weight dropped to 111 pounds. It had been holding at around 114 pounds for the past six months. It could have been due to losing some muscle mass because of her lack of exercise.

The death of a resident was always a sad occasion, but Starr Farm lost a person who really added to the institution. Ken and his wife were both residents of Starr Farm. They had been married well over 60 years. He had just celebrated his 90th birthday, and was as alert and sharp someone much younger. It was always a joy to see them because of the obvious love they had for each other. Their children, grandchildren, and great grandchildren visited on a regular, almost daily basis. It was such a good example to see family members support one another like that. I had known one of the grandchildren for a few years as she had been a student in one of my classes.

I walked in the front door of Starr Farm soon after he had passed away and met the family leaving. One daughter, who had taken the lead in overseeing his care, spoke to me with tears in her eyes.

"He had a full and good life . . ."

When she stopped I said, "Don't try to rationalize his death. When a loved one dies it hurts, no matter how young or old they are." With that she gave me a big hug. I hurt for them and could sense some of their pain. I knew it helped me when I could see that others perceived some of the pain and burden of our situation. It was as if they helped to shoulder the burden with me, and I truly knew I was not alone in this.

Lou-Ann came down with another urinary infection. It took awhile to determine what was wrong so all during that time she had had to suffer with it. Her fever peaked at 102° to 103°. When they confirmed what it was,

I had to face another critical decision. How aggressively should we treat something like this? Besides pneumonia, an infection could be the problem that would take her. This didn't seem to be in that serious category, so I decided we should go ahead and treat it with antibiotic. It took a couple of days until the fever broke, but it was the right decision.

Her regular temperature had been running in the high 90's and didn't come down to what was considered normal. The doctors thought her body was losing its capacity to regulate its temperature. They thought this was where her temperature would probably remain and we shouldn't become concerned unless it went above 100°. She seemed to be failing a little piece at a time. Would the end come when the total of all these little pieces added up to something big?

Tim and Maria left for Egypt to begin their world trip. They planned to be gone for six months, returning the first weekend in March. Since they would be trekking, no one would be able to get in touch with them. Accordingly, they planned on calling home every two to three weeks, alternating contacting his folks and me. There was always the possibility that Lou-Ann could die while they were gone and they weighed that into their decision to leave. She could live for quite a while also, so either they went then or put it off for a long time. If she had died while they were gone, I would have been willing to wait to have her funeral for a week until they could get back, but no longer. I didn't want everything to drag on after she died. This was a risk they had to take. I hoped this wouldn't happen because there was always the possibility that they would feel guilty if they should miss the closure of her life and not be with the family at that time.

September, 1992

Lou-Ann seemed to be grinding her teeth a lot. I talked to our dentist and in her case there wasn't much that could be done. As teeth are worn down, the nerves recede so she shouldn't come to a place where her teeth would become painful. Oral hygiene was a real problem since no one could get into her mouth to take care of her needs.

She hardly moved when I dyed her hair this month. She didn't move either her head or hands during the whole ordeal. I had a hard time getting her to close her eyes while I gave her a shower. What would the dye and soap do to her eyes? Transferring her from the shower chair to the chair on the scales was extremely difficult since she couldn't support any of her weight. She had to be belted into the shower chair to keep her from falling out. Her weight had slipped again, she was down to 110 pounds.

Tim and Maria made their first call from Cairo, Egypt. It was between 105° and 115° and they were feeling the effects of the heat. Maria had been sick twice and Tim once since they left.

While getting my car repaired, I ran into an old friend whom I hadn't seen since my 50th birthday party. We had a nice talk that ended with "We'll have to get together." The next time I saw her would be at Lou-Ann's funeral.

For more than a week, Lou-Ann had an inflamed big toe. No one could figure out what was causing this problem. Foot soaks and keeping her feet elevated didn't help. She was sitting in the geri-chair to keep her feet up when I went to tweak her toes as I was having fun with her. I was astonished when the front of her left sneaker was empty. Her toes weren't where they should have been. I took her sneaker off and discovered that the lining had ripped and every time it was put on, her toes became caught and were turned under. This was causing the inflammation. Out went the sneakers and that solved the problem.

In my entire life, there had never been a time I had known of someone going to Katmandu, Nepal, except for the day Tim and Maria said they would be arriving. On that day, while shaving, half listening to the morning news on public radio, I heard a news bulletin that said a plane from Pakistan had crashed upon landing at Katmandu. The day the kids arrived, a plane crashes. I was 99 percent sure they were not on that plane, but there was always a remote possibility. They shouldn't have gone to Nepal by way of Pakistan, but we didn't have specifics of their travel plans while in India and Nepal since their itinerary had not been established until they arrived in that area.

They were supposed to call when they first arrived, but we didn't hear from them. It didn't make sense that they went to Pakistan to go to Nepal. It also didn't make sense that they wouldn't call when they said they would. Maria called three days later than we expected. They had become involved in making the final preparations for their trek and had not gotten around to calling. They were unaware of the crash since they didn't get any English news and hence weren't aware of our concern.

Lou-Ann's temperature stayed right around 100° for the entire month. Tylenol hadn't made much of a difference in this condition. It had been over three months that this had been happening. At the end of the month, her temperature spiked to 104°. After six hours, Tylenol and cool washcloth compresses brought it down to 101°. She continued to become more apathetic and less aware of her surroundings.

Lou-Ann's roommate had become verbally abusive, which made me very uncomfortable. We knew this person's comprehension of reality wasn't always clear because she would carry on conversations with some teddy bears she had on her bed. She would talk to them in her normal voice but would change her tone as she spoke as if they were responding to her. She wasn't causing Lou-Ann any harm, but I wouldn't be able to put up with her comments if Lou-Ann became critically ill. I doubted that Lou-Ann understood what she said, but I certainly did. I asked for a change in roommates. The administration said they would look into making a transfer.

October, 1992

They moved Lou-Ann's roommate since a bed in another room in the wing had opened. Lou-Ann's new roommate, Helen, was new to the nursing home. She was a delightful person in her 80s who loved to watch the TV programs *Jeopardy* and *Wheel of Fortune*. So much for watching the news during that hour, but it was fun to see Helen enjoying those programs. It was a routine she had started long before coming to Starr Farm, so adjusting to her new environment would be easier if she could continue it. She took an immediate liking to Lou-Ann and became an advocate for her when I was not there. Helen's mind was sharp and she could get around relatively well with a walker, which she called her "Buick." She'd do things like buzz the nurses at night if she thought Lou-Ann might be getting cold. It was nice to have someone to interact with again as we sat watching some TV.

I received a call from the nursing home after I got home from church. Lou-Ann was very congested, had some change in color, and wheezed and moaned with every breathe. She was awake when I arrived and was having trouble breathing. She would clear up for a few minutes then would have trouble again. We got her up in the late afternoon so she would be more upright. She coughed up a lot of phlegm during the afternoon and was more relaxed when I left. But when I called later at 9 p.m., I was told that at 7:00 her temperature had gone up to 104.7° and her breathing had become shallow. She was given Tylenol, which helped because her temperature had dropped to a little over 102° by 10:00 when the nurse called back to give me an update. Her pulse was up to 132 and her respiratory rate was 32 and still shallow. The nurse had expected her temperature to be lower so they proceeded with cold compresses. She thought Lou-Ann was starting to go into pneumonia again.

This was the first time I would have to make the call on using an antibiotic since the kids had left. If they were home I would definitely let the condition run its course, but it was a different situation with them halfway around the world. I wasn't sure what to do. The impact if she should die and they weren't able to get home in time could be significant. Why couldn't I make that decision once and for all? It seemed as if I had to make it over and over.

She was awake and alert at midnight and her temperature had dropped to 100°. She gradually pulled out of this over the next couple of days and returned to where she was before. The crisis had passed. It was so hard to see her go through these sessions and not be able to relieve or lessen her struggle. Even the simplest of tasks, like breathing, were presenting problems.

A few days later she saw Dr. Gomez. She had lost all movement in her arms and legs and had trouble holding her head upright. He ordered a soft neck collar to help support her head. He wanted a reassessment in four months. We set the date for the middle of February.

My mother phoned to tell me my father's brother, Uncle Eddie, had died while he and his wife, Aunt Georgie, were on a vacation. He had worked hard all his life and was finally able to do enjoyable things like traveling. I called Aunt Georgie and she seemed to be doing as well as could be expected. I got a chance to talk to my cousin whom I hadn't seen in about eight years. I made plans to get together with Aunt Georgie the next summer when I visited my mother. We had never been really close, and this would be a chance to share something we sadly now had in common.

Lou-Ann continued to bite her lip, peeling the skin off a small area until it would bleed and become raw. There didn't seem to be any way we could get her to stop.

I now needed help to get her in the shower chair after I dyed her hair. At 111 pounds, her weight was up by one pound. She still had trouble breathing since she continued to be somewhat congested.

We were discussing some important educational issues in our last department meeting at school, and how they would affect our department. I just couldn't get into the discussion. I had absolutely no concern about them. I was making decisions as to whether I should try to keep my wife alive, which made those educational issues seem so unimportant. How did I keep going in my profession when all my energy had been used trying to keep things together regarding my dying wife?

Two weeks after her first call, my mother phoned again to tell me that my Aunt Esther, my father's sister, had died the night before in a nursing home. It wasn't a big surprise since she was 89 and in poor health. This was to begin a stretch of a few weeks where death seemed to permeate my life. The same day a friend of my parents, a woman whom I had known all my life, was killed in an auto accident just a mile from my mother's house. The day after my mother phoned, I called my cousin and his wife to convey my condolences regarding Aunt Esther's death. That morning an uncle of his had also died. The uncle and his wife were the youth group advisors in church when I was a teenager.

Three deaths in three days, four in two weeks, all in my hometown and all people in their later years. These deaths were from a distance, so to speak, but they all represented an end to some connection in my life.

November, 1992

November started like October left off. The son of the elementary school principal where Keith and Maria had gone to school was killed in a plane crash. He was a pilot in the Marines and had been killed on a training mission in California.

Three days later Bill, the husband of Gerry Fitzgerald, a friend from the support group, died in a local nursing home. He had multi-infarct dementia and had been in the home for a couple of years. Gerry and I had been on the Board of Directors of the Vermont Chapter of the Alzheimer's Association and had given talks about dementia together.

Two days after, that I received another call from my mother that my Aunt Georgie was killed when she was struck by a truck while crossing the street in front of her home. It was less than a month since her husband had died. Seven people in 3½ weeks made me ask who was next.

John, a resident at Starr Farm was all upset. He thought his wife was dying. She had passed away a number of years before. He was always such a friendly, tender, and compassionate man whom I enjoyed talking with. It was hard enough to go through the loss of a loved one the first time: this poor man was going through it again.

Lou-Ann's eyes had become red and dry. I wanted the nurses to apply some eye drops to try to relieve this condition. They had to get the doctor to prescribe artificial tears. This would clear up and then return a couple of times over the next month.

She had a bad night in the middle of the month when she began to moan as her temperature rose to 102.4°. It sounded as if she was starting to have a buildup of mucus in the back of her throat, so they put her in a geri-chair and moved her to the nurse's station to keep a close watch on her. They observed her closely for the next day but nothing developed.

Lou-Ann and I spent Thanksgiving together in the nursing home. They served dinner for any immediate family members who wished to eat there. I chose to take advantage of this and had my Thanksgiving meal with Lou-Ann. I stayed all day, so at suppertime, the nurses said I should go out back and help myself to the buffet that was provided for the staff who had to work on the holiday. One of the nurses whom I had known for more than three years brought me an entire turkey meal to take home. She said they had plenty of food from her family's dinner and thought I might like some of it. Gestures like this from people who saw what we were going through were so very encouraging. It also meant that they saw Lou-Ann as more than just a person whom they were required to attend to. In a way, they had chosen to take part in our struggle as a friend, as well as a professional. Lou-Ann was very tranquil all of Thanksgiving and slept a lot. It was a relief to see her so relaxed and breathing without any difficulty.

November is national Alzheimer's month, and as a result, I was asked to be on two radio shows. One program was a taped 15-minute interview that I had done with a research physician who was involved in a drug study for Alzheimer's. The other was a live hour-long call-in show that I did by myself. I liked to do these because it meant that through me, Lou-Ann was able to contribute to educating others about this disease.

December, 1992

This time of the year used to be enjoyable and full of excitement. It had become a time of depression. It seemed that Thanksgiving began the time when more people in the nursing home passed away. Five people had died so far this month.

When I wrote this year's Christmas letter, I had a real sense of Lou-Ann's decline. I read last year's letter to see what I had said about her and realized she was still walking, with help, whereas now she couldn't move. All she could do now was roll her head from side to side and follow people with her eyes. That was the extent of her movement. Except for walks in her wheelchair, she now stayed in a geri-chair by the nurse's station, wearing her neck collar to help keep her head up.

Christmas was quiet. My mother and Keith and Maria were home for the day. It was cold and windy, a wind-chill factor of -16 below zero. I bundled up Lou-Ann for the half-mile trip home, my sweater, her coat, big boots, and a blanket over her legs. She was home from 10 to 5. It was the first time she had left the nursing home since her doctor's appointment in October. We didn't know it then, but it was to be the last time she would leave Starr Farm. She sat up most of the day because when she lay down, her throat tended to fill up, which made breathing difficult. She appeared to be comfortable throughout the day. Denise, her family, and friends came over in the afternoon and sang carols for us. It was a nice pick-me-up for the afternoon. No one said anything, but we were all aware that in all probability, this would be Lou-Ann's last Christmas with us.

Coming home for Christmas really tired her out. For two days she didn't eat much and was lethargic. She tended to look to the side, stare at the wall and not look at me when I visited.

She had a relatively comfortable month, no major incidents. It was good to have some time when she wasn't always fighting to get through the day.

I wheeled her around the nursing home on New Year's Eve. As I pushed, she kept looking up. It wasn't as if she was always looking at me, but she seemed to be trying to keep track of where I was. As we walked, my mind recalled the major events of the year: Keith and Maria's wedding, Tim and Maria's trip, our 30th wedding anniversary, and the loss of her ability to walk. It was good to just be able to be with her and feel her touch. That was still comforting to me. I wasn't sure how aware she was of people around her, so I tried to always be in physical contact with her so she would have some way of knowing I was there.

Chapter 12

The Final Month

January, 1993

The holidays seemed to be a bittersweet time. In many ways I was glad they were over. I felt less depressed.

Helen, Lou-Ann's roommate, fell flat on her face. She zoomed around in her walker, her "Buick," like she was driving a hot rod. Her family said she also drove like that. The front wheel caught on something and over she went, like someone going over the handlebars of a bicycle. Her face was all swollen and black and blue. It looked like someone hit her with a 2 x 4. She had a fairly good attitude about it, even though she hurt.

Someone read a short devotional piece during our choir's warm-up before the worship service. It reflected upon the number we were to sing that morning. It had the theme of "be happy in your troubles." I got so sick of those messages. The writer or person talking was always telling someone else to be happy. It would be more meaningful if someone who was facing severe problems would be the messenger. I was having a hard enough time accepting our situation let alone being happy in it. On the other hand, how many times had I said things like that to people without thinking of the impact it might have had on them at the time?

My annual physical — I went to Dr. Martenis with a list of concerns about myself and Lou-Ann. I felt like I was taking my car into the garage for maintenance: change the oil, check the tire pressure, there's a rattle under the dash, the clutch slips and I'm leaking brake fluid.

Dr. Martenis made his usual rounds at Starr Farm and prescribed more artificial tears. Except for the red and dry eyes, she had not had a bad month. Her temperature rose to around 102° a couple of times over the course of the first two weeks, but other than that she was still relatively stable and comfortable.

I dyed her hair on the 14th and her weight remained at 111 pounds. Her weight had stayed between 110 and 115 pounds for the past 16 months.

Wednesday, January 20, 1993

The telephone rings as I'm about to leave for school. Who would be calling at 7:45 in the morning?

"Lou-Ann woke up congested with a temp of 103° and we want to let you know."

It was the charge nurse at the Starr Farm nursing home. Lou-Ann had had higher temperatures than that before, but they were always able to get it down so there wasn't any reason to panic.

"We will give her Tylenol as we've done in the past. Do you want to also start her on antibiotic?"

"Tylenol has always worked before, but I guess it wouldn't hurt to also put her on the antibiotic. I've got a class at nine so I will call back after that to see how she is doing."

The nurses knew of my decision to not give antibiotic, or initiate any other means of prolonging her life, if she was in a critical situation. Hence, I figured this must not be that critical since they asked about using an antibiotic. By noon she would be starting to feel better, and we could still have a good evening together. I was not able to call until around 11 a.m. because of students' questions after my first class.

"She's on oxygen, her temp is still up, but we've just started the antibiotic so that should help. We've put cold compresses under her arms, neck, and head to try to cool her off and keep her comfortable. She hasn't shown any improvement since I first called you."

By now there should have been some indication that her temperature was on the decline. It had always started down by this time in the past. The nurse didn't say she was in trouble, and her voice didn't seem to indicate they were too concerned, so hopefully she would be better when I called later.

After lunch — She had been on my mind since my last call. I thought about canceling my 4-7 p.m. class, but some students had to travel quite a distance to get to the university. There was no way we could have gotten in touch with everyone anyway since some students didn't register until the first class.

Getting organized for a three-hour class when my mind was somewhere else did not help calm the nerves for a first class. I couldn't concentrate on what I was supposed to be doing. How could I teach when I wanted to be at the nursing home?

Three o'clock — I called again, "There's no change in her condition. Her temp is 104.8°. She's still very congested. She wouldn't swallow any of her lunch, but did take a full glass of water. She's had a pretty hard day."

What to do? Maybe I should cancel my 4-7 p.m. class? It started in less than an hour. The nurses didn't say that I should come, and they knew my desire to be with her if she became really sick, so I started class and planned to call during our break.

5:30 p.m., break time — I could not take my eyes off the clock while teaching. All I could think of was Lou-Ann, and wanting to get to a telephone. "Her temp has come down some, but she is still very congested. Her pulse is 130 and her respiratory rate is 38. This is the worst I have ever seen her. She took some apple juice and water, but we had to suction her mouth to help her breath." That was it, there was no way I could continue this class. I had to get to the nursing home to be with Lou-Ann. I was not sure what to expect when I saw her.

I needed to call Pastor Coffey right away to tell him what was happening since I wouldn't be able to reach him later because he would be at prayer meeting. I called him at his house. He said he would come as soon as the meeting began, and he could get someone else to lead it.

6:30 p.m. — The drive to the nursing home seemed to take forever.

I could feel the concern of everyone as I entered the nursing home. People glanced at me as I walked down the hall to her room but said nothing. There were not the friendly hellos and smiles I usually got when I arrived.

She seemed to be resting relatively comfortably. They had given her 2 mg of morphine, which gave her some relief. One did not need a stethoscope to hear the rasping in her lungs. Even though her temperature was so high, she was cool to the touch. She was lying in bed with her eyes closed. The only movement one could see was the rise and fall of her chest as she struggled for each breath. She looked so helpless.

At 7:00, the doctor on call came to check her. "Lou-Ann's condition is very serious. I am afraid that she is not going to make it."

Did he say what I think he said? Did he really mean she was dying?

"How much time do you think she has?"

"It's hard to say. Each person is different, but I don't think she will make it through the next 24 hours."

As I looked down at her, I could not believe this could be our last night together.

"What about the antibiotic? If I knew she was this serious, I would not have agreed to put her on it."

"The antibiotic is not having any impact on her condition. It won't make any difference one way or another."

After seven years of struggling with this disease, this day had arrived. In my mind I had lived this moment over and over, but I still was not prepared for it to come. I had less than 24 hours to be with my wife of 30 years. How could I say good-bye?

It was so quiet in the room.

I had to let the family know of Lou-Ann's condition. I called Boston and Buffalo to let both sides of the family know what was happening. Tim and Maria were in New Zealand, and would be calling his parents sometime from Friday through Sunday. I had just talked to them the night before and told them that Lou-Ann was doing fine. I had to be sure to get in touch with them, otherwise Tim and Maria would not know what was happening for another two weeks. Fortunately, they wouldn't be trying to reach me since there was no way for them to know to call the nursing home. No one answered the Thibault's phone when I called.

I called Keith and Maria, and they said they would come as soon as they could.

Pastor Coffey arrived around 8:30 after turning the prayer meeting over to an elder. We talked a little, he then took Lou-Ann's and my hands and prayed.

"Lord, we commit Lou-Ann into your care. We pray she will not linger in this state. May you give her comfort and peace, and may her leaving be peaceful and not delayed. Be with Clint and comfort him, give him strength to face the loss of the one he loves, and face the future with hope and assurance of Lou-Ann's rest in you. In your holy name we pray. Amen."

No! No! No! No! I do not want her to die! I was not ready to give her up. I was not ready to say good-bye. The tears ran down my cheeks as I sobbed while he prayed. After seven years of this dreaded disease, knowing this day would eventually arrive, I could not let go of her. I prayed God would give me the strength to be able to let go when the time came. "I don't think she will make it through the next 24 hours," kept ringing in my ears.

I wanted to be with her when she died. The watch started by sitting in a straight-back chair to help me stay awake. Her breathing was less labored although her temperature, pulse, and respiratory rate remained high. All I could do was hold her hand. She was to go on a journey, and I could not go along. There was nothing I could do that would have any effect on what was about to transpire. The only thing I could do was remain by her side.

Around 11:30 p.m., I tried to call the Thibaults again, without any luck. Their phone rang and rang and rang. What if I could not get a hold of them? If Tim and Maria called early they would not know that their mother was dying. I had to get in touch with them!

She slept for a while, then she awoke. Her eyes were wide open, I leaned over to kiss her, she looked at me. She closed her eyes, and fell back to sleep. This sequence of waking and looking around continued throughout the night.

Thursday, January 21, 1993

The nurses offered me a geri-chair, but I knew if I sat in it I would be asleep in no time. My arm was getting tired since all night I had been reaching through the side rails of her bed, holding her hand. At 4 o'clock in the morning, I changed chairs. God knew my desire to be awake with her when the time came, but I had had only 5 hours of sleep in the past 48 hours.

If she died while I was asleep, it would be His timing. The next thing I knew it was 7 a.m., the shift was changing. Lou-Ann's temp had fallen to 101.2°. She was sleeping.

Time to try to reach the Thibaults again. I was getting closer, the phone was busy. I tried again 15 minutes later — no answer. I called Lori, Maria's best friend, to see if she would also try to get in touch with them, this would double our chances.

Since she seemed to be resting comfortably, I decided to go home to shower and call both Lou-Ann's and my mother to bring them up to date on how she was. I also got a few more hours of sleep. When I returned, I noticed that another bed had been moved into the room for me. It was a tight squeeze but they got it in. This was where I would be spending all my time. I was moving in.

Helen, Lou-Ann's roommate had been very concerned. With tears in her eyes she would hold Lou-Ann's hand. Helen had only been at Starr Farm four months, but she had established a relationship with Lou-Ann. Helen had always looked out for Lou-Ann when I wasn't there. I was going to miss watching *Wheel of Fortune* and *Jeopardy* with her every night.

Marlene Thibault called around noon. Thank God Lori had gotten a hold of her. That was one worry that had been taken care of. The phone company had been working on a pole down the road from their house, and had mistakenly disconnected their phone. It was out of order, and they didn't know it. They had been home every time I had called.

Lou-Ann had started on a two-stage cycle that was to continue until her death. She would have a high fever - around 104.5°, rapid pulse — about 140 — and a respiratory rate of around 34 for 24 hours, after which her temperature would decrease to between 100° and 101°, pulse would come down to 100, and her breathing would become so shallow that one would almost have to touch her chest to make sure she was still breathing. She would continue like that for another 24 hours before beginning the cycle again.

Three choir members came to visit after rehearsal. It was good to see them. This was only the second year I had sung in the choir, and for two of the people, it was the first time they had met Lou-Ann. It had always been important to me that people realized Lou-Ann and I were still a couple, regardless of her condition. Many people would be very hesitant to come under such circumstances. Their visit and show of support was extremely encouraging.

That night, I got five hours of sleep because Lou-Ann rested peacefully. The doctor increased her morphine to 30 mg to keep her comfortable. It was the second time the dosage had been increased. Throughout the night I would get up to make sure she was still breathing because she was so quiet.

She was removed from the bottled oxygen and placed on a machine that concentrated oxygen from the air. It was delivered to her through a nosepiece and not via a mask. I didn't know how much the oxygen helped because she was mainly breathing through her mouth and not her nose.

Friday, January 22, 1993

She seemed to be alert when she awoke in the morning. She was still able to follow people with her eyes. She took some fluids, apple juice and water. It was now a day and a half after the doctor said she had 24 hours left, and she was looking around the room. The nurses asked if I wanted to discontinue the antibiotic. To not initiate it at the beginning would have been a decision I could have made at the time, I had done it twice before. But to withdraw it was another matter. I could not do that at this time. I guess I was still not ready to let her go.

Even though her temperature was not extreme, she felt hot to the touch, but her arms and legs were cool. As the day progressed, her temperature rose and she started the cycle all over again. I had never seen anyone with acute bronchopneumonia. Her breathing was so regular, but she was pulling so hard to get air. It was like someone rowing a scull, every pull took so much energy while at the same time the cadence was so consistent. Her stomach muscles rippled with every breath. How much longer could she go on since she was working so hard? I found myself breathing with her. If there was only something I could do to ease her fight. She never was one to give anything but her all in any endeavor. Why should she change now?

No word from Tim and Maria. I couldn't wait to talk with them. I didn't know how much time Lou-Ann had left. I could tell by the way the nurses reacted that they were extremely concerned when Lou-Ann went into the hard phase of the cycle. She took some apple juice and water at noon.

She seemed to have a lot of mucus in the top of her throat so they tried to suction it out to give her a clearer breathing passage. Every time the tube was placed in her mouth, she bit down on it. It seemed her biting reflex was still intact.

Saturday, January 23, 1993

The entire day was spent trying to keep her cool. Her temperature was back up to 104.6° with labored breathing and audible rales. I kept her forehead and neck covered with cool washcloths. I didn't know if it made her feel better or not, but at least I was doing something.

At 11 p.m., I got a call from Marlene Thibault that Tim and Maria had called. They would be calling me shortly. They had only talked for about 5 minutes so I was not sure how much information was relayed concerning Lou-Ann, except that she was very serious.

It wasn't long until I was on the phone with Maria.

"Is this for real or do you think she might pull out of it like she has done before?" she asked.

"I'm afraid she is not going to make it this time. She has already lived more than two days longer than the doctor expected."

"We'll make arrangements to return, and get there as soon as possible."

It was midafternoon, Sunday in New Zealand. They were calling from a pay phone in a shopping mall that was about to close. It would take a 10-hour overnight train ride to get to Auckland, then plane reservations to Los Angeles, with only a one and a half hour layover, before heading to Boston. Arrival time in Boston was Monday, 9 p.m. EST, 46 hours from when we first talked. Talking with them, and knowing they were on their way was reassuring to me. Our family would be together. The only question that remained was whether they would get here before Lou-Ann died.

Sunday, January 24, 1993

During the night, the nurse and I talked about discontinuing the antibiotic, but I still couldn't make the decision to stop. She came in at 5:00 a.m. to give Lou-Ann her medications and morphine. As we talked by the edge of Lou-Ann's bed she said, "This is the antibiotic. Do you want me to give it to her?"

I looked at it, then at Lou-Ann, "No. Let's stop it."

The knowledge that Tim and Maria were on their way home helped to make that decision. It was a major step in letting go. From now on, the only medication she would receive would be for comfort. She was now strictly on her own. She was in God's hands.

Her condition remained the same until just before the sun rose. She started to breath easier, and her vital signs came down to a more reasonable level. One big difference I saw from her previous low ebb was that she no longer looked around. She just stared straight ahead at the ceiling.

Aides attempted to give her some juice and water but she wouldn't take any. She hadn't taken any nourishment since noon on Friday.

Her mother and brother arrived in the late afternoon. There would be a lot of people coming in the next few days, but they would have to fend for themselves. Except for the few hours each morning when I went home to shower and call everyone to update them on how the night went, I was at the nursing home by Lou-Ann's side.

After her mother and brother spent some time with us, they went to the house to settle in. The weather had turned cold. It was snowing outside. This was the first snow of the season to accumulate to where you knew it would last. There was almost a foot of snow on the ground. The view from Lou-Ann's window was starting to look like a scene from *Vermont Life* magazine.

As it became late evening, all the hustle and bustle of the nursing home seemed to quiet down. We were alone together. She was so peaceful, as if sleeping. For a moment it seemed that she couldn't be dying, that when she woke up this whole thing would have just been a bad nightmare.

I was going to miss the touch of her hand, the softness of her cheek. How do people get through this?

Monday, January 25, 1993

In the morning the doctor increased the dosage of morphine to 45 mg. Her temperature started to rise in the afternoon, and her breathing became labored as she entered the cycle for the third time.

We hadn't heard from Tim and Maria so they must have made all of their connections. Tim's parents left for Boston to pick them up. The four-hour drive to Burlington would give them time to adjust and become updated on how things were going.

Keith and Maria, Lou-Ann's mother and brother, Pastor Coffey, and myself were all in the room at night. We had pizza delivered, and everyone seemed relaxed as we ate. It was as if we were getting ready to watch Monday-night football. Lou-Ann's bed had been turned so that there was room on both sides so more than one person could be close to her. It was almost 10 p.m., she was again pulling for every breath. Tim and Maria should have landed in Boston an hour before, and would be on their way home.

As I held her hand it felt very cool, even though she had a high temperature. I noticed her fingers, as well as her lips started to turn blue. Her arms and legs were cool, and her feet were cold. The time of waiting seemed to be over! I really believed she was dying, and I felt a peace and calmness. I was ready to let her go. I turned away for a moment, and as I looked back, color had returned to her lips as well as her fingers. She had returned. Something told me that she would be alive when the kids arrived. She had passed a crisis. I had been ready then to let her go, how would I ever be that ready again?

Tuesday, January 26, 1993

Tim and Maria walked in at 2 a.m. Lou-Ann was sleeping. It had been almost five months since they had left. I wondered if in some way Lou-Ann had been waiting until they returned. My mother arrived during the afternoon.

Lou-Ann seemed comfortable throughout the day even though her temperature, pulse, and respiratory rate were high the entire time.

Wednesday, January 27, 1993

During the night she settled down and went into her less labored state. But this time her eyes were only partially opened and were becoming red and dry. We kept a moist washcloth over them so they wouldn't dry out. It was obvious that she didn't have much fight left.

In the morning everyone had gone except Maria and Tim, Keith and Maria, and myself. Our daughter Maria said, "Here we are now, together as a complete family." Tim and Maria left on their trip two months after Keith and Maria were married, so there was not much time for all of us to be together. Some families measure their time together, after all the children get married, in years. We measured ours in hours.

At 4:30 p.m., her breathing began to become more labored, and in 15 minutes she was back to her extreme condition again. This was the fourth time. I did not see how she was going to pull through this time because she was in such a weakened state.

At 5:00 p.m., aides came in, took some of Helen's clothes, and told us she was being moved to another room. After her dinner Helen came back with her "Buick" crying. "What have I done wrong that they are moving me?" I gave her a big hug. "Helen, Lou-Ann is about to leave, and then I will be going too. That means you will be alone so you need to be with someone else." She had mothered Lou-Ann the entire time they had been roommates. I wished she could have stayed all the way through to the end. When I asked, I was told this was the nursing home decision, and it was final. It was ironic that in four weeks, Helen would also be gone.

At 9:30 p.m., a nurse and aides came in to get Lou-Ann washed and medicated for the night. Everyone left the room to let the staff do their work. As I headed back to her room 15 minutes later, the nurse approached and said Lou-Ann's temperature had risen to 106.6°, and she thought I might want to reconsider whether I still wanted her to remain on oxygen. Lou-Ann's mother sat by the left side of the bed holding her hand. I held her right hand. Our daughter Maria and her husband sat beside me. I looked at Maria, "Do you want to help make the decision regarding the oxygen?"

"No."

"I'm going to remove it."

Maria could not bear to watch me remove the oxygen, so she and Tim left the room for a few minutes.

Lou-Ann was lying slightly on her right side as I took the oxygen tube from around her left ear, and removed it from her nose. There was no resistance from her neck as I lifted her head to remove the tube from around her right ear. I gently placed her head back on the pillow. It was as if her head was on a swivel. There was no resistance to any movement.

The oxygen machine continued to hum. I could not find an on/off switch so I pulled the plug from the wall.

Beep, beep, beep. After two minutes an alarm went off to indicate the machine had lost its power. The machine was large so I wheeled it, still beeping, from the room and started down the hall to the nurse's station. As I got only a few steps from Lou-Ann's door, Maria came rushing from the room. "Come quick! It's Mom, she's stopped breathing!"

I rushed in, and held her hand close to my chest as I sat on the edge of her bed. She breathed, then stopped, then breathed, then stopped.

It was 9:58 p.m., January 27, 1993. My wife had just died. Her journey had ended.

Afterword

The diagnosis of Pick's disease was confirmed by an autopsy. There was marked knife-edged atrophy involving the frontal and temporal lobes of her brain, which was consistent with Pick's disease. There was also marked depletion of neurons in this area of her brain. Lou-Ann was otherwise very healthy.

Life has continued on for our family. Keith and Maria purchased a house about three miles from my home, and Tim and Maria built a home 20 miles away.

Our family has grown; Alexa Richelle Erb was born to Keith and Maria on July 30, 1994. I was privileged to be with them in the birthing room for a couple of hours until the time of delivery arrived. I was more involved with the birth of my granddaughter than the birth of our own daughter. The birth of Alexa was a special moment for the entire family and marked the beginning of a new chapter in our family history.

I went on sabbatical leave from the university the fall after Lou-Ann died. It was an important time for me; a time of healing, and a time to begin to rebuild my life. The writing of this book during that year helped to start the healing process.

As I returned from my sabbatical, I met a graduate student who was a kindergarten teacher at a local elementary school. I had taught a course with her the previous summer. She had heard I was beginning to date and a couple of weeks into the school year she told me about, Pamela, a third-grade teacher whom she taught with who had a lot in common with me. It took me three weeks to get the nerve to contact Pam. That was the start of a new and exciting relationship. The next summer we were married.

In addition to my marriage, our family grew further. After Maria and Tim moved into their home, they announced they were expecting. On August 11, 1995, Daniel Allen was born, our family's second grandchild.

Our family grew close during those final few years of Lou-Ann's life, and we continue to grow close and support each other as life moves on. Lou-Ann never lived to see how well her children turned out as they progressed into adulthood, but successful parenting means that our efforts bear fruit, not that we get to see the fruit. The fact that we can enjoy the results of our efforts is certainly a pleasurable thing and something to be desired, but the experiencing of that pleasure is not necessary in order to be a successful parent.

Lou-Ann's life was shorter than we would have wished, but she lived a full and complete life in the 51 years she was on this earth. Many people live a lot longer and never experience all the things we did in our years together. The knowledge of this is comforting.

Appendix

The following definitions are included to help clarify some of the terms used in this book. These are not thorough medical definitions, but they will help to distinguish the differences between the various terms.

"**Dementia** is the loss of intellectual functions (such as thinking, remembering, and reasoning) of sufficient severity to interfere with an individual's daily functioning. Dementia is not a disease in itself but rather a group of symptoms which may accompany certain diseases or conditions. Symptoms may also include changes in personality, mood, and behavior." (*Alzheimer's Disease and Related Disorders*, Alzheimer's Association: Chicago, IL, 1987). Dementia does not imply irreversibility.

Alzheimer's Disease (AD) was definitively described in 1907 by A. Alzheimer in a 51-year- old woman with a 4½-year course of progressive dementia. "AD is a progressive, age-related brain disease that impairs thinking and behavior.... AD is the most common form of dementing illness, which causes declines in intellectual functions and in the ability to perform routine activities. AD usually has a gradual onset. Problems remembering recent events and difficulty performing familiar tasks are early symptoms. The Alzheimer patient also may experience confusion, personality change, behavior change, impaired judgment, and difficulty finding words, finishing thoughts or following directions. How quickly these changes occur will vary from person to person, but the disease leaves its victims totally unable to care for themselves. An absolute diagnosis can only be made upon examination of brain tissue, usually at autopsy.... Currently there is no treatment available to stop or reverse the mental deterioration characteristic of AD." (*Alzheimer's Disease and Related Disorders*, Alzheimer's Association: Chicago, IL, 1987).

Pick's Disease was first described in 1892 by Arnold Pick in a 71-year-old patient with a three-year history of progressive dementia. "Pick's disease is a rare brain disease which closely resembles AD and is difficult to clinically diagnose. . . . Like Alzheimer's Disease, a definitive diagnosis is usually obtained at autopsy." (*Alzheimer's Disease and Related Disorders*, Alzheimer's Association: Chicago, IL, 1987). "Onset is slow and insidious, involving difficulty in thinking, slight memory defects, easy fatigability, and, often, character changes with a lowering of ethical inhibitions. At first there is a rather circumscribed atrophy of the frontal and temporal lobes; as the atrophy becomes more severe, the mental deterioration becomes progressively greater and includes apathy and disorientation as well as impairment of judgment and other intellectual functions. The disease usually runs a fatal course within two to seven years." (*Abnormal Psychology and Modern Life*, 7th ed., Coleman, James, Butcher, James, Carson, Robert. Scott, Foresman: Glenview, IL, 1984, p. 506).